The full force of the attack, the costly defense, and the disastrous retreat must be read to be believed.
Atlantic Monthly

Mr Macrory tells the story of this dreadful march with such success that the reader feels he is there. He shares the agony of cold as the living huddle together at night without food, warmth or shelter. Around their pathetic camps prowl the Afghans...
The New York Times

The narrative has all the excitement and contention of one of those Erroll Flynn movies about the Khyber Pass and the wild Northwest frontier: officers disguised as natives, wild cavalry charges, massacres, the courageous young captains and the hidebound old generals. In some ways what occurred in Afghanistan (though neglected in history) was something of an overture to the follies and heroism of the Crimean War.
The Los Angeles Times

Everything that could happen to a military force happened to the British, from freezing to death, to falling into chasms, to walking into an endless series of ambushes...Macrory has set the story down in vivid well-documented prose.
World Herald, Omaha

This astonishing drama of intrigue and violence, of heroism and appalling incompetence.
Adelaide Advertiser

Those who like their history larded with horror will be a mass of goose-flesh long before they reach the last terrible chapter.
The Telegraph, Sydney

A brilliant narrative of human heroism, cruelty and suffering.
The Examiner

KABUL
CATASTROPHE

KABUL CATASTROPHE

The Invasion and Retreat, 1839-1842

PATRICK MACRORY

with a new Foreword
by General Sir Michael Rose

This edition published in 2002 in Great Britain by
Prion Books Limited
Imperial Works, Perren Street,
London NW5 3ED

ISBN 1-85375-489-7

TO ELIZABETH

Because she encouraged me to start and
refused to let me stop

Cover design by Bob Eames
Cover illustration by The Illustrated London News

Printed and bound in Great Britain
by Creative Print & Design, Wales

FOREWORD

by General Sir Michael Rose,
KCB.CBE. DSO. QGM.

Standing astride a major route through Asia, Afghanistan has for two centuries been an important element in the long struggle amongst the great powers to gain control of central Asia, - the so called Great Game. In 1839, determined to keep the Russians out of Afghanistan, the British overthrew its ruler, Dost Mohamed, and replaced him with Shah Soojah, - thus opening one of the darkest chapters in British military history. Two years later the people of Afghanistan rose up against the hated foreigners and massacred virtually the entire British army of occupation as it retreated from Kabul. The news of the terrible losses sustained in this retreat shook the establishment of Victorian Britain to its foundations. Hitherto the news from India had been of almost unqualified military success and yet suddenly a powerful British force, which had been peaceably living in Kabul for the past two years, had been brutally attacked and destroyed by seemingly primitive tribesmen armed only with matchlocks and swords.

The principal causes of the disaster were an exaggerated assessment of the strategic risks posed by Afghanistan to India which had led to the ill-conceived attempt to establish a British presence by force in Afghanistan as well as a serious under-estimation of the Afghan capacity for treachery and killing. Political mismanagement of the operation, over-confidence in the British Army's capability, a failure of military command, poor intelligence, and an inadequate provisioning of the expeditionary force, had subsequently combined to make defeat all but inevitable once the uprising in Kabul against the British had begun. As one of the survivors put it, 'Our Kabul Army perished, sacrificed to the incompetency, feebleness and want of skill and resolution of their military leaders'.

Today, the great powers are once again attempting to bring about a change of rule in Afghanistan, and the underlying risk to their mission is much the same as that experienced by all foreign powers that have sought to impose their will on Afghanistan throughout the centuries. For amidst the endless tribal feuding and civil wars that make up so much of the bloody history of that country, the one thing that binds the people of Afghanistan together is a violent hatred of foreign interference. Indeed, the entire history of Afghanistan is one of broken treaties, changing alliances, treachery, torture and killing. In the First Afghan War, so relatively unopposed was the British Army's march to Kabul, that the British administration was lulled into a false sense of security that proved ultimately to be fatal. Fortifications were never properly constructed. the Treasury and most military supplies were housed separately from the army in indefensible places, and scarcely any training was carried out amongst the garrison troops. It was when the British were at their weakest and most ill-prepared that the Afghans struck.

It is, of course, inconceivable that any country or representative foreign power, including the United Nations today, could be so unaware of the risks inherent in a mission to Afghanistan. However, at a political level the present lack of clear strategic objective will make the necessary coordination between the political, humanitarian and military aspects of the international mission difficult to achieve. Any lack of cohesion will surely encourage unscrupulous Afghan warlords to disrupt the international effort, – in the same way as their 19th century forbears were able to do when confronted by the disagreements between Macnaughten, the British Resident, and Elphinstone, his ailing military commander. Today there are many different national agendas being pursued by the countries involved in Afghanistan. Whilst the US works to destroy the al Quaeda organisation, Russia seeks to recover its favourable political position, lost when it invaded Afghanistan. Other nations, such as Britain, may have more altruistic aims. But unless there is clear unity of purpose amongst the entire international community, it is likely that all efforts to create conditions of peace and security in the region will fail.

At a military level, within the Coalition forces currently engaged in Afghanistan, good intelligence, effective command and control, highly professional soldiers and vastly superior military technology will surely prevent a repetition of the defeat of the British Army in the First Afghan War. Since there is, rightly, no intention of imposing any foreign presence in Afghanistan by force of arms, the relationship between the Coalition forces and the militias of the Northern Alliance will be one of friendship not enmity, – at least for as long as there is some tactical advantage to be gained by the Northern Alliance from the continuing presence of the Coalition forces on their territory. However, as the Duke of Wellington put it in 1839, 'the difficulties would begin where the military successes have ended'. Therefore unless some military influence can continue to be exerted in Afghanistan in the longer term through the presence of foreign advisors or military training teams in order to allow humanitarian aid to be delivered and civil reconstruction to take place, – then creating the conditions for peace and security will once again become almost impossible.

In his history of the First War in Afghanistan, the eminent Victorian historian Sir John Kaye wrote 'Throughout the entire period of British connection with Afghanistan, a strange moral blindness clouded the vision of our statesmen: they saw only the natural, the inevitable results of their own measures, and forgot that those measures were the dragons' teeth from which sprang up armed men.' If we are not to repeat the bloody mistakes of the past in Afghanistan, then we must learn about its history, and Patrick Macrory's excellent book *Kabul Catastrophe* is a highly useful and timely reminder of the circumstances that led to the terrible destruction of the British expeditionary force in Afghanistan in the winter of 1841/42.

H.M.R.   December 2001

PREFACE

Folly and cowardice marked the story of the First Afghan War, but there was great heroism too, and astonishing endurance. The life of the British in the India of the early nineteenth century may not have been nasty or brutish but it was certainly apt to be short. Parents at home in England learnt to endure the news that whole families had been wiped out. In a mere eighteen months, for example, between 1840 and 1842, death removed all three Conolly brothers from the scene, two of them violently; in the space of little over a year three Pottinger brothers perished, the eldest only just over thirty. A memorial tablet at Madras to George Broadfoot, killed at the battle of Ferozeshah in 1845, recorded that "He was the last of three brothers who died for their country in the battlefields of Asia"— all of them within four years.

The price was paid uncomplainingly. The courage with which it was paid and, perhaps, above all, the lonely "three o'clock in the morning" courage of such men as Alexander Burnes, Arthur Conolly and Eldred Pottinger, venturing alone into the barbaric and almost unknown wastes of Central Asia, deserves to be remembered.

As one of my sources, Major Broadfoot, says, "the transliteration of Indian names is a vexed and troublesome business". One has the choice, for example, of Kabul, Kaubul, Caubul, Cabul or the older, and pleasantly phonetic, Cabool. I have used the spelling of the period, except where today's version, e.g. Karachi, is so well known to the modern reader that the nineteenth-century spelling ("Currachee") would seem pedantic and almost unrecognisable. When contemporary documents are directly quoted I have left the spelling unaltered.

I must thank Professor Charles Wilson, Professor of Modern History at Cambridge, who was kind enough to read the manuscript in draft and to make a number of helpful suggestions. And I am grateful to Mr. W. J. Reader, whose alert browsing in second-hand bookshops produced not only Lieutenant Eyre's *Journal* but the *Punch* almanack referred to on page 276.

My cartographer, Mr. Sidney Blackhurst, seems to me to have carried out his task admirably.

A list of works consulted is given at the end of the book. But this may be the place to say that quotations, except where otherwise stated or the context makes the source apparent, are from Sir John Kaye's *History of the War in Afghanistan*.

CONTENTS

Maps

PROLOGUE

IT was the autumn of 1839, and General Sir John Keane was preparing to take his leave of Kabul. He had, you might think, every reason to be pleased with life and his achievements. He had successfully led the splendidly-styled "Army of the Indus" up from India into the heart of Afghanistan; his troops had trounced the Afghans wherever they had met them in the field; he had stormed the reputedly impregnable fortress of Ghuznee; he had entered Kabul in triumph.

True, this Irish general was not without his critics. One of the strictest was Major Henry Havelock, who had served on his staff throughout the expedition. In the opinion of the future hero of Lucknow the general's "open parade of private vices and affected coarseness of language and manner were only a cloak for darker features of his character"—whatever that might mean—"and the most malignant personal animosities". He would grant that Keane was a "man of tried courage and an apt clever officer" but added that he "hardly deserved the name of general".

Havelock, however, was well known to be a crank and a bible-thumping teetotaller, and it was not these strictures, even had he been aware of them, that now darkened Keane's thoughts. For by the touchstone of success he had done all that could reasonably be required of him. At a trifling cost in lives—though the financial bill was already causing grave head-shakings in Calcutta—he had led his expedition to a triumphal conclusion. He had brought out of exile the elderly Shah Soojah, the former King and representative of the original royal house of Afghanistan, and restored him to his throne in Kabul. And there Soojah now sat, sustained on the right hand and the left by British political and military advisers. Russia had been beaten to the draw; Afghanistan had passed under British tutelage at last.

Keane's part had now been played and he was to return to an honourable retirement at home, there to be raised to the peerage as Baron Keane of Cappoquin, in the County of Waterford, and of Ghuznee, in Afghanistan. And yet his thoughts were sombre. Havelock may have been right in thinking that he hardly deserved the name of general, but he had sufficient perception to grasp a

13

fact to which his colleagues left behind in Kabul remained obstinately blind. He had seen all too plainly that the British were about to give a striking demonstration of the impossibility of sitting on bayonets. And to young Lieutenant Durand,[1] who was to accompany him back to India, he observed:

"I cannot but congratulate you on quitting the country; for, mark my words, it will not be long before there is here some signal catastrophe!"

A mere two years saw Keane's prophecy amply fulfilled. Then, having looked on helplessly while the British Resident was butchered by the city mob, having stood by in idleness when the British Envoy was shot by the Afghan leader at a parley and his dismembered corpse hung up in triumph in the Kabul bazaar, the remnant of the Army of the Indus marched to its doom. Four thousand troops, twelve thousand followers, and a number of British wives and children who had been blithely brought into the hornets' nest, set out from Kabul in the depths of the Afghan winter, under a shameful capitulation and an illusory safe conduct. From the ramparts of a fort ninety miles nearer India and safety a British garrison was keeping anxious watch for the first signs of the retreating army. Seven days after the march had begun the watchers saw far up the Kabul road a solitary horseman, a man bruised and bleeding, who came slowly towards them astride a pony as weary as its rider. Officers rushed to bring him in and when they heard his story, orders were given that for three nights long a great light should be kept burning above the Kabul gate and that every half hour four buglers should sound the advance. But there were no other survivors[2] to see the guiding light; the friendly bugles were sounding only to the dead. For what had been witnessed was one of the great dramatic moments of history; it was indeed the remnants of an army; it was the 13th January, 1842, and Surgeon Brydon had come to Jalalabad.

The news of the disaster made a tremendous impact upon young Queen Victoria's England. The official despatches from India, having taken two months to reach home, were laid before the Queen within the hour by Lord Fitzgerald and Vesci, the President of the Board of Control, with his most humble duty and the comment that they unhappily confirmed "to an appalling

[1] Later Major-General Sir Henry Marion Durand, K.C.S.I.; d. 1871.

[2] Or so it was at first thought. Some days later a few Sepoys and camp followers straggled in. Brydon, however, was the only European who was not either killed or captured.

degree, the disastrous intelligence from Afghanistan". "Appalling" was indeed the word. For generations the British had been accustomed to hear from India a story of almost unbroken success, a story of campaigns against great odds and often hard-fought, but always won. Now the despised Asiatics had wiped out a British army almost literally to the last man. It was almost inconceivable, it was certainly unparalleled. Eight years later Kaye, the first historian of the war, was still aghast. "There is nothing more remarkable in the history of the world," he wrote, "than the awful completeness, the sublime unity of this Caubul tragedy." Nor were the British alone in seeing the significance of the defeat. The spark of the realisation that the hitherto invincible English could, after all, be beaten was to smoulder in secret in many an Indian breast for another fifteen years until, with the Great Bengal Mutiny, it burst into angry flames.

There were Englishmen ready to admit that the disaster was a fit punishment for a policy as inept as it had been immoral, as stupid as it had been unjust. Nor was this just the wisdom of hindsight for, even before General Keane's deceptive initial success, there were those in high places, the great Duke of Wellington among them, who had foretold that the policy could lead only to shame and disaster. A few years later Havelock's kinsman and biographer, John Clark Marshman, was to denounce the war as an expedition "which began in injustice and ended in the most signal disaster, and which stands forth in the history of British India as the most stupendous act of fatuity to be found on its pages . . . an expedition memorable in our Indian annals as having inflicted on us the most astounding disaster which had ever befallen our arms . . . a war in which every principle of equity and justice was sacrificed to considerations of policy, and that policy so fatally false that its success served only to augment our danger."

The more they thought about it, the more convinced were the British that the stars in their courses had deservedly fought against them. "In the pages of a heathen writer," wrote Kaye, "over such a story as this would be cast the shadow of a tremendous Nemesis. The Christian historian uses other words; but the same idea runs, like a great river, through his narrative: 'For the Lord God of recompense shall surely requite.' "

In Heaven's name, the British began to ask, what had they been doing in Afghanistan in the first place, to lay themselves open to so terrible a stroke of Divine retribution? To find the answer they had to go back forty years.

PART I

THE APPROACH MARCH

I

At the dawn of the nineteenth century Zemaun Shah reigned in Kabul over the Afghan Empire. Brief and bloodstained had been its history since his grandfather, Ahmed Shah, had welded it out of a host of petty city states, some of them the nominal vassals of the Great Mogul in Delhi, others owning a vague allegiance to the Shah of Persia. The boundaries of Ahmed's empire ranged far beyond those of modern Afghanistan. Scinde was his, and Baluchistan. Over Kashmir he had cast out his shoe, Peshawar was his washpot. Such was his glory that there was bestowed upon him the honorific title of *Durr-i-Dauran*—"Pearl of the Age"—and the Abdali tribe, of which he was the head, changed its name to Douranee.

In the days of its greatness the Douranee empire was bounded north and east by immense mountain ranges, to south and west by vast sandy deserts, a country for the most part of wild and forbidding aspect, of gloomy rock-strewn passes and lonely glens, inhabited in popular belief by ghouls and demons. The inhabitants were suited to the country, a nation of hardy vigorous mountain men. There were between four and five million of them, a mixture of races. About half were Pathans, the true Afghans. For the rest, there were Hazaras, Tartar by origin, Parsiwans of Arab descent and Kuzzilbashis, whose ancestors had been immigrant mercenaries from Persia. And there were those who claimed Greek or Macedonian blood, a legacy from the soldiers of Alexander the Great, who had passed that way in his invasion of India. Centuries later, to British eyes, "the European features, fair complexions and, sometimes, blue eyes and red beards of the people, especially of those from Kabul, were very striking".[1]

The Afghans themselves proudly believed themselves to be of Israelite origin and their own historians, as men stating an established fact, refer to them as *Ben-i-Israel*—the Children of

[1] Mackenzie. Sir Olaf Caroe (*The Pathans*), while doubting the legend of Macedonian blood, agrees that "there are young Pathan warriors . . . whose strong classical profile and eagle eye recall the features of Alexander himself".

Israel. The link was variously traced, by some to a legendary grandson of King Saul named Afghana, by others to the lost Ten Tribes, whom the Assyrians had deported from Palestine.[1] There were indeed a number of resemblances between Afghan customs and physical characteristics and those of the Jews, and certainly the Afghans displayed towards their foes a ferocity equal to anything to be found in the Old Testament. The enemy who fell into their hands need expect no mercy, and the prophet Samuel, hewing Agag in pieces before the Lord, would have saluted the skill of fellow-practitioners in the art of dismemberment if he had seen the Afghans and their womenfolk going delicately to work with their long knives upon the squirming bodies of their prisoners.[2]

Human life was not greatly valued. A British officer who assumed a suitably reverent expression when his Afghan guide pointed out a roadside grave at which the faithful were required to pray and make offerings, was somewhat surprised when his guide added casually, "That is the grave of my father-in-law. I killed him shortly after my marriage, as his head was full of wind"; in other words he had given himself airs intolerable to his son-in-law. The slaughter was sometimes on a larger scale. Colin Mackenzie was told of a chief who "some years ago invited some sixty of his kith and kin to dine with him, having previously laid bags of gunpowder under the apartment. During the meal, having gone out on some pretext, he blew them all up."[3]

The Afghans were Moslem by religion and on occasions could work themselves into paroxysms of enthusiasm for the Faith, when frightful feuds would break out between the rival sects of

---

[1] The most recent account of this theory is Sir Olaf Caroe's (*The Pathans*; Macmillan, 1958); he rejects it.

[2] Hence the advice that Rudyard Kipling later gave to *The Young British Soldier*:

> *When you're wounded and left on Afghanistan's plains,*
> *An' the women come out to cut up what remains,*
> *Jest roll to your rifle an' blow out your brains*
> *An' go to your Gawd like a soldier.*

[3] Killings of this kind could often be satisfied by the payment of blood money, but not always. Justice, patriarchal in administration, could be savage in execution. Mackenzie was present on an occasion when a woman, complaining bitterly to the King's son that her husband had been murdered by his second wife's lover, shrilly refused to be appeased by the payment of the appropriate fine. The assassin was therefore led forth, his hands tied behind his back and his breast bared. A large knife was handed to "the gentle widow", as Mackenzie sarcastically called her, and she instantly plunged it into the victim's heart.

Sunni and Shia. But in general they were lax in their observance of the rules laid down by the Prophet. There was, for example, plenty of locally produced wine, euphemistically referred to as "grape juice". It was purified in clay vats by the addition of a chalky marl, then boiled and poured into goatskins, and drunk in secret by the faithful. It was said to improve after two years' keeping and Mackenzie, when he presently sampled it at the house of the British Resident in Kabul, found that it tasted like "small Madeira".

The Afghans indeed wore their religion lightly. When young Lieutenant Rattray, commanding a troop of irregular Afghan horsemen, considerately stopped his march at the appropriate hour so that the men might turn to Mecca and pray, the troopers were amused. "You surely do not take us for clowns or pedlars," said one; "we are soldiers, and never pray." "Indeed," added another, "I have only prayed twice in my life; once a thief took advantage of it to steal my saddle, and the other time a favourite horse got loose and damaged himself, which has determined me never to do anything so foolish again."

This cynically humorous outlook appealed to the British, who found the Afghans cheerful and lively, despite the outward gravity of their long beards and sober dress. It was true, as the indignant Mackenzie recorded, that "they can sneak, lie, cheat and practise any other of the smaller virtues to attain an object", yet, as Kaye said, "side by side with other Asiatic nations, their truthfulness and honesty were conspicuous". The feudal chieftains were kind and considerate to their dependants who, in consequence, followed them with a loyal devotion in the interminable vendettas and warlike forays that racked the land. And through all their turbulence and feuds there shone one passion above all others, a love of independence and a violent hatred of outside interference. It was a characteristic that the British were presently to underrate, with consequences disastrous to themselves.

Afghanistan was not a wealthy country. The inhabitants made their living as soldiers, as farmers or as shepherds, despising the life of the tradesman. The business of getting and selling in the bazaars was left to despised Hindoos and other aliens, except when it was on a scale enough to warrant the attractions of the life of a wandering merchant. Trade was mainly with Persia and Russia, though occasionally a venturesome trader would make his way up from Bombay with a caravan of British goods, in particular with scarlet cloth which, manufactured in England, found a ready sale as uniforms for the royal bodyguard. Exports were few, but important. The shawls of Kashmir and the gaudy chintzes of Mooltan were highly regarded all over the civilised world. Dyestuffs (madder, indigo) and assafoetida sold well in Persia, and the dried fruits of the Afghan orchards were in demand in all neighbouring countries; for most of the year the flat roofs of the houses were spread with grapes, the small white Kishmish variety and the long red Munakers, as big as small plums, being dried off into raisins. And there was, too, a considerable through trade in horses, the animals being brought from Balkh and Turkestan for fattening in the Kabul region and then taken down to India for sale.

Alas, this agricultural and mercantile activity did not produce a revenue sufficient to support the empire or—what came to the same thing—to pay the army. The troops were there, had the money been available to pay them, for the Afghan was a natural soldier. He was a marksman, he knew by instinct how to make the best use of cover, he could flit from rock to rock of his mountain country as nimbly as a goat. Since the country had no navigable rivers and was too steep for wheeled traffic, most Afghans perforce became good horsemen, and when the army took the field, its strongest arm was the cavalry. In the time of Ahmed Shah the Douranee horsemen alone mustered some 6,000 strong, while the other western tribes and the Persian mercenaries about doubled that total. The troops were raised under a rough form of feudal levy, each Douranee being obliged, in theory at least, to contribute one cavalryman for each parcel of his land demanding the services of a single plough.

Under the military genius of Ahmed Shah the system worked well enough. He had founded his empire with the fortuitous wealth that he had gained as loot as a cavalry commander under Nadir Shah of Persia, last of the great Asiatic conquerors, and had replenished his treasury from time to time by incursions into India, in one of which he captured Delhi and put it to the sack. But in 1773 the Pearl of the Age died and was succeeded by his son Timur, degenerate bearer of a terrible name, and at once the Douranee Empire began to disintegrate. Timur managed to lose Scinde; Khorassan and Kashmir seethed in revolt; Balkh and other parts of Afghan Turkestan became virtually independent. Worst of all, Timur, when he died after a reign of twenty years, left behind him twenty-three sons, who now entered with ferocious zest upon a struggle for the succession.

The Royal Family of Ahmed Shah were Suddozyes, one of

the leading clans of the great Douranee tribe. Next to them in importance stood the Barukzyes, a close-knit Douranee family of whom the chief was one Poyndah Khan. A warrior-statesman of considerable ability, who had served Timur well, Poyndah now gave his support to Timur's fourth son, Zemaun, who with this backing was able to ascend the throne as Zemaun Shah, but with foolish ingratitude failed to reward Poyndah with the office of Vizir. The disappointed Barukzye plotted treason, was detected and put to death. A crop of dragon's teeth were to spring from his blood. For Poyndah had almost rivalled Timur in philo-progenitive prowess and had sired twenty-one sons. From this moment on, under the resolute leadership of the first-born, Futteh Khan, the family were implacably resolved to avenge their father's death upon the royal house of Suddozye.

First and most obvious target of their revenge was Zemaun Shah himself, and he had laid himself open to their thrust. Chronically hard up, and contemplating the usual remedy of Afghan monarchs, an invasion of Hindustan, he had led his army off towards Lahore. In so doing he not only exposed his back to a stab from Futteh Khan but drew upon himself the anxious and formidable frown of the British rulers in Calcutta, a thousand miles away.

2

British India was ruled by the Honourable East India Company, a commercial enterprise that after being reluctantly forced into political activity now found itself directly governing the three great Presidencies of Bengal, Bombay and Madras. Under the remote control of a Court of twenty-four directors sitting in London and annually elected by the shareholders, the Company levied taxes, collected revenue and administered justice. It had raised, equipped and trained a large and powerful army to enforce its will, an army mainly composed of Indian mercenaries officered by British, but containing some wholly European regiments and supplemented by the hiring from the Crown of British regiments on their tour of foreign service. Addiscombe, a country house near Croydon, had been converted into a military academy for the training of British cadets for the Company's army, while early in the nineteenth century a college was established at Haileybury for the education of its embryo civil servants. Promising young officers who showed a gift for Eastern languages were seconded to the Political Branch, the Company's diplomatic service, where

—at times with "an exaggerated estimate of their own ability and their own importance"[1]—they drafted minutes on foreign policy and negotiated treaties and alliances with independent potentates. And all this great engine of government had evolved not from grandiose ambitions for conquest and empire, but because it seemed the only way in which the Company could establish the conditions necessary for the achievement of its prime object, the earning of a commercial profit for its shareholders.

Towards the end of the eighteenth century the British Parliament had intervened to exert some measure of control over this peculiar dominion. It established a Board of Control in London over which a member of the Government presided, acting in effect as minister for East India Company affairs. The Board was given power "to superintend, direct and control all acts, operations and concerns which in anywise relate to the civil or military government or revenue of the British territorial possessions in the East Indies"[2] and could insist upon its orders being transmitted to India whether or not the Court of directors consented. In secret matters it dealt with an inner committee of three directors whose proceedings were unknown to their colleagues. A Governor-General was appointed for Bengal and given supervisory powers over the other two Presidencies. The appointment still lay in the Company's gift, but behind the scenes the wishes of the British cabinet played an increasing part. Political power in India, in short, was passing more and more from the hands of the Court of directors into those of the British Government of the day.

Yet so long and so slow was the line of communications between Calcutta and Whitehall that policy in India, both in its formulation and its execution, must inevitably rest mainly upon the character and talents of the man selected for the key post of Governor-General. Stepping into this appointment in 1797, that resplendent proconsul, Richard, Marquess of Wellesley, found that he had inherited from his predecessor the most alarming stories of a threatened Afghan invasion of India. The wisdom of hindsight would presently show that the fears aroused by the irresolute marchings and counter-marchings of Zemaun Shah upon the north-west frontier were largely unreal but for the British, who were too far away to perceive the basic weakness of Afghanistan, but who nevertheless retained vivid memories of the military exploits of Ahmed Shah forty years earlier, distance and ignorance exaggerated the danger. In truth, Zemaun himself was

[1] Fortescue.   [2] Pitt's India Act, 1784.

of a gentle and unwarlike character, and if indeed he planned invasion, it was largely because he knew of no other way to rescue his kingdom from bankruptcy. By now, however, he could not even raise the initial revenue that was a pre-requisite to a successful invasion. Men said, and rightly, that he could have put 200,000 men in the field if he had the money to pay them. But money was the one thing he did not have, and so his "Grand Army" could muster a mere twelve thousand men, most of them miserably equipped. His troops, exasperated at the mounting arrears of their pay, had the disconcerting habit of deserting at crucial moments, and although his artillery consisted of twelve brass field-guns and five hundred little zumboorucks, or camel guns, many of the camels lacked drivers and many of the zumboorucks would no longer fire. The cavalry, traditional strength of the Afghan army, had hardly five hundred good horses between them. And Zemaun himself was doomed. His own country was about to rise in revolt behind him and his short and troubled reign was soon to be brought to a tragic end.

The British, to whom none of this comforting intelligence was available, continued to be alarmed, and not without reason, for India was seething with excitement and, if the Afghan invader struck in earnest, he would find friends and allies within the gates. From Oude in the north to Mysore in the south invitations and large promises of aid both in money and men had gone to Zemaun Shah. Wellesley, describing the threatened invasion as "creating the liveliest sensation throughout India", reported that "every Mahomedan, even in the remotest region of the Deccan, waited with anxious expectation for the advance of the champion of Islam".

Behind the Afghan threat loomed another peril, vaguer and more remote, but potentially more formidable, the shadow of Napoleon. French agents were active in Persia and expected in Kabul and it was no secret that Napoleon was contemplating an offensive alliance between France, Persia and Afghanistan that would pave the way for a French invasion of India. There seemed at the time no limit to what the Corsican Ogre might dare and, having dared, achieve. Already he had brought a French Army as far as Syria and Egypt. Might he not strike still further to the east and, emulating Alexander the Great, plant the eagles of France upon the banks of the Sutlej?

Faced with this alarming thought, the British in Calcutta went into contortions of diplomatic activity. They wove elaborate networks of defensive alliances, playing off one ruler against

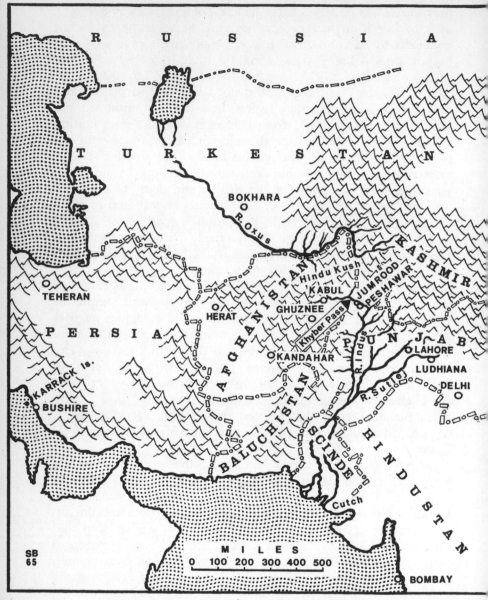

Central Asia at the time of the First Afghan War

another and cajoling others into playing the thankless role of buffer state. The nearest potential enemy to the north-west was Afghanistan, and therefore every effort must be made to enlist the support of the states that lay between that country and the British dominions. Scinde was an obvious choice. It was now independent, a state somewhat chaotically governed by a family oligarchy known as the Talpoor Amirs, but it had earlier been incorporated by Ahmed Shah into the Douranee Empire and, although the Afghan yoke had been thrown off in the reign of the degenerate Timur, the Amirs went in constant fear of an attempt by Kabul to reassert its suzerainty. An even more promising ally might be found in the Punjab, where a strange new race of men, the Sikhs, were in the process of establishing a military state. As warriors the Sikhs were no less formidable than the Afghans; the natural antipathy of plainsman for highlander was sharpened by the difference of religion; and the Sikhs were beginning to cast covetous eyes upon the Afghan cities of Peshawar and Lahore.

The second leg of the British plan varied as the point of danger veered from one quarter to another. When Afghanistan seemed the chief peril the counter was to seek the alliance of Persia, well placed to assault the Afghan rear. When a few years later it seemed as if the main threat lay in Persia itself, egged on by Russia, the adaptable British began to court the Afghans as a bulwark against Persia and the greater European power at her back.

First, however, a British alliance had been concluded with Persia, enshrined in a treaty whose flowery language gave no indication of the scenes of undignified farce that had led to its conclusion. "Praise be to God," it proclaimed, "the All-Perfect and All-Sufficient! These happy leaves are a nosegay plucked from the thornless garden of Concord and tied by the hands of the plenipotentiaries of the two great states in the form of a definitive treaty in which the articles of friendship and amity are blended." The plucking of this nosegay had, however, been preceded by an unedifying episode; indeed, thought Kaye, "no treaty before or since was ever interchanged under such extraordinary and unbecoming circumstances".

Sir Harford Jones, the British legate, was a brash and blustering man with odd notions of diplomatic behaviour. On his arrival at Teheran in 1808 as the accredited envoy of the Court of St. James, his temper, never equable, had been exasperated by the jealous hostility of the Calcutta Government, whose own representative, Colonel Malcolm, had followed him to the court of the Shah and was now spitefully reporting that he should despair "from his knowledge of Sir Harford's character and petty animosities . . . of maintaining unanimity on the Gulf one hour after his arrival".[1]

It was therefore in no very amiable frame of mind that Sir Harford, who had already insolently defied an order from the Governor-General to close his mission and retire from the scene, now found himself negotiating with the Persian prime minister, Meerza Shefee, an ancient statesman who believed that his age and rank gave him licence to speak with a freedom unusual in polite society. The bleary eye of this greybeard having lit on an article of the preliminary treaty which had been intentionally left vague (it was intended to be referred to the British government for final adjustment), he blurted out that the British envoy was trying to "cheat" him. The expression he actually used, says Kaye primly, "is gross and offensive, and the word I have employed but faintly expresses the force of the insult". To the astonishment and terror of the aged Persian the choleric Jones instantly jumped to his feet, bellowing that the Vizir was a stupid old blockhead to dare to use such words to the representative of the King of England; nothing but his respect for the Persian monarch, roared Sir Harford, restrained him from knocking out the old fool's brains against the wall; and "suiting the action to the word", as he later complacently reported, "I then pushed him with a slight degree of violence against the wall which was behind him, kicked over the candles on the floor, left the room in darkness, and rode home without any of the Persians daring to impede my passage."

The Persians, tolerantly supposing this extraordinary and uncouth envoy to be either drunk or mad, duly exchanged the preliminary agreement which, five years later, was to be confirmed by the nosegay plucked from the thornless garden of Concord. The Persians undertook not to allow any European army to enter Persia or proceed towards India and the British promised that, should any European nation invade Persia, the Governor-

[1] Malcolm, later to become famous as Sir John Malcolm, Governor of Bombay, had his own plan for bringing the Persians to their senses. He recommended the despatch of an expedition—under his own command—to seize the island of Karrack in the Persian Gulf and there "form an establishment". This, he pointed out, would be "a central position, equally well adapted to obstruct the designs of France against India as to assist the King of Persia . . . against his European enemies". Malcolm therefore blandly described this proposed attack on Persia as "entirely defensive, and intended even to be amicable".

General on request would support his allies with the necessary force, complete with officers, ammunition and warlike stores, or in lieu with a subsidy in cash. It was solemnly stipulated that this subsidy should be paid in as early instalments as possible since—and this must have raised covert smiles among the British —"it is the custom in Persia to pay the troops six months in advance".

As to the Afghan threat to India, it was provided that "should the Afghans be at war with the British nation, his Persian Majesty engages"—at the British expense—"to send an army against them in such manner and of such force as may be concerted with the English Government". But this, the original object of the British in seeking the Treaty, had been overtaken by events. The Afghans were no longer a serious threat. Civil war and bloody fraternal strife had torn them in pieces.

3

Zemaun Shah, marching his twelve thousand men irresolutely up and down the north-west frontier of Hindustan, had reached Peshawar when the news reached him that Afghanistan was in flames behind him. Futteh Khan, the Barukzye leader, burning to avenge his father, had leagued himself with Zemaun's elder brother, Mahmoud, who ruled in the far west over the principality of Herat. Mahmoud, unpleasant father of an unpleasant son, Prince Kamran, willingly raised the standard of rebellion and advanced eastwards, where his followers, though described to Malcolm as "men of low condition and mean extraction", succeeded in capturing Kandahar. When Zemaun hastened back to crush the revolt, his commander, to save the life of a brother captured by Futteh Khan, went over to the insurgents. The royal army disintegrated and the King fell into the hands of his brother. It was unnecessary to put him to death, for in a Mahomedan country there was no political distinction between a blind king and a dead one. As Zemaun was being hurried under guard to Kabul he was met by a brother of Futteh Khan and when he saw that the Barukzye was accompanied by a surgeon, he knew his fate and accepted it with dignified resignation. There and then, with delicate skill, the surgeon punctured his eyeballs with a lancet, he was cast into prison and *de facto* ceased to reign. Shah Mahmoud, propped by the strong arm of Futteh Khan the King-Maker, reigned in his stead.

In command at Peshawar at this time was a twenty-year-old

brother of Zemaun, Prince Soojah-ool-Moolk, who had been described as an appendage to Shah Zemaun—"his constant companion at all times".[1] His constancy did not fail at this dark hour. Since Zemaun, being blind, could never reign again, there was no disloyalty in Soojah's proclaiming himself king and, when he eventually fought his way to the throne, he cared for Zemaun with a solicitude that, whatever his other failings, was wholly admirable. "In a country where fraternal strife is the rule and not the exception," comments Kaye, "it is worthy of record that these two brothers were true to each other to the last."

At first, Soojah was repeatedly defeated by Mahmoud's troops under the leadership of Futteh Khan. But after two years, with the growing unpopularity of the detestable Mahmoud, the tide turned. There was a day-long battle outside Kabul, at the end of which Mahmoud was defeated. Futteh Khan fled; Soojah entered the capital in triumph; and Mahmoud, throwing himself at the conqueror's feet, was shown the mercy that he had denied to Zemaun. Soojah spared his eyes, and lived to regret it.

The historians' judgement on Soojah has been harsh. True, he was born under an unlucky star and all his life anything to which he turned his hand crumbled sooner or later, and usually sooner, into failure. He was often inept. "He wanted vigour," says Kaye; "he wanted activity; he wanted judgement; and above all, he wanted money." Yet he was to impress the British with his shrewd intelligence, his charm of manner and a considerable natural dignity. He showed a readiness to extend mercy to a defeated enemy, as in Mahmoud's case, which was to his credit as a man, however impolitic in an Afghan ruler. And through a long series of heartbreaking defeats and disappointments his pertinacity in clinging to, or seeking to regain, his throne was worthy of Robert the Bruce himself.

Effectively, his earlier reign lasted a mere six years, from 1803 to 1809, and it was racked by rebellion and civil strife of every kind. No sooner had he set out with his army to overawe Peshawar and Kashmir (amusing himself en route, as he recorded in his memoirs, by "enjoying the beautiful scenery and the diversion of hunting"), than rebellion broke out behind him, again instigated by Futteh Khan who, on this occasion was backing the claim of the King's nephew, a son of the blind Zemaun. Soojah was victorious, and again showed mercy to the vanquished. But in 1812 the ungrateful Mahmoud was up

[1] Zemaun and Soojah were whole brothers, born of the same mother. Mahmoud was their half-brother only.

28

in arms again, with the indefatigable Futteh behind him, and this time Soojah's cause was hopeless. He retreated to Peshawar, but the citadel was stormed by his enemies and he was carried off prisoner to Kashmir, where he was offered his freedom at the price of the great Koh-i-noor diamond.[1] To his honour he refused to surrender this magnificent heirloom of the Crown of Kabul, but it was soon to be wrested from him by a shrewder and more determined plunderer.

After a curious incident, when Mahmoud appears to have been moved to rescue his brother from his Kashmiri gaolers—though the real object may well have been to bring back the somewhat independent Kashmiris under the firm rule of Kabul—Soojah foolishly let himself be persuaded that he should now pay a visit to the greatest of all the Sikhs, Maharajah Runjeet Singh, the Lion of Lahore. He therefore set out with a Sikh escort for Lahore, where it soon became clear that what Runjeet really coveted was the Koh-i-noor.[2] Soojah temporised and Runjeet applied pressure. "We then," says Soojah gloomily, "experienced privations of the necessaries of life, and sentinels were placed over our dwelling." After a month of this sort of treatment, Soojah agreed to hand over the Koh-i-noor for 50,000 rupees and a treaty of friendship under which the Sikhs were to assist him with men and money to regain his throne. Runjeet Singh came in person to seal the compact and Soojah records that, like Rugby football players exchanging jerseys after a hard-fought game, "Runjeet Singh then proposed himself that we should exchange turbans, which is among the Sikhs a pledge of eternal friendship . . . we then gave him the Koh-i-noor."

Having got his hands on the great diamond, Runjeet Singh showed no great enthusiasm about fulfilling his side of the bargain. He started out with Soojah on a half-hearted expedition towards Peshawar, but then abandoned him to be further plundered by Sikh chiefs. In something like despair, Soojah returned to Lahore, where the Maharajah now proceeded to strip him

[1] The Koh-i-noor—"Mountain of Light"—came from the Golconda mines. It had been taken from the Mogul Emperor by Nadir Shah of Persia, when he sacked Delhi in 1739, and on Nadir's assassination fell into the hands of Ahmed Shah of Afghanistan. After the British annexation of the Punjab in 1849 it became one of the Crown jewels of England.

[2] The Sikh version, which may well be true, is that at the request of Soojah's senior wife, and in return for her promise of the Koh-i-noor, Runjeet's troops rescued Soojah from Kashmir and saved him from falling into the hands of Mahmoud and Futteh Khan. (Khushwant Singh: *Ranjit Singh, Maharajah of the Punjab*.)

of everything worth taking, and "even after this" says Soojah, "he did not perform one of his promises". Instead, Runjeet began to heap new indignities upon his captive, setting spies to watch his movements and sentries to guard his dwelling. After five months of this wretched existence Soojah began to remember the friendly overtures of the British government and to sigh for a peaceful refuge under the shelter of the great Feringhi power beyond the Sutlej. "We thought," he says, "of the proferred friendship of the British Government, and hoped for an asylum in Ludhiana."

But escape from the clutches of the Sikh Maharajah was not to be so easy. Soojah managed by bribery to smuggle the members of his seraglio safely away to Ludhiana, and "when we received accounts of their safe arrival, we gave sincere thanks to Almighty God!" Runjeet, outwitted to this extent, redoubled his precautions over the ex-King. "Seven ranges of guards;" says Soojah, "were put upon our person, and armed men with torches lighted our bed." In this critical hour he showed considerable resource. Seven rooms were tunnelled through until the outside of the building was reached; an attendant was persuaded to take the Shah's place in the royal bed (history does not record the fate of this brave fellow when the ruse was discovered nor yet what the armed men with torches were doing at the time) and Soojah escaped into the street and thence from Lahore by crawling through the main sewer, which ran beneath the city wall.

Having evaded Runjeet's iron grip in this adventurous fashion, Soojah managed to raise another army with which, "tired of an idle life, we laid plans for an attack on Kashmir". A two days' snowstorm brought this adventure to total disaster and at last he decided to give up the struggle and join his family at Ludhiana under the protection of the British Raj. He therefore made his lonely and perilous way along the snow-clad mountains of Tibet, insulted and ill-treated by hill tribes as he went, until to his joy the red houses of the British residents at an English hill-station came in sight. "Our cares and fatigues were now forgotten," he recorded, "and, giving thanks to Almighty God who, having freed us from the hands of our enemies and led us through the snows and over the trackless mountains, had now safely conducted us to the lands of friends, we passed a night for the first time with comfort and without dread." Friendly hands received him and escorted him onwards to Ludhiana, "where we found our family treated with marked respect, and enjoying every comfort after their perilous march from Lahore".

Soojah settled down to a well-earned rest. The British, for their part, were well content to provide the accommodation and the pension that sustained the ex-King, his blind brother Zemaun, and the members of the seraglio. It had occurred to them that some day, somehow, as a pawn for their diplomatic chequer-board, he might come in useful.

4

During the years while Soojah had been experiencing these adventures the British had patiently continued to weave their diplomatic tapestry. At about the time when Sir Harford Jones was kicking over the candles in Teheran as the best means of cementing Anglo-Persian friendship, Calcutta had sent out three other diplomatic missions, charged to bring the border states on what was then the north-west frontier of the British dominions into a grand alliance against the threatened French invasion. The first had been despatched to the Punjab, to negotiate with the wily Runjeet Singh. The second headed for Scinde and the third, on the hopeful assumption that Afghanistan itself might yet be won to the British side, was making its way slowly to Peshawar.

Scinde was duly brought into alliance under a vague agreement of general friendship and amity, the Talpoor Amirs promising that they would never allow "the tribe of the French" to settle in their country. Runjeet Singh was a harder nut to crack, but the British envoy to the court of Lahore,[1] though only twenty-three years old, was already a skilled and determined negotiator. Charles Metcalfe[2] played his cards well, the British strengthened his hand by quietly moving troops forward to the frontier between Runjeet's dominions and their own, and events on the world stage were working in their favour. The French threat to India vanished for ever as, far away in the Spanish peninsula, Wellington began to smash the armies of France, and the value of the Sikh alliance dwindled in proportion. Runjeet became noticeably more friendly and when he heard the British celebrating the news of Vimeiro with an artillery salute he ordered it to be repeated by all the guns in his own camp, "a circumstance which, whether

[1] Runjeet Singh had been confirmed in the possession of Lahore by Zemaun Shah in 1799. Thenceforth Lahore was a Sikh city.

[2] Charles Theophilus Metcalfe, 1785-1846 (later Lord Metcalfe) Acting Governor-General of India 1835-38. Governor of Jamaica 1839-42. Governor-General of Canada 1843.

it be attributed to politeness towards the British commanders with whom he was in treaty, or to a general condemnation of the system of Buonaparte, was felt equally agreeable". A treaty was duly signed at Amritsar, in 1809, which made no more mention of the French than if the threat of Napoleon had never existed. It was to endure until the outbreak of the first Sikh War in 1845, and it brought stability to the whole of the Punjab. For although the Lion of Lahore was always one to exploit a bargain to the uttermost and would presently show that he could outsmart the British when it came to getting one's allies to pull the chestnuts out of the fire, yet for thirty years, until his death in 1839, the Sikh ruler remained faithful to his new friends after his fashion.

Meanwhile the third British mission had been making its way to Peshawar, to the Court of Shah Soojah, who was now in the sixth year of his reign and about to experience the disasters and hair-breadth escapes that have just been recounted. It was led by Mountstuart Elphinstone, fourth son of the head of an ancient Scottish house, now in his thirtieth year. He had served in India since he was seventeen and before he died, aged eighty, would twice refuse the Governor-Generalship on health grounds.

His mission was received with marked civility in every Afghan town and village through which it passed, though the British soon found it necessary to grow beards and moustaches in order to win proper respect from their hairy-faced hosts. Great crowds thronged the streets of Peshawar to stare at them and the royal bodyguards lashed at the citizens with whips and officiously tilted their lances at spectators who were looking on with quiet gravity from the balconies of their own houses, before a way could be cleared to the royal guest house. Here the visitors, seated on rich carpets, were fed with sweetmeats and regaled with sherbet while Soojah, a true host though perpetually hard up, sent in provisions for two thousand men.

A few days later the British were ceremonially presented to the King, who "in a loud and sonorous voice" declared, "They are welcome."[1] Soojah received his guests seated upon a gilded throne, crowned, plumed and arrayed like a peacock. He was ablaze with jewellery and the great Koh-i-noor diamond glittered in a splendid bracelet on his arm.[2] Elphinstone, who found the

---

[1] Elphinstone (*Account of the Kingdom of Caubul*, 1815).

[2] Soojah's appearance was so dazzling that at first the British thought that he was wearing an armour of jewels. On closer inspection they found that he was wearing "a green tunic, with large flowers in gold, and precious stones, over which were a large breast-plate of diamonds, shaped like two fleur-de-lis,

King "a handsome man . . . his address princely", reported that it would scarcely be believed "how much he had of the manners of a gentleman, or how well he preserved his dignity, while he seemed only anxious to please". The Shah declared impressively that England and Kabul were designed by the Creator to be united by bonds of everlasting friendship and professed himself eager to hear the British proposals. These, however, had become strangely vague, for with the removal of the French threat instructions from the Governor-General had overtaken Elphinstone, urging him if possible to avoid contracting any firm commitment with Kabul.

Meanwhile Soojah had presented him and his officers with dresses of honour and, in return Elphinstone, not to be outdone in generosity, produced a mass of presents, "curious and costly". Soojah shouted with naïve delight and his face shone with pleasure as he took first pick, while his unmannerly courtiers, making no attempt to conceal their greed, scrambled eagerly for any gifts not appropriated by their royal master. The memory of these splendid presents lived on for a generation in Afghan minds, and thirty years later the failure of another British envoy to match them was to form one of many nails in the coffin of British hopes.[1]

A treaty was now concluded, decreeing eternal friendship between the two states and sonorously declaring that "the veil of separation shall be lifted up from between them, and they shall in no manner interfere in each other's countries". They also bound themselves to concert active measures to repel an imaginary Franco-Persian confederacy allegedly aimed against Kabul, the British "holding themselves liable to afford the expenses necessary for the above-mentioned service to the extent of their ability". But Soojah was no longer able to give his attention to foreign affairs and new treaties, for his country was unsettled and his throne was tottering. He was collecting an army, he told Elphinstone; he was projecting a great military expedition. He hoped to see more of the English gentlemen, he said, in more prosperous times; at present the best advice he could give them was to retire

---

large emerald bracelets on the arms (above the elbows), and many other jewels in different places". (Elphinstone.)

[1] The cost of the presents was to earn Elphinstone a thunderous rebuke from the Governor-General, who recorded "his deliberate opinion that the actual expenditure has far exceeded the necessity of the occasion . . . and that the provision of articles for presents to an extent so enormous as that exhibited in the accounts has been regulated by a principle of distribution unnecessarily profuse".

beyond the frontier. The British Mission took the hint and withdrew to Hindostan. Within a few months Shah Soojah had been driven from his throne, eventually, as we have seen, to find refuge beneath the flag of the British Raj at Ludhiana.

5

By the year of Waterloo, therefore, the British in India had advanced their rule to the borders of Runjeet Singh's Punjab empire; and they had signed up in treaties of friendship of varying degrees of warmth not only the Sikh Maharajah but the Amirs of Scinde, the Shah of Persia and the King of Afghanistan. But the Afghan King with whom they had made their alliance was now an exile under British protection, dreaming of the day when he would recover his royal inheritance, and it was doubtful to what extent the present ruler, Mahmoud, would regard himself as bound by the obligations entered into by his brother Soojah; but as the British themselves had been at pains to see that the obligations were of the vaguest possible nature, this did not greatly signify.

Over the next fifteen years two new factors emerged to complicate the situation. First, in place of the long-dreaded French menace, often imaginary and always exaggerated, there now appeared the very real threat of a Russian push to the south-eastwards; the "Great Game" of nineteenth-century Central Asia was about to begin in earnest. Secondly, the Afghan kaleidoscope was given another violent shake, and when it settled down into its new pattern the rule of the Suddozyes everywhere, except in the far west, had been replaced by that of the Barukzyes; and presently there emerged as the strongest of the Barukzye clan a ruler whose name was to become very familiar to the British over the years. Dost Mahomed, a younger brother of the great Futteh Khan, was brought to the top by a series of explosions set in train by the brutal murder of Futteh Khan himself. Nearly twenty years earlier the execution of his father, Poyndah Khan, had shaken the Suddozye dynasty to its foundations; his own assassination was now to bring it down in ruins.

Fate overtook Futteh Khan at a time when he had become the virtual ruler of Afghanistan, for Mahmoud, weak, indolent and debauched, had been content to leave the government in his hands. The Vizir accordingly took an independent decision to lead an army out to repel Persian encroachment upon the western borders of Afghanistan and, while he was about it, to bring

34

into Barukzye hands the city of Herat, where one of Mahmoud's brothers was the governor. This part of the plan was entrusted to his young brother, Dost Mahomed, and Dost Mahomed went too far. The Suddozyes might have turned a blind eye to his massacre of the palace guards, his seizure of the governor and his looting of the treasury. But he could not be forgiven for his violation of the harem, where he had the effrontery to tear a jewelled waistband from the body of a Suddozye princess. Prince Kamran, Mahmoud's son, swore vengeance, and kept his word. But the blow fell not on Dost Mahomed but on Futteh Khan.

The Vizir, returning from his Persian expedition, was seized by the Prince and, in traditional style, his eyes were put out with a sharp dagger. (Soojah, in his memoirs, says that Kamran added an original touch to the torture by first performing on his victim "an operation similar to the African mode of scalping".) But honour and vengeance were not yet satisfied, and Kamran and his father decided that the prisoner, the man above all to whom Mahmoud owed his throne, must die. A tent pitched outside the walls of Herat was appointed for the shambles and Futteh, blind and bleeding, was led into a circle of his mortal enemies. He was told to write to Dost Mahomed and his brothers, who had taken refuge in Kashmir, ordering them to surrender to the Shah. He steadfastly refused; he was but a poor blind captive, he said; his career was run and he had no longer any influence, nor could he consent to betray his brethren. The enraged Mahmoud turned down his royal thumb and the killers moved in. The mercy of a quick death was not, however, to be granted. After insults and abuse had been heaped upon the victim the ringleader, Atta Mahmoud Khan, stepped forward and hacked off his ear, specifying some injury once done him by Futteh Khan as justification for this mutilation. A second assassin sliced off his other ear, a third cut off his nose. Each in turn named the wrong for which he was now exacting vengeance, "thus depriving Futteh Khan of the highest consolation the mind of man can possess under torment—the conscience void of offence". His right hand was amputated and then his left, the blood gushing from the stumps. Futteh Khan bore these mutilations without cry or murmur, but when next his beard, symbol of honour and manhood, was derisively cut off, he burst into tears. Mercifully, his torments were now drawing to a close. After each foot had been hacked off with a sabre, Attah Mahmoud, who had begun the butchery, finished it by cutting the victim's throat.

So, cut to pieces in the prime of his age and the fullness of his power,[1] perished the great Vizir, the King-Maker, the head of the Barukzye clan. The vengeance of the Barukzye brethren was swift and sure. With Dost Mahomed ever in the lead, their troops took the field and captured Kabul—where they had the sweet satisfaction of putting out the eyes of Attah Mahmoud—and within a short time had captured the whole country, except for Herat. Here Mahmoud and, later, Kamran reigned precariously, last representatives in Afghanistan of the royal line of Ahmed Shah. There was still, of course, the indefatigable Soojah in retreat at Ludhiana, and Soojah, with his usual optimism, had more than once emerged from exile to see if he could glean any pickings from the struggle. His interventions, however, ended in the usual failure and he had returned to Ludhiana and his pension.

The Barukzyes now parcelled out the realm among themselves. Dost Mahomed reigned at Ghuznee, another brother at Kabul, a third at Peshawar, and a whole team of them ruled collectively over Kandahar under the generic title of "the Kandahar Sirdars". Before long the brothers were all fighting each other for a larger share of sovereignty until at last, in 1826, after the affairs of the Afghan empire had been thrown into frightful confusion, the shifting pattern of battle, murder, treachery, plot and counter-plot settled down to reveal that the strongest had come to the top and that Dost Mahomed was reigning in Kabul as Amir of Afghanistan. Those of his brothers who had survived the fraternal struggle now acknowledged his supremacy and held rank under him as Sirdars at the various key points of the country.

Dost Mahomed's youth had been wild and dissolute but power brought responsibility, and, like the young Henry the Fifth, he became a reformed character. He renounced wine, of which he had been inordinately fond; he learnt, belatedly, to read and write; he studied the Koran; and he made a public confession of past errors and a promise of reformation for the future. This promise was kept. His head was not turned by power and he remained simple in his way of life, affable of manner and accessible to all.[2] When he rode abroad the humblest citizen might stop him to lay before him any grievance or fancied injustice, in the sure know-

[1] The remains of Futteh Khan were collected in a sack and buried at Ghuznee.
[2] When he was first urged to assume the titles of royalty, he replied that as he was too poor to support his dignity as a Sirdar, it would be preposterous to think of converting himself into a king.

ledge that the Amir would listen patiently and give redress if he could. "Is Dost Mahomed dead," ran the rhetorical question, "that there is no justice?"

The two great dangers confronting him at the outset were the treachery of his brothers and the aggressive designs of the Sikhs, two threats which combined in 1834 to inflict a heavy blow. His brother, Sultan Mahomed Khan, the Sirdar of Peshawar, entered into treasonable plots with Runjeet Singh to destroy the Amir. A Sikh army, advancing to Peshawar ostensibly as the friends of its Sirdar, seized the city. Sultan Mahomed Khan ignominiously fled and Peshawar was lost to the Afghans for ever.

Dost Mahomed was not the man to submit tamely to the loss of one of the greatest of Afghan cities. Proclaiming himself Amir-al-Mominin—"Commander of the Faithful"—he declared a Holy War against the infidel Sikhs. Thousands streamed to his banner. From Turkestan they came, from Kohistan and the hills beyond, from the grim country of the Hindu-Kush, Ghilzyes, Kuzzilbashes and rugged Uzbegs, horse and foot, all who could lift a matchlock or wield a sword in the name of the Prophet. General Josiah Harlan, an American adventurer in the service of Runjeet Singh, vividly described the motley horde: "Savages from the remotest recesses of the mountainous districts, who were dignified with the profession of the Mahomedan faith, many of them giants in form and strength, promiscuously armed with sword and shield, bows and arrows, matchlocks, rifles, spears and blunderbusses, concentrated themselves around the standard of religion, and were prepared to slay, plunder and destroy, for the sake of God and the Prophet, the unenlightened infidels of the Punjab."

This Harlan (his rank of General was a Sikh one) was a dubious character who had arrived in India as supercargo on a merchant vessel. Having originally entered the Company's service on the medical establishment, he had transferred to the artillery and had served in Burma. But he had not earned a very good name in the Company's army and soon left to take employment under Runjeet Singh; his own rather unlikely boast is that he was engaged in making himself King of Afghanistan when he was taken prisoner by the Sikhs; whereupon Runjeet is supposed immediately to have recognised his talents and to have said to him: "I will make you Governor of Gujerat. If you behave well, I will increase your salary; if not, I'll cut off your nose."

Runjeet Singh, preferring to defeat Dost Mahomed's mighty

host by guile rather than force, wisely employed this clever and unscrupulous American as his instrument. Harlan, arriving as an envoy in the Afghan camp on the pretence of negotiating, found his task absurdly easy. He played on the jealousy of the Barukzye brothers, he exasperated their family feuds, he hinted at large bribes for the feudal lords. Sultan Mahomed Khan, the traitor of Peshawar, promptly betrayed his brother once more and at nightfall suddenly quitted the Amir's camp, taking with him 10,000 men. Dost Mahomed's camp was thrown into disarray by this large scale desertion and, in Harlan's words, broke up "without beat of drum or sound of bugle or the trumpet's blast, in the quiet stillness of midnight. At daybreak no vestige of the Afghan camp was seen, where six hours before 50,000 men and 10,000 horses, with all the host of attendants, were rife with the tumult of wild emotion."

Dost Mahomed withdrew to Kabul to meditate upon the Koran and inveigh against the emptiness of military fame. But almost at once he heard that his traitor brother was now plotting with Runjeet for the advance of a Sikh force through the Khyber Pass. To forestall this aggression the Amir despatched an army under his sons, Afzul Khan and Akbar Khan, who laid siege to Jumrood. A relieving Sikh army came up from Peshawar and after a fierce struggle was driven back, and Akbar, elated by victory, wished to press on to Peshawar. But his father had attached to him, as adviser, one of his ministers, Meerza Samad Khan, who during the battle had "secreted himself in some cave or sheltered recess where, in despair, he sobbed, beat his breast, tore his beard and knocked his head upon the ground". He now emerged, smugly announcing that his prayers had been accepted, and "entreating the boasting young man to be satisfied with what he had done". Akbar listened to the voice of caution and the Afghan army withdrew to its own country. The battle of Jumrood was long celebrated by the Afghans as a great victory, though in truth it had served only to confirm the Sikhs in their possession of Peshawar.

Dost Mahomed was in no mind to try another fall with the formidable Runjeet Singh, at any rate not without allies to assist him. He thought now of the Persians as possible allies, now of the British, but meanwhile the pace of events was quickening towards the climax. By the autumn of 1837 it was rumoured in Kabul that a British emissary was about to arrive at the capital and that a Persian army was advancing from the west towards the Afghan frontier. For once rumour was true. Before the first snows had fallen Captain Alexander Burnes was in Kabul and Mahomed Shah of Persia was laying siege to Herat. Both events stemmed from the same root cause, the implacable expansionist urge of mighty Russia.

6

For more than a hundred years Russia, steadily pursuing her dream of a great eastern empire, had been unrelenting in her aggression towards her eastern neighbours and by 1800, after a series of bloody wars, had managed to wrest Georgia from the Persians and incorporate it in the Empire of the Czar. The Persians continued to kick against the pricks until, in 1813, with Great Britain using her good offices, a treaty was signed under which Persia ceded to Russia all her acquisitions south of the Caucasus. An uneasy peace prevailed for thirteen years until, in 1826, the quarrel again flared into war. Russian misrule in Georgia had wantonly outraged the religious feelings of the Moslem inhabitants and now, with one voice, the Mullahs of Persia called upon their Shah to defend the faith. The Shah, thus threatened with the loss of all his hopes of paradise, was compelled reluctantly to order his armies into the field.

They were repeatedly and disastrously defeated, and after both Erivan and Tabriz had fallen to the Russians. Great Britain hastily came forward to mediate once more. The treaty of 1813 was replaced by a still more humiliating agreement under which, as that redoubtable old diplomat Sir Harford Jones commented, "Persia was delivered, bound hand and foot, to the Court of St. Petersburgh." The British had made no move to assist their Persian allies. Under that treaty whose foundations had been laid by Sir Harford himself twenty years earlier they had promised, in the event of war between Persia and any European state, to support the Shah with an army from India or an annual cash subsidy. They did neither, pleading a condition in the treaty that the war should have been in no way provoked by Persian aggression. There was little doubt that the real *casus belli* was the Russians' continued aggression, but technically it could be argued, and was so argued by the Russians, that the Persians had been the first to resort to arms. While the British were debating, the Russians acted, and the war was over before the British had made up their minds. *The Foreign Quarterly Review* was bitterly critical of the vacillations of the British Prime Minister, Canning. "Though Persia had fairly executed all her share of the treaty in question, the English minister, when called upon to fulfil this condition, hesitated, hung back, negotiated and delayed under every possible pretext, while he could not deny the faith or the claim of Persia. It was clear, however, to all the parties that Mr. Canning only sought a means of escaping the fulfilment of the stipulation."

British reluctance to fulfil obligations had thrown Persia, "bound hand and foot" as Sir Harford Jones had said, into the arms of the Russians, who now began to use her as a stalking-horse to cover their own further advance to the eastward. They hinted that in the east lay Persia's consolation prize for the territory lost to the Czar, and the Persians, smarting from their defeat and understandably exasperated by the inaction of their British allies, greedily swallowed the bait. The old Shah, who had always had a soft spot for the British, had been succeeded in 1834 by a young grandson whose ambition for military fame and conquest made him listen readily to the Russian suggestions. And so, with Russian encouragement being whispered in his eager ear and Russian military advisers at his elbow, Mahomed Shah of Persia began to lay plans for the conquest and annexation of Herat.

Herat lay in a plain so fertile that it was known as the "Granary of Central Asia" and by the conventions of contemporary strategy it was agreed to be the "Gate of India". There was much to support this view. All the great routes to India from the West converged upon Herat, and it was the start of the only road to the Indian frontier that was practicable for an army equipped with baggage and heavy artillery. As an assembly area it was a quartermaster's dream. It produced ample supplies of grain and fodder, and there were mines to furnish lead, iron and sulphur; the topsoil nearly everywhere was rich in saltpetre, while willows and poplars, from which the best charcoal could be made, grew in abundance. Given pay or the press-gang, there were plenty of tough yet docile soldiers available among its inhabitants from whom the troops of an invading army might find reinforcement.

The city of Herat, fortified by a moat and a solid outer wall, was a pleasant enough sight to the traveller who approached it across the great plain. Cornfields alternated with vineyards, orchards and gardens, and the landscape was patterned with sparkling brooks and streams. But it was only distance that lent enchantment, for on closer acquaintance the city itself turned out to be little better than a vast midden. The medieval streets were narrow, dirty and roofed across; they were indeed little better than dark tunnels, where every conceivable kind of filth was left to collect and rot. There being no drains, rainwater collected in stagnant ponds dug in different parts of the city. Household refuse was simply thrown into the streets and dead cats and dogs were to be seen lying on heaps of the vilest filth. One English visitor, expressing tactless surprise that people could endure to live in such dirt and stench, was cheerfully answered: "The climate is fine; and if dirt killed people, where would the Afghans be?"

The climate apart, the forty-five thousand inhabitants of Herat had little to be cheerful about. They groaned under the tyranny of Shah Kamran, son of that Mahmoud—now happily gathered to his fathers—who had supervised the torture and murder of Futteh Khan. It could reasonably be claimed that Kamran was even worse than Mahmoud—that he was indeed the worst of the whole rotten race of Suddozye princes. As a young man he had brutally enforced a promiscuous *droit de seigneur* and terrorized the citizens with the bands of murderous followers whom he led round the town after dark in the fashion of the London Mohawks of the seventeenth century. By now years of debauchery had turned him into a feeble old man before his time. His appearance was as nasty as his character. He was short and thick set, with misshapen limbs and a shambling gait, and a face pitted with smallpox. Yet he had a kind of courage and, when he chose, could assume the charm and dignity of which all Suddozyes were capable. And he was still something of a sportsman, as the Afghans understood sport; he was a crack shot with the matchlock; he could cleave a sheep in two with a single sabre cut, and with a Lahore bow send an arrow clean through a cow.

Kamran left most of the affairs of state in the hands of his Vizir, Yar Mahomed Khan. "Of all the unscrupulous miscreants, in central Asia," says Kaye, "Yar Mahomed was the most unscrupulous." He was a stout square-built man, of medium height, with a lowering countenance, thick negroid lips, bad straggling teeth and a receding forehead. He was avaricious, brutally cruel and utterly treacherous. Yet, like his master, he had some redeeming qualities. His unpleasant appearance was saved from utter repulsiveness by his fine eyes and comely beard. His conversation was civilised and affable, and he kept his temper under an iron control. Neither his courage nor his ability could be questioned. But, on balance, he was thoroughly

41

evil. "If there was an abler or a worse man in Central Asia," says Kaye grimly, "I have not yet heard his name."

This was the man to whom, early in 1836, Mahomed Shah of Persia addressed an ultimatum, demanding hostages and tribute. A legitimate pretext for the demand had been easily found, for Herat, under Kamran's rule, lived largely by slave-dealing and the supply of slaves had been frequently replenished by raids into Persia. Yar Mahomed returned a defiant answer. "You demand hostages," he wrote; "we gave no hostages during the reign of the late Shah, and we will give none now. You demand a present; we are ready to give as large a present as we can afford. If the Shah is not satisfied with this, and is determined to attack us, let him come. We will defend our city as long as we can; and if we are driven from it, it will of course remain in your hands till we can find means to take it back again from you."

Mahomed Shah took the winter to reflect upon this unmannerly reply, and meanwhile Kamran and Yar Mahomed conceived the ingenious thought of enlisting the help of the Persian Shah to recover Kabul and Kandahar from the Barukzye brothers. The King of Kings crushingly replied that he was claiming both cities for himself and, for good measure, intended to possess himself of Herat on the way. Then, so ran his plan, when he had reduced Dost Mahomed of Kabul to his proper station in life, that of vassal of the Persian Empire, he would be graciously pleased to join him in a religious war against the Sikhs.

The Shah, backed as he was by the Russians, expected Herat to be an easy prey. The forces of Kamran could hardly match the might of Persia and it was not to be supposed that the citizens of Herat would fight with any great enthusiasm for their brutal master. The neighbouring petty states, having all suffered from the slave-raiding habits of the Heratis, would no doubt gladly follow like jackals in the path of the Persian lion, and while the Barukzye rulers had little love for the Persians, they had less for Kamran. To Kamran and Yar Mahomed the outlook seemed grim and gloomy. Safety could be bought only by abject surrender to the Shah's demands, which were becoming increasingly imperious; Kamran was now told that he must give up his regal titles, that prayers in Herat would in future be said in the name of the Shah of Persia, and that coinage would be minted bearing the head of Mahomed Shah. Kamran, base as he was, could not bring himself to swallow pie so humble. Yar Mahomed returned a defiant answer on his behalf and the precious pair settled down to an anxious winter, looking now to the west for the first signs of a Persian advance, now to the east in the hope that somehow, somewhere, some help, some ally might be found. Not in their wildest dreams could they have guessed the form that the help would take or who that ally was to be, but already he was on his way. A young Ulster subaltern of the Bombay Horse Artillery, spending an adventurous local leave exploring Afghanistan in the disguise of a native horse-dealer, was making his solitary way up the road to Kabul and, beyond Kabul, to Herat.

7

The Shah of Persia, wrote Mr. Ellis to Lord Palmerston, "had very extended schemes of conquest in the direction of Afghanistan. . . . In common with all his subjects, he conceives that the right of sovereignty over Herat and Candahar is as complete now as in the reign of the Suffarean dynasty." Ellis had been sent by Palmerston to Teheran to offer official condolences to the Shah on his grandfather's death and at the same time "especially to warn the Persian Government against allowing themselves to be pushed on to make war against the Afghans". The Persians, however, far from being impressed by Palmerston's warning, informed Ellis that the rightful dominions of the Shah extended to Ghuznee, that an expedition against Herat would be undertaken in the following spring, that the capture of Kandahar would shortly follow; their royal master would then launch into new fields of military enterprise among the Baluchis and the Turkomans.

It was plain to Palmerston that the real threat was not Persia (there were always plenty of Englishmen in the mould of Sir Harford Jones who would kick over the Persian candles at any time, and that would be that), but Russia. Nor was it only in Central Asia that the growing power of the Czar was giving cause for anxiety. In 1828-29 Russia had defeated Turkey, annexed Turkish territory in Asia Minor and secured the practical independence of the Danubian principalities which were later to become Rumania. Before long, it seemed, the Russians would control the whole of the Near and Middle East. Warnings of a Russian threat to India now began to be heard in high places, and Palmerston moved into a diplomatic counter-offensive. The steady support of the Turks against Russian encroachment became, and remained for sixty years, a main plank in the platform of British foreign policy. But Palmerston's fertile and imaginative mind ranged further afield. The Russians, he observed, could alarm the British in India by moves in Persia; let the British in turn alarm the Russians by moves in Afghanistan. Let a pro-Russian ruler in Persia be balanced by a pro-British ruler in Afghanistan, a ruler who would not only keep Persia in her place but exercise influence on affairs beyond the Pamirs in Turkestan. It was a typically Palmerstonian concept, but it took for granted the willingness of the Afghans, most fiercely independent of nations—"the Spaniards of Asia" they had been called—to play their part as British pawns in the Great Game.

With the international scene so threatening and Palmerston in this frame of mind, much would depend upon the calibre of the man holding the office of Governor-General. Lord William Bentinck's term of office had ended in the spring of 1835 and Sir Charles Metcalfe was acting head of the government, pending the appointment of a permanent successor. Had Metcalfe been confirmed in office it is reasonably certain that there would have been no invasion of Afghanistan, no retreat from Kabul and no signal catastrophe. But his liberal outlook had been too much for the directors of the Company; his repeal of a long-standing rule requiring printers to obtain a licence before publishing a newspaper had so alarmed the Court of Governors that he forfeited his chance of a permanent appointment.

The post was now offered to his old colleague, Mountstuart Elphinstone, who declined on grounds of health. Wellington's short-lived Tory Government then appointed Lord Heytesbury to the office, and Heytesbury's friends were loud in their prophecies of a memorable and successful Governor-Generalship. But before Heytesbury could do more than acquire the large and expensive outfit necessary to uphold the gubernatorial dignity, the Tories were out and the Whigs were in. The new Government rudely cancelled Heytesbury's appointment and in his stead selected a safe and steady-going placeman, George Eden, 2nd Baron—and later 1st Earl—of Auckland.

Auckland was a bachelor, forty-nine years old, when he became Governor-General of India. His father had been a prominent politician at the turn of the century, holding office under Pitt and Addington and in Granville's ministry of "All the Talents". Through his mother, a sister of Lord Minto,[1] he already had a family connection with the supreme post in British India. He was, in the words of Kaye, "quiet and unobtrusive in his manners, of a somewhat cold and impassive temperament, and

[1] Governor-General, 1807–12.

44

altogether of a reserved and retiring nature". In the modern idiom, a bit of a Grey Man, a bit of a cold fish. A perceptive young British officer,[1] two years before Auckland's Afghan policy had collapsed in ruin, pronounced him "a good well-intentioned hard-working man, of shallow judgment" and condemned the premises of his decisions as "vague surmises, almost all—to my knowledge—unfounded". He was certainly well-meaning, he had no delusions of military grandeur, and he was undoubtedly sincere when, at the farewell banquet at which he was entertained by the Governors of the East India Company before sailing for India, he declared that he "looked with exultation to the new prospects opening out before him, affording him an opportunity of doing good to his fellow-creatures, of promoting education and knowledge, of improving the administration of justice in India, of extending the blessings of good government and happiness to millions of Indians". This worthy mediocrity was not the man to stand up against the ambitious designs of Lord Palmerston, backed as they were by the Governor-General's own immediate staff, who were soon to show themselves too clever by half.

Auckland had been specifically charged to look to Afghanistan, and the first news from that country was encouraging. He received from Dost Mahomed a letter of congratulation couched in friendly and flowery language. "The field of my hopes," wrote the Dost, "which had before been chilled by the cold blast of wintry times, has by the happy tidings of your Lordship's arrival become the envy of the garden of paradise." After this splendid over-statement Dost Mahomed went on to ask Lord Auckland's advice on the best means of dealing with "the conduct of the reckless and misguided Sikhs, and their breach of treaty". With true Oriental courtesy he concluded by expressing the hope that "your Lordship will consider me and my country as your own," little thinking that within three years Lord Auckland would have taken the compliment literally and given his country to Shah Soojah.

For the moment, however, Auckland contented himself with a friendly reply to the friendly overture. It was his wish, he said, that the Afghans "should be a flourishing and united nation". As for the Dost's hint that he might be given some British help against the Sikhs, Auckland sententiously reminded him: "My friend, you are aware that it is not the practice of the British Government to interfere with the affairs of other independent

[1] Mackenzie.

45

states," words which the Dost may have remembered with a wry smile three years later, when a British army marched on Kabul to depose him and put the despised Soojah in his place.

But in 1836 this still lay three years in the future, and meanwhile Auckland hinted in his letter to Dost Mahomed that he would probably soon "depute some gentleman" to discuss commercial topics at Kabul. This innocent-sounding proposal was Auckland's first step in the execution of a directive sent to him by the secret committee of the Company's directors, which had instructed him to "judge as to what steps it may be proper and desirable for you to take to watch more closely than has hitherto been attempted the progress of events in Afghanistan; and to counteract the progress of Russian influence in a quarter which, from its proximity to our Indian possessions, could not fail, if it were once established, to act injuriously on the system of our Indian alliances, and possibly to interfere even with the tranquillity of our own territory". The means of accomplishing the task were left to Auckland's discretion, "whether by dispatching a confidential agent to Dost Mahomed of Caubul merely to watch the progress of events, or to enter into relations with this chief, either of a political or merely, in the first instance, of a commercial character". The Governor-General was also told that he was free to adopt "any other measures that may appear to you desirable in order to counteract Russian advances in that quarter". But he was left in no doubt that once he was satisfied "that the time has arrived at which it would be right for you to interfere decidedly in the affairs of Afghanistan . . . such an interference would undoubtedly be requisite, either to prevent the extension of Persian dominion in that quarter or to raise a timely barrier against the impending encroachments of Russian influence".

Auckland decided that, in the first instance, it would suffice to send a confidential agent to Kabul to "enter into relations of a political or merely . . . of a commercial character." The young man whom he selected to head what was officially known as the "Commercial Mission" to Kabul (though, as Kaye remarks, commerce in the vocabulary of the East is only another name for conquest) was Captain Alexander Burnes of the Company's service. The appointment would bring Burnes a knighthood at the age of thirty-five, and a gruesome death three years later.

8

Alexander Burnes, the fourth son of the provost of Montrose, had served in India since the age of sixteen. He had won rapid promotion, largely because of the determination with which he mastered the native languages, Hindi, Persian, and presently Arabic. At eighteen he had become regimental adjutant and was gaily writing to his parents in Scotland: "Behold your son Alexander the most fortunate man on earth for his years! Behold him Lieutenant and Adjutant Burnes of the 21st Regiment, on an allowance of from five hundred to six hundred rupees a month." By 1828 he had transferred to the Political Branch as assistant to the Company's Resident in Cutch "and on the high road, though I say it myself, to office, emolument and honour". Two years later he was chosen by Lord Ellenborough, President of the Board of Control, to take a letter of compliments to Runjeet Singh with a batch of fine horses, a present from His Britannic Majesty to the Sikh Maharajah.

Burnes' career was turning out to be almost spectacularly successful, a reward for hard work and enthusiasm. "I like the country amazingly," he wrote to his parents, "and as yet am not at all desirous of a return to my own land." Not that he did not adore his family: "How dearly should I like to see little Charley or Cecilia trudging into my canvas abode but, ah! that is far beyond probability. However, I may yet see Charley in India, for he seems a boy made for it." Years later the old Provost of Montrose may have re-read that letter with mixed feelings when the news came that little Charley had been killed at his brother's side by the Kabul mob.

Burnes had been instructed, while escorting the horses to Lahore, to carry out some thinly-veiled espionage en route to the Punjab, a subterfuge which drew a trenchant minute from Sir Charles Metcalfe, then a member of the Governor-General's Council: "The scheme of surveying the Indus, under the pretence of sending a present to Runjeet Singh, seems to me highly objectionable. It is a trick, in my opinion, unworthy of our Government, which cannot fail when detected, as most probably it will be, to excite the jealousy and indignation of the powers on whom we play it." The Amirs of Scinde did indeed see through the trick from the outset, and went to great lengths to prevent Burnes from spying out the nakedness of their land. "They first drove us forcibly out of the country," he wrote; "on a second attempt they starved us out." But he got through eventually and the congratulations and the horses were safely delivered to Lahore, where he received something of an ovation.

Reporting in person to the Governor-General on his return, Burnes took the opportunity to ask Lord William Bentinck's sanction for an ambitious piece of exploration that had long been simmering in his mind, nothing less than a project to cross the Indus and the Hindu-Kush and then travel by way of Balkh, Bokhara and Samarkand to the Aral and Caspian Seas; he would then move southwards until he reached the Persian coast, whence he would return by sea to Bombay. The proposal came at a moment more timely than he had guessed. "The Home Government," he wrote to his sister, "have got frightened at the designs of Russia, and desired that some intelligent officer should be sent to acquire information in the countries bordering on the Oxus and the Caspian; and I, knowing nothing of all this, come forward and volunteer precisely for what they want. Lord Bentinck jumps at it, invites me to come and talk personally, and gives me comfort in a letter."

Thus encouraged, Burnes and his little party set out at the beginning of 1832, and by May they were in Kabul. They made no attempt to conceal their nationality but, perhaps to avoid attracting attention from covetous strangers, they travelled rough, without tent, chair, table or bed. They wore native dress and Burnes had his head shaved and his beard dyed black. "I now eat my meals with my hands, and greasy digits they are. . . . I frequently sleep under a tree, but if a villager will take compassion upon me I enter his house." The Afghans knew him as "Sekundur", the Persian version of his Christian name, "and a magnanimous name it is," he wrote, for it had been famous in those parts since the days of Alexander the Great.

With all the instincts of a good intelligence officer, Sekundur Burnes lost no chance of gathering useful information. With a slightly unpleasant air of superiority at the naïvete of the Afghans he described how "I tell them about steam-engines, armies, ships, medicine and all the wonder of Europe, and in return they enlighten me regarding the customs of their country, its history, state factions, trade, etc., I all the time appearing indifferent and conversing thereon *pour passer le temps*'." But he felt a genuine affection for the people, who "are kind-hearted and hospitable; they have no prejudices against a Christian, and none against our nation. When they ask me if I eat pork, I of course shudder and say it is only outcasts who commit such outrages. God forgive me! for I am very fond of bacon, and my mouth waters as I write the word. I wish I had some of it for breakfast, to which I am now about to sit down." In Kabul he was the guest of a brother of Dost Mahomed, the Newab Jubbur Khan, in whose house breakfast, though baconless, was no mean meal. It consisted of "pillaw (rice and meat), vegetables, stews and preserves, and finishes with fruit, of which there is yet abundance, though it is ten months old. Apples, pears, quinces and even *melons* are preserved, and as for the grapes they are delicious. They are kept in small boxes in cotton, and are preserved throughout the year." As Burnes commented, "they understand gastronomy pretty well".

Eventually Burnes said good-bye to Jubbur Khan—"I do not think that I ever took leave of an Asiatic with more regret than I left this worthy man"—and moved on from Kabul through the mighty Hindu Kush to Balkh and thence to Bokhara, where his party was received with kindness and hospitality very different from the treatment that would be given ten years later to two less fortunate British officers. "Sekundur," said the Vizir of Bokhara on Burnes' departure, "I have sent for you to ask if anyone has molested you in this city, or taken money from you in my name, and if you leave us contented." Burnes replied gratefully that his party had been treated in every way as honoured guests, that "their luggage had not even been opened nor their property taxed". And so, with every kind of safe-conduct that Bokhara could provide, the travellers passed on across the great Toorkoman desert to Merv and Meshed, and so to the shores of the Caspian; they then turned southwards to Teheran and thence to Bushire, where they took ship for Bombay.

What Burnes had to tell seemed to the Governor-General, Bentinck, so important in the light of the Russian threat that he at once sent him back to England to report in person to the authorities at home. On this, his first visit home since he had sailed for India as a boy of sixteen twelve years before, Burnes found himself the celebrity of the season. On his first evening in London he dined with the Court of Directors at the London Tavern, and from then on life became a whirl of excitement. "I have been inundated by visits," he wrote to his mother, "from authors, publishers, societies and what not. . . . All, all are kind to me. I am a perfect wild beast."

"Bokhara Burnes" was indeed the lion of the day. The great Whig lords sought him out and the Prime Minister, Lord Grey, talked to him at length and in confidence. To crown all, he was summoned to the Pavilion at Brighton to meet His Majesty,

William IV. Expecting to meet a jolly-looking laughing sailor-king, Burnes found instead an old man who looked grave, care-worn and tired. But William was at his most affable and garrulous best. "Really, sir," he told the young Lieutenant, "you are a wonderful man. . . . I had heard you were an able man, but now I know you are *most* able. I trust in God your life may be spared, that our Eastern Empire may benefit by the talents and abilities which you possess." Then, with owlish anxiety, perhaps having heard that Burnes was writing a book, he added, "You are in-trusted with fearful information: you must take care what you publish." Finally, Burnes was dismissed graciously with the remark that, "I think, sir, that your suggestions and those of Lord William Bentinck are most profound; you will tell Lord William, when you return to India, of my great gratification at having met so intelligent a person as yourself."

Mindful or not of the royal command to take care what he published, Burnes produced his book at speed and found that it caught the public fancy in a timely moment. Fear of Russian designs in Central Asia was fast gaining ground in England, and many felt sure that soon, somewhere in that waste land, Cossack and Sepoy must meet face to face. Burnes' account of his travels was therefore widely acclaimed; he was awarded the gold medal of the Geographical Society and elected, without a ballot, to membership of the Athenaeum.

After such exciting success it must have come as an anti-climax to find himself, in the spring of 1835, returning to his old subordinate post of assistant to the Resident at Cutch. But he had been marked out by higher authority for early advancement. During his leave he had met, at Lord Lansdowne's house, the man who had now unexpectedly become Governor-General, and Auckland had not forgotten him. Burnes presently received orders from the Supreme Government in Calcutta to hold himself ready to take charge of the "commercial mission" which it had been decided to send to Kabul. His terms of reference were to "work out the policy of opening the River Indus to commerce", but for the British in India it was a case of the flag following trade, and his real task was one of political negotiation. "I came," he wrote privately, "to look after commerce, to superintend surveys and examine passes of mountains, and likewise certainly *to see into affairs and judge what was to be done hereafter*; but the hereafter has already arrived."

9

The Amir Dost Mahomed, peering forth from his citadel at Kabul, could see nothing but storm-clouds building up on every side. To the east the implacable Sikhs were remorselessly amputating and devouring large segments of the once-great Dourance Empire, and were now in possession of Peshawar, one of the fairest and greatest of Afghan cities. The recent battle of Jumrood, despite the loud boastings of the Amir's son Akbar, had made it plain that they would not lightly be ejected. Westwards the outlook was hardly less grim. Mahomed Shah of Persia, with Russian support, was moving up against Herat, and although the Dost would shed no tears if the hated Suddozye Kamran came to an unpleasant end, Herat was nevertheless an Afghan city and it was abundantly clear that the Persians had no intention of halting there. Moreover, true to Afghan form, there was treason afoot within the gates. The Amir's brothers, the Kandahar Sirdars, were ripe for treachery as black as that of Sultan Mahomed, the traitor of Peshawar, and already were showing signs of selling out to Persia.

Dost Mahomed, in desperate need of a reliable and powerful ally, was more than ready to see the British in this role, with the result that Burnes, reaching Kabul in September, 1837, found himself greeted "with great pomp and splendour". Akbar Khan met him at the head of a fine body of cavalry and escorted him into the city, mounted on an elephant beside his own. Soon the British envoy was in private midnight conference with the Amir, and the commercial aspect of the mission was quickly abandoned. Indeed, the Amir took the lead in shedding the pretence. Burnes having dutifully said his piece about the navigation of the Indus and the benefits that this would bring to Afghanistan's trade, the Amir replied that his resources had been so crippled by his wars with the Sikhs that, in his efforts to raise revenue, he had been compelled to take measures injurious to commerce. To this obvious hint for help against Runjeet Singh, Burnes warily replied with some observations about the ability and strength of the Sikh leader. Dost Mahomed readily agreed that he was not strong enough to cope with so powerful an adversary. "Instead of renewing the conflict," he said, "it would be a source of real gratification if the British Government would counsel me how to act; none of our other neighbours can avail me; and in return I would pledge myself to further its commercial and political views." He was ready, he said, if the British could persuade

Runjeet to restore Peshawar, to hold the city as vassal to Lahore and pay the customary tribute of horses and rice. He could hardly have done more to show his willingness to follow the British line and this was perhaps the more remarkable in view of the disappointment and shock to his dignity that he had experienced at the start of the conversations when Burnes had presented the customary gifts. Memories of the lavish presents bestowed upon Soojah by Mountstuart Elphinstone nearly thirty years before were still green in Kabul, and the Amir's hopes ran high. But there was an economy campaign afoot in India, and Burnes, having been directed to "procure from Bombay such articles as would be required to be given in presents to the different chiefs", had been enjoined that "they ought not to be of a costly nature, but should be chosen particularly with a view to exhibit the superiority of British manufacture". As a result, the eagerly awaited gifts consisted of a pistol and a telescope for the Dost himself and a few trumpery pins, needles and toys for the inmates of the Zenana.

The Amir, though he thought that this niggardliness of the British Government boded no good, politely hid his disappointment and Burnes was soon convinced that he was sincere and that the right course was to make him the friend of Britain and maintain him on the throne of Kabul. But when it came to giving the Amir some reassurance against the Sikh power, the British envoy's hands were tied. Auckland and his advisers cannot be blamed for having determined that under no circumstances would they jettison the firm alliance of Runjeet Singh for the sake of the more problematical friendship of Dost Mahomed. This meant, however, that Burnes was compelled to content himself with vague and general assurances of goodwill and he turned more hopefully to deal with the Kandahar Sirdars, whose senior member had not only declared his willingness to accept alliance with Persia, but had decided to send his son with gifts to the Shah and the Russian Embassy.

Dost Mahomed had already protested. "Oh, my brother," he wrote, "if you do these things without my concurrence, what will the world say to it?" Burnes now weighed in and wrote the Kandahar Sirdars a stern letter, "such a Junius as I believe will astonish them". At the same time he was reporting to his own government ever more warmly of Dost Mahomed. "Russia has come forward with offers which are certainly substantial. Persia has been lavish in her promises, and Bokhara and other states have not been backward. Yet . . . the Chief of Caubul declares that he prefers the sympathy and friendly offices of the British to all these offers, however alluring they may seem, from Persia or from the Emperor—which certainly places his good sense in a light more prominent and, in my humble judgement, proves that by an earlier attention to these countries we might have escaped the whole of these intrigues, and held long since a stable influence in Caubul."

But his masters would still let him offer Dost Mahomed no more than vague assurances of sympathy and goodwill, and when the Amir offered publicly to demonstrate his wish to strengthen his relations with the British Government and to do all in his power to get his Kandahar brothers to adopt a wiser course, Burnes could only reply that, while he was delighted to hear such sentiments, he must distinctly state "that neither the Amir nor his brothers were to found hopes of receiving aid from the British Government". The fact was that the British alliance with Runjeet Singh had placed Burnes in a cleft stick. He was a bold, even a brash, diplomat, always ready to use any latitude given to him—"it is this latitude throughout life that has made me what I am, if I am anything," he wrote to a friend—but even he did not dare to hold out any hope to Dost Mahomed for the recovery of Peshawar. He thought, however, that he might safely use his own discretion to put a stop to the machinations of the Kandahar Sirdars. The "Junius" letter that he had already sent to the senior brother, Kohun Dil Khan, seemed to have worked, for Kohun Dil now declared that he had dismissed the Persian Ambassador, had changed his mind about sending his son to the Persian Court and was anxious above all things for the advice and assistance of the British Government and of his brother, Dost Mahomed.

There were already signs that Mahomed Shah of Persia, instead of rewarding Kohun Dil with Herat as promised, intended instead to rob him of Kandahar. Burnes saw in this the opportunity for a master-stroke, and on his own initiative wrote at once to Kohun Dil to assure him that, if the Persian threat materialised, he—Burnes—would go at once to Kandahar, accompanied by Dost Mahomed, and give every assistance to the Kandahar Sirdars in their resistance to Persian aggression, even to the extent of paying their troops. To a friend Burnes wrote—"The chiefs of Candahar had gone over to Persia. I have detached them and offered them British protection and *cash* if they would recede and if Persia attacked them. I have no authority to do so; but am I to stand by and see us ruined at Candahar?"

Before long Lord Auckland was to admit, with admirable candour, that Burnes had taken the best possible action under the circumstances, but the Envoy's immediate reward was a pompous rebuke, delivered from a great height by the Chief Secretary, William Macnaghten. "It is with great pain," he wrote, "that his Lordship must next proceed to advert to the subject of the promises which you have held out to the chiefs of Candahar. These promises were entirely unauthorised by any part of your instructions. They are most unnecessarily made in unqualified terms and they would, if supported, commit the Government upon the gravest questions of general policy. His Lordship is compelled, therefore, decidedly to disapprove them." The Chief Secretary went on to explain that, to save Burnes' face, he would not be openly disavowed but that he must feel himself bound in good faith to inform the Kandahar Sirdars that he had exceeded his instructions and held out hopes which he had now found could not be realised. "After what has been stated," ended Macnaghten's lecture, "his Lordship feels that he could not enlarge on his strict injunction that you in future conform punctually on all points to the orders issued for your guidance."

With this clumsy intervention the Kandahar brothers at once relapsed into negotiating an alliance with Persia, and entered into a formal treaty with the Shah under a Russian guarantee. So long as Burnes was forced to follow Macnaghten's line it could only be a question of time before Dost Mahomed followed his brothers' example. And prompt upon his cue a new actor now appeared upon the Kabul scene, ready to pick up for Russia what the British seemed so determined to reject.

Major Rawlinson,[1] an officer on the staff of the British Minister at Teheran, was bivouacking one night in the wild desert country about a hundred miles west of Herat. On his way with a message from his minister to the army with which Mahomed Shah was now moving towards Herat, he had missed the road in the dark and, when dawn broke, he found another party camping nearby. Some of them he saw with surprise, wore Cossack uniform. They were plainly anxious not to attract attention and soon made off, but Rawlinson, his curiosity aroused, followed, and overtook them breakfasting beside a stream. Their officer, a young slightly-built man of fair complexion, bright-eyed and

[1] Later to become famous as Sir Henry Rawlinson, 1810-95, the great Orientalist who deciphered the Behistun inscription and the cuneiform writings of Persia, Assyria and Babylonia.

lively-looking, rose and bowed politely in silence. Rawlinson addressed him in French, but he shook his head. The Englishman tried his own language and was answered in Russian. Rawlinson then switched to Persian and the stranger replied in halting Uzbeg-Turkish, of which the British officer knew just enough to carry on a simple conversation, but not enough to probe very deep. All that he could make out was that the other was an officer of the Russian army, carrying gifts from the Czar to Mahomed Shah. The two officers then smoked a silent friendly pipe together and Rawlinson rode on his way.

He reached the Persian camp ahead of the Russian and had an immediate audience of the Shah, to whom he mentioned this chance encounter in the desert. The reply made him prick up his ears. "Bringing presents to me?" exclaimed Mahomed Shah; "why, I have nothing to do with him! He is sent direct from the Czar to Dost Mahomed of Kabul, and I am merely asked to help him on his journey."

Two days later the young Cossack officer rode into the Persian camp and at once greeted Rawlinson in excellent French, with the smiling comment that "it would not do to be too familiar with strangers in the desert". Rawlinson, realising that this was the first evidence of direct communication between St. Petersburg and Kabul, immediately posted back the 750 miles to Teheran to report to his Minister that he had met a Russian emissary to Dost Mahomed and that his name was Captain Vickovich.

This attractive character, who makes but a fleeting appearance on the scene and whose brief life ended in tragedy, was a Lithuanian whose participation in a student demonstration on behalf of Polish independence had led to his being banished to Orenburgh, a military colony in the Urals, where he was employed in a sort of honourable exile. He soon distinguished himself by his intelligence and daring, taking part in several exploring expeditions and learning a number of native languages. His career was curiously parallel to that of Burnes, and he was for the Russians as obvious a choice to head their mission to Kabul as Burnes had been for the British.

Dost Mahomed's behaviour, when he heard of Vickovich's approach, was exemplary. He inquired of Burnes whether he was to receive the Russian at all, declaring that he did not want to have dealings with the agent of any other power so long as he had hope of any sympathy from the British. He offered to have Vickovich expelled from his realm, or detained on the road, or treated in any other way that Burnes might advise. Burnes suggested that he should receive the Russian, but could show his friendly feelings for the British by making a full disclosure to them of any proposals that Vickovich might make. To this the Amir "most readily assented".

"We are in a mess here," wrote Burnes to a friend; "the Emperor of Russia has sent an envoy to Caubul to offer Dost Mahomed Khan money to fight Runjeet Singh!!! I could not believe my eyes or ears; but Captain Vickovich arrived here with a blazing letter, three feet long, and sent immediately to pay his respects to me. I, of course, received him and asked him to dinner. This is not the best of it. The Amir came over to me sharp, and offered to do as I like, kick him out or anything; and since he was so friendly to us, said I, give us the letters the agent has brought; all of which he surrendered sharp; and I sent an express at once to my Lord A., telling him that after this I knew not what might happen, and it was now a neck-and-neck race between Russia and us."

It was a race which, at the outset, the British had every chance of winning. The personal relationship between Burnes and the Amir was a warm one and, wrote Vickovich, "all this has occasioned Dost Mahomed to conduct himself very coldly towards me; and then, as he daily converses with Burnes, from my arrival here to the 20th of February, I have been hardly two or three times in his presence". Burnes was doing his best for his Afghan friend. Reporting how Dost Mahomed had rejected the overtures of Persia, and now of Russia, he wrote that "the Amir of Caubul has sought no aid in his arguments from such offers, but declared that his interests are bound up in an alliance with the British Government, which he will never desert as long as there is a hope of securing one."

But all hopes of such an alliance foundered on the future of Peshawar. The furthest that Auckland would go was that this city should be handed back, not to Dost Mahomed but to his brother Sultan Mahomed, who was hand in glove with the Sikhs, who had already twice betrayed the Amir and who was now in treasonable negotiations with the ex-King, Shah Soojah, in his exile at Ludhiana. "As for the ex-King himself," said the Amir, "I fear him not; he has been too often worsted to make head, unless he has aid from the British Government, which I am now pretty certain he will never receive." But the thought of the traitor Sultan Mahomed ruling again at Peshawar was more than he could stomach and he argued, reasonably enough, that he might find "that in expressing my satisfaction at his restoration to Peshawar, I have been placing a snake in my bosom". Dost Mahomed preferred the Sikhs, who at least were open enemies.

The negotiations dragged on at Kabul through the first three months of 1838, with Dost Mahomed leaning over backwards to secure British friendship and studiously ignoring Captain Vickovich, and Burnes making the strongest representations to Calcutta on his behalf. But the "do-nothing" policy of Government, as Burnes later called it, put the British envoy in the position of one who asked for everything and promised nothing. Towards the end of March the Amir made a last despairing effort, imploring Auckland to "remedy the grievances of the Afghans and to give them a little encouragement and power". It was all useless. The Governor-General—and who could blame him?—was not going to risk antagonising Runjeet Singh. The resourceful Vickovich had already offered to visit the Sikh ruler to press the claims of Dost Mahomed, and cunning old Runjeet had taken care to let the British know of this overture, making them more anxious than ever to avoid giving him cause for umbrage by negotiations with the Amir of Kabul. Dost Mahomed was given a flat refusal and Alexander Burnes, with a heavy heart, took his leave of Kabul. "Thus closed a mission," recorded Masson, the British writer in Kabul, "one of the most extraordinary ever sent forth by a government, whether as to the singular manner in which it was conducted, or as to its results." Unable to resist a scorpion sting at Burnes, whose rapid advancement and abounding self-conceit precluded his receiving much sympathy in this setback, he added, "the government had furnished no instructions, apparently confiding in the discretion of a man who had none".

Vickovich now reaped his reward. Dost Mahomed, feeling that he now had no choice but to turn to the Czar, made much of the Russian envoy and paraded him in triumph through the streets of Kabul. Vickovich, less scrupulous than Burnes when it came to undertaking what he might not be able to fulfil, promised everything. There would be money galore for the Barukzye chiefs, there would be help from Persia and help from Russia. A treaty was made between the Shah of Persia and the Kandahar Sirdars, guaranteed by the Russian Ambassador, by which the Sirdars were promised Herat, so soon as it had been captured by the Persians. The shallow minds of the Kandahar brothers were filled with glee, but the Amir Dost Mahomed was already full of misgivings. His insistence on the Peshawar problem had lost him the friendship of the British and now he began to doubt whether the Russians could give him any solid help. The Baruk-zyes had been promised Herat, but the Persian army, though commanded in person by the Shah and directed by Russian military advisers, was already hopelessly bogged down before that city. For Shah Kamran's unlooked-for ally had arrived at last. The Persian artillery roared and thundered at the gates and the Persian storming-parties repeatedly charged the fortifications; but from within the walls a young subaltern of the East India Company's army was setting them at defiance.

10

Eldred Pottinger, whom Auckland was to dub "the Hero of Herat", came of an Ulster family whose tradition of service in India would continue unbroken through the generations down to the present day. Commissioned into the Bombay Horse Artillery in 1827, at the age of 16, he presently transferred to the Political Department and joined the staff of his uncle, Colonel Henry Pottinger,[1] that same Resident in Cutch to whom Alexander Burnes had been assistant. The Politicals were anxious to collect intelligence about Afghanistan and young Pottinger volunteered to undertake a solitary exploration of those parts. With his uncle's blessing, but with even less official backing than Burnes had enjoyed on his journey to Bokhara, without a single British companion, disguised first as a Cutch horse-dealer and later as a 'Syud' or holy man, he attached himself to a small party of Afghans returning to their own country and made his lonely way up through Kabul and on to Herat, where he arrived in August, 1837.

The city was buzzing with rumours of the approach of the Persian army and Pottinger, abandoning his disguise, was welcomed almost literally with open arms by the crafty Vizir, Yar Mahomed. The Vizir saw at once the benefit that might result from associating a British officer with the defence and cordially invited Pottinger to remain for the siege as his military adviser. In those days subalterns, with no swift line of communications from Regimental Headquarters to say them nay, were prepared to take great decisions on their own responsibility and Pottinger, knowing how seriously the British regarded the Russo-Persian threat to Herat, saw no reason to refuse.

[1] Sir Henry Pottinger, Bart., 1789-1856; first Governor of Hong-Kong, 1843, and subsequently Governor of the Cape of Good Hope and ultimately of Madras.

In the last week of November the Persian advance guard arrived and took up positions in the gardens and enclosures west of the city. The siege of Herat, which was to last until the following September, had begun. Already the inhabitants of the outlying villages had been brought into the city and crammed in somehow, five or six families to a house. They had brought with them all the grain and forage that they could carry and a scorched earth policy was applied to the rest, the crops being destroyed and the fruit trees cut down. They now awaited the worst that the Persian invader could do.

The Persians conducted the siege in a desultory fashion. They bombarded the city with all the arms at their disposal, including the discharge of rockets whose fiery flight overhead struck terror into the hearts of the besieged, but which were too inaccurate to do much damage. They fired their guns, but Pottinger, a trained artilleryman, noted that the shots often passed clean over the city to fall harmlessly in the countryside beyond and that the fire was so wild as to suggest that every gun was pointing in a different direction and every gunner firing at some individual mark of his own choice. In February the siege train was augmented by a huge sixty-eight pounder cannon, firing eight-inch shells and confidently expected to batter down the walls of Herat as if they had been glass, but with typical Persian incompetence the great gun was so badly mounted that after five or six rounds the carriage collapsed and the dreaded weapon became a useless hulk. The mortars, lobbing their shells down vertically upon the city, were more accurate, but Pottinger observed that "great numbers of these shells are carved out of slate-rock and their chamber contains little more than a bursting charge. Hence they are unable to do much execution"— though they did execution enough for those unlucky enough to be in the direct line of descent; one dropped on the house next to Pottinger's billet, where a baby was asleep; the terrified mother, flinging herself protectively over her child, was beheaded by the missile and the baby was suffocated by its mother's corpse.

The siege had its bloody moments, as when the defenders would return from their sallies with the bleeding heads of their enemies, to claim the reward that Yar Mahomed had offered for these gory trophies. "I never could speak of this barbarous, disgusting and inhuman conduct with any temper," wrote Pottinger indignantly, and recorded with obvious pleasure that on at least one occasion avarice led to the Vizir's being cheated. One hero having been rewarded with money and a cloak for turning in a pair of ears, another arrived half an hour later with a head. In the very act of paying over the reward the sharp-eyed Vizir noticed that the head lacked ears, and on closer inspection found that the missing ears were those for which he had a few minutes earlier paid blood money; what was more, it was not even the head of an enemy, but of a member of the garrison who had been killed in a sortie the previous night.

There were spectacular moments, as when the Herat cavalry rode forth to engage the enemy while the citizens applauded from the walls with excited cries of "Shabash! Shabash! Chi Roostum-any!" ("Bravo! Bravo! Conduct worthy of Rustum himself!") There were ludicrous moments, as when the garrison, alarmed by a strange noise which they thought must indicate that the besiegers were digging a particularly dangerous mine, spent some months in laborious countermining, only to discover at last that the mysterious hum was caused by nothing more formidable than "a poor woman who was in the habit of using a hand-mill to grind her wheat, in an excavation at the back of the mound". And there were truly barbarous moments, as when the Heratis sent off all their prisoners to be sold into slavery and the Persian Monarch retaliated by having the bellies of all his prisoners ripped up.

Despite Persian incompetence and lethargy, it was not long before the inhabitants of Herat were suffering great hardship and Pottinger noted that by January, 1838, "scarcely a shop had escaped destruction. The shutters, seats, shelves—nay, even the very beams and door-posts had been torn out for firewood." Business was almost at a standstill and food was running short. When, on the great feast day of Eyd-i-Ramzan, Shah Kamran made the customary distribution of sweetmeats among the Mullahs, it was noted as a sure sign of the times that these ancient holy men scrambled for the delicacies with a most unusual agility. As the year wore on, famine conditions prevailed. Houses were pulled down for fuel, horses were killed for food, the air was polluted by the stench of corpses, fever and scurvy were rife. Yet even more than famine, disease and the enemy mortars, the average citizen dreaded the myrmidons of Yar Mahomed, who swaggered round the city bullying, arresting and torturing the unhappy Heratis to make them disgorge their hoarded wealth so that the Vizir might meet the troops' clamorous demands for their pay. If the torture proved fatal the corpse, wrapped in a blanket, would be flung down on the threshold of the victim's house as a warning to others.

Both sides showed a flattering readiness to employ British officers as their envoys. Pottinger was sent under flag of truce with a message from Kamran to Mahomed Shah and was received by the Persian army with enthusiastic shouts of "Bravo! Bravo! Welcome! The English were always friends of the King of Kings." The Persians presently riposted by sending as their emissary a Major D'Arcy Todd, a Bengal Artillery officer who had for some years been on secondment to the Persian army. Todd aroused the unbounded admiration of the Afghans by entering the beleaguered city on horseback and wearing full regimentals, tight-fitting frock coat, glittering epaulettes, cocked hat—the lot. Despite this impressive finery he was no more successful than Pottinger in effecting a reconciliation. Pottinger continued to do his indefatigable best to keep up the spirits of the besieged; never, he urged the Vizir, must Kamran submit to be called the servant of Persia, nor on any account admit the interference of the Russians. But among the Heratis, who were understandably beginning to wonder if the game was worth the candle, a movement was gaining ground to send a deputation to the Russian Ambassador, who was in the Persian camp, to offer Herat to the Czar; if he would accept, it was argued, the Persians would not dare to continue the siege nor the British to interfere. This imaginative scheme failed to gain acceptance.

The crisis came on 24th June, when the Persians for once made a really determined effort to storm the city. After a heavy bombardment five storming columns advanced to the assault, and although four were repulsed, the fifth managed to breach the defences. The Afghan reserve was thrown in and a desperate hand-to-hand struggle began in the breach, with both sides fighting with the utmost determination and bravery. The fate of Herat was trembling in the balance when Pottinger, hurrying to the scene, met Yar Mahomed going on the same errand. The closer they came to the breach, the plainer were the signs of impending defeat. The garrison were beginning to skulk off by twos and threes, making their way to the rear under the skrimshanker's usual pretext of carrying away the wounded. To Pottinger's dismay the Vizir's morale wavered, he walked slower and slower and finally sat down on the ground. The young Ulsterman urged him on and finally got him to his feet again, and with sudden valiance, from his Plaza Toro point of vantage, Yar Mahomed now roared at the Afghans, in God's name, to stand and fight. Again, however, they wavered, and again the Vizir's heart failed him. He turned back, vaguely muttering something about going to get help, but Pottinger saw plainly that he was looking round for the place where he had previously sat down. In a fury of rage, the Ulsterman shouted insults at the Vizir and finally, grabbing his arm, began to drag him forward to the breach. Whereupon, suddenly and surprisingly, Yar Mahomed went berserk. Snatching up a large staff, he rushed like a madman upon the hindmost defenders and began to belabour them and drive them forward under a shower of blows. The Afghans, cooped up in a narrow space, were unable to avoid this assault from their rear. With bellows of pain and fright scores of them, taking the only way of escape from the Vizir's great cudgel, leapt wildly over the parapet. The momentum of their jump carried them on down the slope at full tilt upon the attackers, and the effect was magical. The Persians, in a panic at what they mistook for a desperate sortie, turned and fled. The crisis was over and at the eleventh hour Herat had been saved.

It had been a close run thing and Pottinger (who was later to express the view that besiegers and besieged were thoroughly afraid of each other, and that a single British regiment could have stormed the town with ease) might well have said, with Wellington, that, by God, it would not have been done if he had not been there. Never again would the Persians come so close to taking Herat, although the siege was to drag on for two or three more weary months and there would be times when the defence would be very close to collapse. The persistent bombardment, the grinding famine, and above all the brutal extortions of Yar Mahomed, had brought morale to the lowest ebb and Pottinger found many who "preferred . . . the ultimate prospect of the city being taken and sacked, to the raising of the siege and the prospect of Kamran's and Yar Mahomed's paternal government". He could only express his surprise that "not a man is to be found among them bold enough to terminate their miseries by the death of their oppressors".

Now, at long last, the British, thousands of miles away, were roused into taking counter-measures. Palmerston lodged with the Russian Government a strong protest against their meddlings in Afghanistan and Persia, and St. Petersburgh gave way. The unlucky Vickovich was promptly disowned. He had carried out his mission for Russia with skill and courage, but when, full of hope, he returned to the capital to report to the Foreign Minister, Count Nesselrode refused to see him. Instead, a flunkey was sent out to him with a crushing message to the effect that Nesselrode "knew no Captain Vickovich except an adventurer of that name who, it was reported, had been engaged lately in some unauthorised intrigues at Kabul and Kandahar". Vickovich realised that he was to be a sacrifice on the altar of appeasement. He went back to his hotel, wrote a few bitter and reproachful messages, burnt the rest of his papers and blew out his brains.

The Calcutta Government too had become active. Auckland mounted a small expeditionary force, detachments of the 15th, 23rd and 24th Regiments, with a battalion of Marines. The steamers *Semiramis* and *Hugh Lindsay*, with escorting warships, picked up the troops at Bombay at the beginning of June and sailed for the Gulf. A fortnight later they landed on Karrack, that strategically placed island which Sir John Malcolm had so coveted thirty years before. The Persian Governor, when he had got over his initial fright, obsequiously declared that the island and everything in it, including himself and the inhabitants, were at the disposal of the British.

This demonstration in force, insignificant in itself, had been made a few days before the great Persian assault on Herat, but the news took several weeks to reach the camp of the besiegers. By that time rumour had been at work and the British force had multiplied like Falstaff's men in buckram. A powerful British fleet, it was said, had sailed up the Gulf, had destroyed every port along the coast, had captured Bushire and had landed a mighty army which was now advancing remorselessly through the mainland, capturing town after town. M'Neill, the British ambassador at Teheran, saw his opportunity and at once ordered his military aide, Colonel Stoddart, to ride post-haste to Mahomed Shah's camp outside Herat with what amounted to an ultimatum. The King of Kings was to be plainly informed that the occupation of Herat or any other part of Afghanistan by the Persians would be considered a hostile act against England; he was to be reminded that a naval expedition was already in the Gulf and troops landed on Karrack; and he must be told that failure to withdraw at once from Herat would be to court immediate danger to Persia. "The fact is," commented Mahomed Shah chattily, when Stoddart paused for breath in the delivery of the message, "the fact is, if I don't leave Herat, there will be war, is not that it?" "It is war," replied Stoddart portentously; "all depends upon your Majesty's answer—God preserve your Majesty!" His Majesty took two days for reflection and then caved in completely. "We consent to the whole of the demands of the British Government," he told Stoddart; "we will not go to war. Were it not for the sake of their friendship, we should not return from before Herat. Had we known that our coming here might risk the loss of their friendship, we certainly would not have come at all."

Within two or three weeks of this remarkable volteface the Persian preparations for departure from Herat were unmistakable. The guns were withdrawn from their advanced positions and limbered up; the baggage-cattle were collected for the march; the tents were struck and packed. On the morning of 9th September the Shah mounted his charger and set his face towards Teheran. The memorable siege of Herat, which had lasted all but ten months, was over.

And what had they all got out of it? For Mahomed Shah and the Persians it had been a mortifying failure and a lamentable exposure of their weakness. It was, however, a weakness in their high command rather than in the fighting qualities of their troops, and Pottinger in his official report gave it as his opinion that the Shah might have carried the city by assault on the very first day that he arrived at Herat or within twenty-four hours, at any time thereafter, by a proper use of the means at his disposal. "His troops were infinitely better soldiers, and quite as brave men, as the Afghans. The non-success of their efforts was the fault of their generals." The Shah, however, did his best to patch up the rents in his tattered reputation by issuing a magnificently face-saving proclamation in which he declared that he had raised the siege because the winter was approaching and "if we protracted to a longer period our stay at Herat, there appeared a possibility that our victorious army might suffer from a scarcity of provisions; the tranquillity of our provinces was also a matter of serious attention to our benevolent thoughts; and thus, in sole consideration of the interest of our faith and country, and from a due regard to the welfare of our troops and subjects, we set in motion our world-subduing army and prepared to return to our capital." No doubt there were a few ingenuous souls who believed this orotund nonsense.

The garrison of Herat, on the other hand, was entitled to a measure of credit for the successful outcome of the siege. Their courage and perseverance may have been patchy, and more than once had only been screwed to the sticking point by the determination of Eldred Pottinger, but there had been times when even Pottinger's bold spirit could not have saved the city without a reasonably heroic response from the defenders. Yar Mahomed too had done great things, and is entitled to praise for his energetic conduct of the defence, however unscrupulous the means he employed to sustain it. For the civilian inhabitants of Herat it had been almost unmitigated disaster; they had suffered famine, pestilence and enemy attack, they had been brutally ill-used by their own Vizir, and at the end of it all they were still under the detestable rule of Kamran and Yar Mahomed.

For the Russians it was not so serious a set-back as might appear at first sight, for their bet had been cleverly hedged and, win or lose so far as Herat was concerned, they might look for some advantage. "If Herat fell," wrote the *Calcutta Review*, "then Candahar and Caubul would certainly have made their submission. Russian influence would thus have been brought to the threshold of India; and England, however much she might desire peace, could not avoid more serious dangers. If, on the other hand, England interfered to save Herat, she was compromised—not with the mere Court of Mahomed Shah, but with Persia as a nation. Russia had contrived to bring all Persia to Herat, and to identify all Persia with the success or failure of the campaign."

The British had been given a great fright. But thanks partly to the ineptitude of the Persian generals, partly to the determination of Yar Mahomed and the Herat garrison, partly to the despatch, albeit belated, of their expedition to Karrack, and above all to the efforts of Eldred Pottinger, things could hardly have turned out better. The Russian-backed threat to Afghanistan had melted like the snow in summer. Now was the time for the British to let well alone. But the raising of the siege of Herat, though it had removed the last justification for the desperate policy on which they were just embarked, did not deter them from carrying it into execution. For the Government of India had taken a momentous decision. It had decided that the Amir Dost Mahomed of Kabul was no longer to be trusted. He was to be put down from his place, and in his stead the British proposed to put the pensioner of Ludhiana, the now elderly and ever luckless Shah Soojah.

PART II

THE TRIUMPH

I

"WHAT?" Lord William Bentinck was to exclaim when he heard that his successor had launched an army against Afghanistan; "Lord Auckland and Macnaghten gone to war? The very last men in the world I should have expected of such folly!" He expressed himself as mystified that such a course could have been adopted.

It had all stemmed from that directive with which the harassed Governor-General had been saddled by the secret committee of the Court of directors. While leaving it to him to decide the moment "at which it would be right for you to interfere decidedly in the affairs of Afghanistan", this directive had made it abundantly clear that "such an interference would doubtless be requisite, either to prevent the extension of Persian dominion in that quarter or to raise a timely barrier against the impending encroachments of Russian influence". With Mahomed Shah's Russian-backed attack on Herat both contingencies had come to pass simultaneously, and Auckland must now do something about it.

The Governor-General may well have been bewildered by the multiplicity of counsels that he received. M'Neill, over in Teheran, was strongly supporting Burnes' recommendation to back Dost Mahomed. Persia, he wrote, must no longer be permitted "to open the way to India for another and far more formidable power", and the Amir of Kabul was in his view the man to keep the way closed. "Dost Mahomed Khan, with a little aid from us, could be put in possession of Candahar and Herat. I anxiously hope that aid will not be withheld. A loan of money would possibly enable him to do this and would give us a great hold upon him." The Amir, he added, must be made to agree to transact all his business with foreign powers through the British agent in Kabul.

Claude Wade, however, the Governor-General's agent on the north-west frontier, was urging a policy of divide and rule. To unite Afghanistan under Dost Mahomed would be, said Wade, "to play into the hands of our rivals and to deprive ourselves, as it were by a *felo-de-se*, of the powerful means which we have in

66

reserve of controlling the present rulers of Afghanistan". In any case, to try to persuade the jealous and eternally squabbling Barukzye brothers to accept the dominion of Dost Mahomed was to "attempt to impose upon them a yoke of a ruler to whose authority they can never be expected to yield a passive obedience". True enough, maybe, but Wade's own solution was no less open to the charge of over-optimism. He was all for the *status quo*; "our policy ought not to be to destroy, but to use our endeavour to preserve and strengthen the different governments of Afghanistan as they at present stand; to promote among themselves a social compact and to conduce by our influence to the establishment of that peace with their neighbours which we are now endeavouring to produce between them and the Sikhs on one side, and the Sikhs and the Sindians on the other".

Auckland clung fast to one basic principle; on no account would he jeopardise the British alliance with Runjeet Singh and the well-trained Sikh army. This consideration in itself was enough to bring him down against the course that was being urged by Burnes and M'Neill. In May, 1838, when the fall of Herat was daily expected, the Governor-General put his thoughts on paper. There were, as he saw it, three possible courses. The first was "to confine our defensive measures to the line of the Indus, and to leave Afghanistan to its fate". In the event this might well have been the soundest policy but at the time it seemed to Auckland that it "would be absolute defeat, and would leave a free opening to Russian and Persian intrigue upon our frontiers". This brought him to Wade's solution, "to attempt to save Afghanistan by granting succour to the existing chiefships of Caubul and Candahar". This, however, "would be only to give power to those who felt greater animosity against the Sikhs than they did against the Persians, and who would probably use against the former the means placed at their disposal." And so, by an enormous and illogical jump in the reasoning, he arrived at the third possibility, "to permit or to encourage the advance of Runjeet Singh's armies upon Caubul, under counsel and restriction, and as subsidiary to his advance to organise an expedition headed by Shah Soojah". It was to this course that the Governor-General gave his vote, on the grounds that it was one "which in the event of the successful resistance of Herat would appear to be most expedient, and would if that state were to fall into the hands of the Persians have yet more to recommend it".

It was an extraordinary proposal. The Afghans were to be persuaded to become a bulwark against Persia and Russia by arranging for them to be conquered by their hated enemies, the Sikhs, it being optimistically supposed that they would be reconciled to this fate by the appearance in their midst of their former king, whom most of them despised as a failure and whom all of them believed to have been born under an unlucky star. Auckland's plan so complacently ignored, or brushed aside, these formidable difficulties, and was so divorced from the realities of the situation, that one feels it could only have been dreamed up by someone "inexperienced in men and ignorant of the country and people of Afghanistan . . . neither practised in the field of Asiatic intrigue nor a man of action". Just such a one, so Durand tells us, was the man whose strenuous advocacy of the Soojah plan weighed so heavily with Auckland—the Chief Secretary of the Calcutta Government, William Hay Macnaghten.

Macnaghten, whom we have already briefly met rebuking Burnes for going beyond his instructions, came from yet another of those Ulster families who, like the Lawrences and the Pottingers, were to send their sons to the India of the early nineteenth century. His father had been a judge of the supreme courts of Madras and Calcutta, and he had himself entered the Company's army as a cadet in 1809, when he was sixteen years old. He had brilliant linguistic gifts and at the age of twenty-three transferred to the Political branch where, with his great industry and a penchant for writing copious but well-turned memoranda, he rose steadily from desk to desk. Auckland was greatly impressed by the experienced bureaucrat whom he found waiting to serve him when he arrived in India. At the age of forty-five Macnaghten, bespectacled, sharp-nosed and heavily moustached, seemed a true elder statesman—"*our* Lord Palmerston" said Auckland's sister, Emily Eden. What then could have led this cautious diplomat to advise a course so reckless that many of his contemporaries prophesied at once that it must end in disaster? Perhaps the urge to prove himself as a man of decisive action, something more than a chair-borne warrior, played its part. Almost certainly he had his eye on the rewards that might come his way if this daring attempt to reduce Afghanistan to a British protectorate should prove successful. "His ambition was great," wrote Durand, "and the expedition, holding out the promise of distinction and honours, had met with his strenuous advocacy." In pursuit of his goal he was ready to shut his eyes in purblind optimism to any difficulty or danger, and to dismiss as "croakers" any who counselled caution.

Yet in justice to his memory it must be recognised that those young officers who worked closely with him regarded him with respect and affection, almost with love. Colin Mackenzie was "convinced of his worth, both as a public servant and a private gentleman", and his personal assistant, George Lawrence, brother of the more famous Henry and John, would write of him many years later as "the man I loved and revered as a father" and describe his "beloved and ever-to-be lamented chief" as one who was "above all, an upright, high-minded, chivalrous gentleman, a fitting representative of the British Government from his brilliant talents, entire devotion to the honour and interests of his country and his undaunted personal courage". It should be remembered, too, that when he was overwhelmed by the tempest in Kabul, to whose approach he had so obstinately shut his eyes, he would so conduct himself as to win from Kaye the tribute that "there was but one civilian at Caubul; and he was the truest soldier in the camp".

Meanwhile, as he urged upon Auckland a course of action that would bring Macnaghten himself to a hideous death at the age of forty-eight, he received every encouragement from his lieutenants, Henry Torrens, the Assistant-Secretary, and John Colvin, the Governor-General's private secretary. Their imaginations had been fired by the grandeur of the project of a great army's advancing into Afghanistan to forestall Russian penetration and establish British influence in that No-Man's-Land, and when presently Alexander Burnes came in to report in person the two young officers "came running to me and prayed me to say nothing to unsettle his Lordship; they had had all the trouble in the world to get him into the business, and even now he would be glad of any pretext to retire from it". All three, Macnaghten, Torrens and Colvin, had taken full advantage of the opportunity to influence Auckland at a time when, unluckily, he was insulated from the advice of the members of his Council in Calcutta, being on his way to the hill-station of Simla, bitterly described by Kaye as "that pleasant hill Sanitarium where our Governor-Generals, surrounded by irresponsible advisers, settle the destinies of empires without the aid of their legitimate fellow-counsellors, and which has been the cradle of more political insanity than any place within the limits of Hindustan".

Macnaghten's plan originally contemplated that the brunt of any necessary fighting would be borne by Runjeet Singh's Sikh army and such levies as Soojah himself might be able to raise. The British would supply officers for the Shah's troops but would otherwise remain in the background, limiting their contribution to advice and money. "Shah Soojah-ool-Moolk and Maharajah Runjeet Singh," wrote Auckland, "would probably act readily upon such a plan." Macnaghten was accordingly despatched to the Sikh Maharajah's court to verify this assumption.

Runjeet Singh was now fifty-eight years old, and within a year of the end of his remarkable life. He had won his first victory in the field at the age of ten; he was barely thirteen when, treacherously attacked by a jealous Khan, he had impaled the assailant on his lance, cut off his head, and ridden back in triumph with the gory trophy fixed to his spear-point. He was still only twenty-one when, after a series of brilliant campaigns, he brought unity to the country of the Five Rivers and was crowned Maharajah of the Punjab.

He had lived hard and played hard. Though never averse to using cunning rather than brute force, he was himself quite fearless, and had often led his troops into battle in person, sword in hand. He loved beautiful women, fine horses and strong drink. He was small of stature and an attack of smallpox in childhood had deprived him of the sight of his left eye. Now, though still under sixty, he seemed to Havelock "an old man in an advanced state of decrepitude, clothed in faded crimson, his head wrapped up in folds of cloth of the same colour". Emily Eden thought him "exactly like an old mouse with grey whiskers and one eye". But, as Havelock would soon observe, that single eye was "still lighted up with the fire of enterprise", and when Macnaghten arrived at the Sikh court he was subjected to a quickfire cross-examination by the insatiably curious Runjeet. "The Maharajah," Macnaghten reported, "passed from war to wine, and from learning to hunting, with breathless rapidity. He was particularly anxious to know how much each member of the Mission had drunk of some ardent liquor he had sent them the night before." This was presumably the same spirit as that which Emily Eden described as "a sort of liquid fire . . . and in general Europeans cannot swallow more than a drop of it". Runjeet, indeed, showed an engaging curiosity about the drinking habits and capacity of the English and another member of the Mission faced a barrage of questions on the subject. "Do you drink wine? How much? Did you taste the wine which I sent you yesterday? How much of it did you drink? Does Lord Auckland drink wine? How many glasses? Does he drink it in the morning?"

Mixed up in all this chatter about drink were shrewd questions about the strength and discipline of the Company's army, their artillery and its ammunition, the distance at which shrapnel could do execution and so on. When he could, he checked the answers. Macnaghten, for example, having claimed to know Arabic and Sanskrit, was instantly ordered to prove it by reciting a couplet in the former language. Runjeet then began to approach the heart of the matter by asking about Dost Mahomed, Herat, the Persian army and its connection with the Russians, and the possibility of their invading India. Macnaghten discreetly replied that this question would be better discussed in private.

Having got the Maharajah to himself, Macnaghten explained that while the main object was to put Shah Soojah in the place of Dost Mahomed, there were two courses by which this might be achieved; Runjeet might either act independently or in co-operation with the British. The Maharajah burst in impatiently that he was only interested in acting in concert with the British and Macnaghten therefore asked whether he wished the British Government to join in a tripartite treaty with himself and Soojah. "That," purred Runjeet, "would be adding sugar to milk." It would be arranged, said Macnaghten, and the British would no doubt supply Soojah with money and officers for his troops. The strategic plan, he explained, was for Soojah to advance up through the Bolan Pass and by way of Kandahar, while Runjeet's troops would move upon Kabul through the Khyber. There then peeped out the first hint that British troops might take a more active part than had yet been contemplated. "Circumstances might arise," said Macnaghten, "to render it necessary for the British Government to send some of its own troops down the Indus, to repel any threat of aggression in that direction." "How many?" snapped Runjeet. "As many," replied Macnaghten suavely, "as the exigencies of the occasion may require; but their employment in that direction will only be temporary."

The Maharajah was beginning to think that he was to get too many of the kicks and too few of the halfpence. In particular he doubted his troops' capacity to perform their allotted task of forcing the Khyber Pass. He had the most rudimentary notions of this type of warfare, and no thought of crowning the heights or of turning the pass by a flanking movement entered his mind. Instead, he believed that forcing the Khyber meant pushing a column of troops into it, rather as he would push them over a narrow bridge, the men in the rear stepping over the bodies of their slaughtered comrades. He had never tried his men at such work, he told the British Mission, and he doubted whether

The area of the army's advance on Afghanistan. The routes marked are the main trade routes and lines of communication.

they could be persuaded to march over the corpses of their countrymen. Macnaghten now hinted—and this was June, 1838, and the siege of Herat at its most critical phase—that if necessary the British might go it alone, that "if it seriously threatened us we might be compelled to arrest the advance of the Persians by the advance of our troops, and in this case we might find it expedient to support the cause of Shah Soojah". This argument plainly made a deep impression on Runjeet.

The Sikhs and their British guests now moved on to Lahore. Here they were joined by Alexander Burnes, who added fuel to the fire by maliciously telling the Maharajah that Dost Mahomed had said of him: "I can't do that brute Runjeet Singh any real harm, but I will torment him a good deal yet before I have done with him." And another Political officer, Lieutenant Mackeson, again warned him that, if pushed to it, the British would act on their own. Runjeet made up his mind: if it had been determined that Shah Soojah was to be restored to his ancestral throne, it had better not be a Soojah beholden solely to the British; he decided to participate in the venture and in his usual quick emphatic manner told Mackeson to have the treaty prepared for his signature.

The pact was a tripartite "treaty of alliance and friendship executed between Maharajah Runjeet Singh and Shah Soojah-ool-Moolkh, with the approbation of and in concert with the British Government". Runjeet took care to see that the treaty included provisions by which Soojah specifically renounced all claims to Kashmir, Peshawar and a number of other places that had been lopped by the Sikhs from the Douranee empire. He was also to send annual gifts to the Maharajah, "55 high-bred horses of approved colour and pleasant paces", scimitars and poniards, twenty-five mules, and a mouth-watering list of fruits, "musk melons of a sweet and delicate flavour, grapes, pomegranates, apples, quinces, almonds, raisins, pistales or chronuts, an abundant supply of each". In return Runjeet would send a rather more niggardly assortment—shawls, pieces of muslin and scarves, and fifty-five loads of rice. Soojah must also promise to send the Maharajah two lakhs of rupees each year, an obligation guaranteed by the British Government. This was thinly-disguised tribute, but to make it more acceptable to Soojah, the Sikhs undertook in return to keep a force of at least 5,000 troops stationed in the Peshawar area, who would be sent to Soojah's assistance "whenever the British Government, in concert and counsel with the Maharajah, shall deem the aid necessary". It was also stipulated that Soojah must not attack or molest his nephew

Kamran, whose continued resistance at Herat presumably secured the insertion of this saving clause in his favour.

Runjeet signed the treaty without demur, but Auckland decided that he could not properly add his own name until it had been agreed and signed by Soojah, who up to this point had not been officially informed of the negotiations or of the commitments which the British were drafting in his name. It was doubtless assumed that as a beggar he could not be a chooser, and so it turned out. Macnaghten moved on to Ludhiana where Soojah received him with a becoming cordiality and listened attentively to his proposals. It was now five years since his last bid to recover the throne of Kabul. In 1833 he had persuaded Lord William Bentinck to pay him four months' pension in advance, and with the money he had raised a force for the invasion of Afghanistan and the overthrow of Dost Mahomed. He had indeed endeavoured to persuade the British to play a more active part in the enterprise, but Lord William, quietly smiling, had sententiously told him: "My friend, I deem it my duty to apprise you distinctly that the British Government religiously abstains from interfering with the affairs of its neighbours when this can be avoided." Soojah, undismayed, had raised his own levies, had been unable to resist the temptation to inflict a swingeing defeat upon the Amirs of Scinde, and in turn had himself been as resoundingly defeated by Dost Mahomed.

He was now about fifty-eight years old and therefore, by the standards of the time, referred to as an old man. Havelock describes him as "rather a stout person of the middle size, his chin covered with a long, thick and neatly-trimmed beard, dyed black to conceal the encroachments of time . . . his complexion is darker than that of the generality of Afghans and his features, if not decidedly handsome, are not the reverse of pleasing; but the expression of his countenance would betray to a skilful physiognomist that mixture of timidity and duplicity so often observable in the character of the highest order of men in Southern Asia". His manner towards the English was gentle, calm and dignified, and however timid and double-faced he may have been, there was no mistaking his delight when he learnt from Macnaghten that Lord William Bentinck's policy of non-interference had gone by the board. But he was particularly anxious that the reconquest of his realm should be carried out mainly by his own troops, pointing out, sensibly enough, that "the fact of his being upheld by foreign force alone could not fail to detract, in a great measure, from his dignity and consequence". He was optimistic of success, for he had already written secretly to a number of influential chiefs in Afghanistan and they, with the Afghan's ingrained love of plots and intrigue, had returned encouraging answers. "The faggots are ready," they said; "it merely requires the lighted torch to be applied." Soojah was all for pressing on. He urged Macnaghten that the advance should begin while Herat was still holding out, and disclosed that a few days earlier he had sent a message to Kamran, exhorting him for the honour of the Afghans to hold out for two short months, when he would hear of miracles worked in his favour. Soojah accepted the strategic plan for a Sikh advance through the Khyber while his own force moved up through Kandahar, and agreed that his eldest son, Timour, should accompany the Sikh army. After some understandable but unavailing protests at having to renounce Peshawar and pay an annual subsidy to Runjeet Singh, he even agreed to sign the tripartite treaty as it stood.

With the signatures of both Runjeet and Soojah safely affixed to the treaty Macnaghten had brought off the double. But before leaving Ludhiana he and his Mission paid a courtesy call upon Soojah's elder brother, the blind old ex-King Zemaun Shah. Zemaun had spent many sightless years as an appendage to his brother's court, dreaming of the glories of many years ago. Now he rejoiced greatly to hear that there was a plan afoot by which at long last he might return home. "He seemed filled with delight," Macnaghten reported, "at the prospect of being permitted to revisit the land of his ancestors." The British officers, touched by his gratitude, could hardly believe that this pathetic old blind man was the same as he whose warlike movements on the northwest frontier had filled their predecessors with anxiety and alarm forty years before, and who had brought fear even to the hearts of the redoubtable Sikhs when, as the young ruler of the Douranee empire, he had "moved from his native land and spread his owl-like shadow over the Punjab".

2

From the outset the British plan had only the barest chance of success, for the intervention of the hated Sikhs would certainly rouse the Afghans to a fury of patriotic resistance. But between July and October of 1838 the plan was given a new twist that was to make ultimate failure quite certain. Somewhere along the line, in those summer months, the decision was taken that British troops should take part in the campaign, and to a major degree.

With Herat under siege it could reasonably be argued that only a British force was capable of advancing into the far west of Afghanistan to repel the Persians, possibly even the Russians, but with the raising of the siege this argument had vanished. There remained the further argument that even a project limited to the restoration of Soojah would end in disaster if it were left entirely to Soojah and the Sikhs; and this too was plausible, considering Soojah's long record of failure, the lukewarm enthusiasm of Runjeet Singh and the hatred of the Afghans for the Sikhs. The puzzled Auckland consulted his military expert, the commander-in-chief, Sir Henry Fane, and this sturdy old warrior had no doubts. He disliked the policy of interference in Afghanistan, but he disliked half-measures even more. If interference there must be, then let it be such as to secure the success of the operation. He added truculently that it was for him alone, as the first military authority in the country, to determine the number of British troops to be employed, and the manner of their employment.

Burnes was again consulted. He would still himself have backed Dost Mahomed—"if half you must do for others were done for him, and offers made which he could see conducted to his interests, he would abandon Russia and Persia tomorrow"—but if the removal of Dost Mahomed must be accepted, then, with his usual optimism, Burnes thought that the restoration of Soojah would be an easy task. "Of Shah Soojah-ool-Moolk personally," he had written, "I have, that is as ex-King of the Afghans, no very high opinion." On second thoughts he scored the words out and substituted: "As for Shah Soojah-ool-Mulk personally, the British Government have only to send him to Peshawar with an agent, and two of its own regiments as an honorary escort, and an avowal to the Afghans that we have taken up his cause, to ensure his being fixed for ever on the throne." But it was essential, he added, for the British to take a direct part, "for the Afghans are a superstitious people and believe Shah Soojah to have no fortune —but our name will invest him with it".

Once Sir Henry Fane and the regulars had been brought into the discussion, Burnes' modest proposals of an agent and two regiments were swept aside. Fane was determined to make sure, and presently the order went forth for the assembling of a grand army—the 'Army of the Indus'—which early in the coming cold weather was to cross that great river and march upon Kandahar in support of Soojah and his levies.

In August the commander-in-chief warned the selected

regiments for field service. The two components, one from the Bengal army and one from Bombay, were in due course to meet and merge under Fane's personal command. The Bengal contingent would consist of a brigade each of artillery and cavalry and two infantry divisions, the Queen's army being represented by the 16th Lancers, 13th Foot and 3rd Buffs; with them would march the Company's European Regiment, two regiments of native light cavalry and twelve battalions of the Company's sepoys. The Bombay contingent was to assemble under Sir John Keane, commander-in-chief of the Bombay army, and would comprise a brigade of cavalry, a brigade of artillery and a brigade of infantry; it would include, of the Queen's cavalry, the 4th Dragoons and, of Queen's infantry, the 2nd Royals and the 17th Foot. All in all, six regiments of cavalry, eighteen battalions of infantry, two brigades of artillery, and ancillary units. So much for Captain Burnes' two regiments and an agent.

The recruitment of Soojah's levies was meanwhile going busily forward; it was to be made clear that they were to be Soojah's army, and his alone, but there was no hiding the fact that they were to be raised in the Company's territories, commanded by the Company's officers, and paid in the Company's coin. There were plenty of volunteers in the Upper Provinces and British officers had already been detailed to supervise the raising and training of the Shah's regiments. Captain Wade was hard put to it to prevent Soojah's interfering with the work, for the Shah, understandably anxious not to appear a mere puppet in British hands, was constantly turning up on parade to superintend personally the payment and enlistment of his men. Wade tactfully ordered that he should be greeted by a royal salute whenever he appeared and Soojah, naïvely delighted with this tribute, urged the work of recruitment eagerly forward.

Auckland had next to select Political Officers to accompany the various armies. Wade was an obvious choice for the Sikh force, and it had already been settled that he should take with him Soojah's eldest son, Prince Timour, "a man of respectable character but not very brilliant parts". There remained the question of a Political to accompany Soojah and the main British force. Burnes had no doubt who deserved this appointment on merit. "What exact part I am to play I know not," he wrote to his brother, "but if full confidence and hourly consultation be any pledge, I am to be chief." Nor, at first, was he prepared to accept any lesser position. "I can tell them plainly that it is *aut Caesar*

77

aut nullus, and if I get not what I have a right to, you will soon see me en route to England." But Auckland had decided that, at the outset, Soojah needed the guidance of an older and more experienced hand, and it was presently announced that the Chief Secretary, Macnaghten himself, would accompany the Army as "Envoy and Minister on the part of the Government at the Court of Shah Soojah-ool-Moolk". To Burnes was given the minor, though important, role of going on ahead to smooth the way for the British force with the Amirs of Scinde and other chieftains along the projected line of advance. Auckland, who was a kindly man, provided a certain amount of sugar to help Burnes to swallow the pill. He let it be understood that as soon as Soojah had been successfully replaced on his ancestral throne, Macnaghten would return to India and that Burnes might expect to succeed him as permanent representative at the Shah's court. He also wrote to Burnes, handsomely admitting that the latter's plan to support the Kandahar Sirdars against Persia, which had attracted Macnaghten's thunderous rebuke, had now been pronounced by the British Government at home to have been right all the time. Burnes crowed with glee. "They would not be guided by me," he wrote, "and sent me a laudatory wig (reprimand), and as sure as I had been a prophet, my predictions are verified. Russia is upon us, and the home Government has pronounced me right and his Lordship wrong! This is the greatest hit I have made in life."

The sweetest sop came to him in a private letter from Auckland, in which the Governor-General told him that he was "glad that a just tribute has been paid to your ability and indefatigable zeal. The superscription of this letter will, in case you have not received direct accounts, explain my meaning to you." A glance at the envelope showed Burnes that it was addressed to "Lieutenant-Colonel Sir Alexander Burnes, Kt." and he realised that at the age of thirty-three he had been promoted by his Sovereign two ranks in the military grade and advanced to the honour of knighthood.

Auckland and his advisers had now to justify to the world the invasion of Afghanistan on which they were resolved, and so, on 1st October, 1838, there was published at Simla a portentous document of which the full title was "Declaration on the Part of the Right Honourable the Governor-General of India" but which was always known as the Simla Manifesto. This masterpiece of *suppressio veri* and *suggestio falsi* began by stating that the troops of Dost Mahomed had made a sudden and unprovoked attack upon those of our ancient ally, Maharajah Runjeet Singh. (It will be recalled that this ancient ally, shortly before this "unprovoked" attack, had seized the Afghan city of Peshawar.) Captain Burnes, continued the Manifesto, had been instructed to use his good offices to reconcile the Sikh Maharajah and the Afghan Amir and thus prevent the "peaceful and beneficial purposes of the British Government" from being frustrated by the outbreak of war. The Maharajah, "with the characteristic confidence which he has uniformly placed in the faith and friendship of the British nation", had at once assented, but the wicked Amir had behaved very differently. "Chiefly in consequence of his reliance upon Persian encouragement and assistance, he persisted, as respected his misunderstanding with the Sikhs, in urging the most unreasonable pretensions . . . he avowed schemes of aggrandizement and ambition injurious to the security and peace of the frontiers of India; he openly threatened, in furtherance of those schemes, to call in every foreign aid which he could command." Dost Mahomed, who had spent months trying to secure the support of the British through Alexander Burnes, could have been forgiven for failing to recognise himself in this description of his behaviour. However, said the Manifesto, his hostile policy "showed too plainly that, so long as Caubul remained under his government, we could never hope that the tranquillity of our neighbourhood would be secured, or that the interests of our Indian Empire would be preserved inviolate".

The siege of Herat, which was still in progress, was now dragged into the story and described as "a most unjustifiable and cruel aggression". As to its gallant defenders, "the Governor-General would yet indulge the hope that their heroism may enable them to maintain a successful defence until succours shall reach them from British India". The opportunity was taken for another side swipe at the Barukzyes by pointing out that the Amir's brothers, the Kandahar Sirdars, had been flirting with the Persians and openly assisting in their operations against Herat. As a result of all this "the Governor-General felt the importance of taking immediate measures for arresting the rapid progress of foreign intrigue and aggression towards our own territories".

The Manifesto now departed even more wildly from the facts. "It had been clearly ascertained," it announced, "from the various officers who have visited Afghanistan, that the Barukzye chiefs, from their disunion and unpopularity, were ill fitted under any circumstances to be useful allies to the British Government." The truth was that, of the "various officers" who knew the Afghan

79

scene, Burnes had repeatedly urged support for Dost Mahomed, M'Neill had strongly supported Burnes, and Wade, though he did not agree with the notion of making Dost Mahomed sole ruler of the country, had been strongly in favour of maintaining the Barukzye brethren in their various strongholds.

The Manifesto, blandly ignoring where it did not falsify the recommendations of officers with first-hand knowledge of Afghanistan, went on to explain that with the Barukzye family written off as hopeless, the Governor-General's attention had naturally been drawn "to the position and claims of Shah Soojah-ool-Moolk, a monarch who, when in power, had cordially acceded to the measures of united resistance to external enmity which were at that time judged necessary by the British Government . . . and whose popularity throughout Afghanistan had been proved to his Lordship by the strong and unanimous testimony of the best authorities". Obviously Runjeet Singh, "no less from his position than from his undeviating friendship towards the British Government", must be invited to take part in the proposed operations; the Amirs of Scinde would be offered a guarantee of independence and the integrity of Herat, under the rule of Shah Kamran, would be fully respected.

And so, the Manifesto triumphantly concluded, "His Majesty Shah Soojah-ool-Moolk will enter Afghanistan surrounded by his own troops, and will be supported against foreign interference and factious opposition by a British army. The Governor-General confidently hopes that the Shah will be speedily replaced on his throne by his own subjects and adherents; and when once he shall be secured in power, and the independence and integrity of Afghanistan established, the British army will be withdrawn." The Governor-General added that he rejoiced that "in the discharge of his duty, he will be enabled to assist in restoring the union and prosperity of the Afghan people. . . . British influence will be sedulously employed to further every measure of general benefit, to reconcile differences, to secure oblivion of injuries, and to put an end to the distractions by which, for so many years, the welfare and happiness of the Afghans have been impaired."

The Manifesto, bearing Macnaghten's signature and no doubt very largely drafted by him, was seized upon by the press, both in India and Britain, and torn to shreds. It was damned as a collection of absolute falsehoods, a highly disingenuous distortion of the truth. "The views of Dost Mahomed Khan," wrote Sir Herbert Edwardes later, "were misrepresented with a hardihood which a Russian statesman might have envied," and Durand commented bitterly that the words "justice" and "necessity" had been employed "in a manner for which there is fortunately no precedent in the English language". The Persian attack upon Herat might have allowed the British to advance to its relief with some semblance of acting in self-defence; but it was by no means clear that because Mahomed Shah of Persia was making war upon Herat, the British were justified in making war upon Dost Mahomed of Afghanistan. In any case, before the Manifesto had been fully circulated, the only plausible excuse for invasion vanished with authentic reports of the raising of the siege of Herat. The officers of the Army in India, though few felt in their hearts that the British cause was just, feared that this would mean the disappearance of their chances of active service and promotion. But a further Proclamation by Macnaghten, a kind of supplement to the Manifesto, put the matter beyond doubt. Dated 8th November, it announced the raising of the siege and added that "the Governor-General deems it proper at the same time to notify that . . . he will continue to prosecute with vigour the measures which have been announced, with a view to the substitution of a friendly for a hostile power in the eastern provinces of Afghanistan and to the establishment of a permanent barrier against schemes of aggression upon our north-west frontier". In short, the Soojah plan and the invasion of Afghanistan were still to go forward.

Back in England, the Court of directors of the East India Company were writhing in anguish at the prospect of the war that was now to be waged in their name; but the law compelled their Secret Committee to give a blind approval to the despatches laid before them by the Board of Control, whose President would later admit that, beyond the mechanical act of signing the papers laid before them, they had had no part in the recommendation or authorisation of the war. Many other experienced heads were being shaken in disapproval and foreboding. Wellington commented laconically that the difficulties would begin where the military successes ended. His brother, Wellesley, spoke contemptuously of the folly of occupying a land of "rocks, sand, desert, ice and snow". Sir Charles Metcalfe repeated the opinion he had expressed in Council at Calcutta two or three years before: "Depend upon it, the surest way to bring Russia down upon ourselves is for us to cross the Indus and meddle with the countries beyond it." Mountstuart Elphinstone, now retired, gave the truest of forecasts in a letter to a friend: "You will guess what I think of affairs in Caubul," he wrote; "you will remember when

F

I used to dispute with you against having even an agent in Caubul, and now we have assumed the protection of the state as much as if it were one of the subsidiary allies in India. If you send 27,000 men up the Bolan Pass to Candahar (as we hear is intended), and can feed them, I have no doubt you will take Candahar and Caubul and set up Soojah; but for maintaining him in a poor, cold, strong and remote country, among a turbulent people like the Afghans, I own it seems to me to be hopeless. If you succeed, I fear you will weaken the position against Russia. The Afghans were neutral and would have received your aid against invaders with gratitude—they will now be disaffected and glad to join any invader to drive you out. *I never knew a close alliance between a civilised and an uncivilised state that did not end in mutual hatred in three years.* If the restraint of a close connexion with us were not enough to make us unpopular, the connexion with Runjeet and our guarantee of his conquests must make us detested."

Elphinstone added modestly that "these opinions, formed at a distance, may seem absurd on the spot"; they would prove to be accurate almost to the letter. But long before such gloomy though well-founded doubts could make their slow way back to India, the cumbrous wheels of the military machine had clanked into motion and the Army of the Indus was mobilising.

3

The British, who confidently believed that the invasion of Afghanistan would be no more than "a grand military promenade", decided that proceedings should start with a ceremonial meeting between Runjeet Singh and Lord Auckland. Ferozepore, about a hundred miles south-east of Lahore, was chosen as the site of the Durbar, and there the Bengal contingent of the Army of the Indus arrived towards the end of November. All went smoothly. "A force," said Havelock, "had never been brought together in any country in a manner more creditable and soldier-like than was the Bengal portion of the Army of the Indus." The Sikh forces marched in from the opposite direction and the first meeting between the Governor-General and the little wizened one-eyed ruler of the Punjab took place "amidst a scene of indescribable uproar and confusion". Indeed, so great was the throng and such the tumult that some of the Sikhs suspected a plot against the life of their venerable ruler and "began to blow their matches and grasp their weapons with an air of mingled distrust and ferocity". However, trouble was averted and for two days great festivities were held in the huge pavilion tents. The Sikhs put on a splendid show. Their horses were gorgeously caparisoned with the riders wearing glittering steel casques and corselets of chain mail, the great ones arrayed in scarlet and yellow and their tents gleaming with crimson and gold. A Sikh band gave a painful rendering of the British National Anthem and the guns of the Khalsa roared forth their salute at frequent intervals.

There was an awkward moment when Auckland presented Runjeet with two 9-pounder guns and the Maharajah, in his eagerness to inspect the gifts, stumbled and fell in front of the muzzles. His entourage gave a murmur of horror at the ominous sight of their ruler prostrate before British guns until some born diplomat relieved the tension by remarking, "Well, if his Highness did fall before the British guns, the highest representatives of the British Government restored him to his feet." Reassured, the little old Maharajah, in his usual faded crimson, pressed hospitality upon his British guests, in particular his own special drink, alleged to be compounded of emeralds, grape spirit and oranges, and rather unconvincingly recommended as good for the digestion. Emily Eden found it "a horrible spirit, one drop of which actually burnt my lips", but luckily she was on Runjeet's blind side and was able to keep pouring it on the carpet, thus greatly impressing her host with her capacity as he continually refilled her goblet. For entertainment the guests were regaled "with an unseemly display of dancing girls and the antics of some male buffoons". And with pursed lips Kaye adds that "the evening entertainments were still less decorous".

By day the allies went through their paces for each other's benefit. Sir Henry Fane put the British force through some reasonably complicated manoeuvres and "the consummate skill with which he attacked an imaginary enemy was equalled by the gallantry with which he defeated it".[1] The Sikh generals contented themselves with simpler movements but their troops carried them out with an efficiency that impressed the British. The Sikh army was interesting. Early in his career Runjeet had realised that the secret of the success of the Company's troops lay in their discipline and training, which he had therefore faithfully copied. Deserters from the Company's regiments were employed as drill sergeants, supplemented by young Punjabis who had been sent

---

[1] William Nott, however, an experienced but embittered officer of the Company's service, was not impressed by the competence of the brigade and divisional commanders. "Oh, how I wished to have done in half an hour what they all bungled at from six to ten o'clock."

across the border to enlist in British service and learn the methods. Presently he began to employ Europeans in his higher commands, such as the American Harlan, a tough Italian called Avitabile and two French officers who had served with distinction under Napoleon. By insistence on high standards in march, manoeuvre and marksmanship he had created an army that was the most formidable in India save for the Company's. Both cavalry and artillery were of good quality and the infantry, tall thin men in scarlet tunics, blue linen trousers and blue turbans, who marched barefoot to drum, bugle and fife, were capable of amazing feats of endurance. The British, unaware that Sikh muskets, manufactured at the Lahore arsenal, had a very limited range and were apt to burst on anything approaching rapid fire, were very satisfied with what they saw of their new allies.

There being now no Persian army to be repelled from Herat, it was decided that the British force could be reduced in size, and the Bengal army was cut from two divisions to one. Faced with the problem of selecting which regiments should go and which be left behind, Sir Henry Fane settled the issue rather oddly by drawing lots. At the same time he decided that with both the task and the force reduced, he no longer wanted to command the Army of the Indus himself. He had for some time been anxious to retire for reasons of health, and he was far from enthusiastic at the prospect described by Auckland; Soojah's forces would lead the advance, wrote the Governor-General, the Bengal army would follow in the rear and the reception of both would be 'welcome with general gladness". "I do not think," replied Fane, "that for this my service is needed." And he had misgivings about the authority to be wielded by Macnaghten; "I think too," he added "that your instructions to Sir William Macnaghten and to me are such as an officer of my rank could hardly submit to serve under."

Fane therefore bequeathed supreme command of the expedition to Sir John Keane, who was bringing the Bombay army round by sea from Bombay to Karachi; the Bengal force would be led to its rendezvous with Keane by Sir Willoughby Cotton, a roly-poly old general of the Queen's service who used to bore his brother officers with the tale of how he had been expelled from Rugby for leading the great school mutiny forty years before. He had served far too long in India and Fane had no great confidence in his ability. "I don't think that Cotton has a mind which carries away much of verbal instructions," he had written, leaving his reader to deduce that what he really meant was that Cotton was

84

both slow and stupid.

With the Ferozepore festivities at an end, and, no doubt, a few sore British heads as the aftermath of Runjeet's fearsome digestive cocktail, the Maharajah led his army back to Lahore, accompanied by Auckland, who was to pay a state visit to the Sikh capital. Willoughby Cotton meanwhile prepared to march the Bengal army south-west, along the line of the Indus, to its meeting with Sir John Keane. Instead of moving straight to its first objective, Kandahar, which lay some six hundred miles due west of Ferozepore, the Bengal army was to cover nearly double that distance by marching round two sides of a triangle. The first leg covered nearly six hundred miles to the south-east, almost to the city of Hyderabad, capital of the Amirs of Scinde; the route then turned north-west across the Indus, up through the formidable Bolan Pass to Quetta, and so on to Kandahar. A political reason had dictated the choice of this circuitous journey; it had been decided that on the way to Afghanistan the opportunity of cowing the unfortunate Scinde Amirs back into subjection under Soojah was too good to be missed.

Soojah's British officers had worked overtime and Cotton was now joined by the Shah's levies, a sizeable and fairly well trained force consisting of two regiments of cavalry, four of infantry and a troop of horse artillery, about 6,000 men in all. Added to the 9,500 fighting troops of the Bengal army they made up a reasonably compact and manageable force, but the ludicrously inadequate administrative plan for the army's maintenance in the field added a nightmare complication. It had been gaily decided that the army should to a great extent live off the land, with little thought whether the land would be capable of supporting it. For the rest, it must move self-contained, driving its meat on the hoof—slaughter cattle for two and a half months—and carrying thirty days' allowance of grain. Hence a vast unwieldy tail of camp-followers, no less than 38,000 of them.

A great part of the enormous quantity of baggage consisted of the personal gear of the British officers, a subject upon which Fane had apparently thought it indelicate to go to the extreme of issuing orders. He had, however, appealed to all officers to travel light and urged that the troops should be able to move "disencumbered of every article of baggage which could, without compromising the efficiency of the corps, be dispensed with". His appeal was totally ignored, and even junior subalterns advanced to war with as many as forty servants apiece. A whole retinue of grooms, cooks, bearers, dhobis and sweepers straggled along behind their sahibs. One regiment allocated two camels for the carriage of cigars for the officers' mess, while jams, pickles, potted fish, hermetically-sealed meats, plate, glass, crockery, wax candles and table linen were all, it seemed, thought necessary for "the efficiency of the corps". Many young officers, said General Nott's biographer, "would as soon have thought of leaving behind them their swords and double-barrelled pistols as march without their dressing-cases, their perfumes, Windsor soap and eau-de-Cologne". Their seniors, however, were in no position to reprimand them. One brigadier had no less than sixty camels to carry his personal belongings and General Keane himself was rumoured to have appropriated two hundred and sixty of the beasts for the use of himself and his staff.

The fact was that while British officers were ready to display personal courage of the highest order when it came to the actual conflict, they had no intention of being uncomfortable on their approach to the battlefield. Few thought this unreasonable. "It is natural," wrote Kaye, "that with the prospect of a long and wearisome march before him, he (the British officer) should not be entirely forgetful of the pleasures of the mess-table, or regardless of the less social delights of the pleasant volume and the solacing pipe. Clean linen, too, is a luxury which a civilized man, without any imputation upon his soldierly qualities, may in moderation desire to enjoy." "The fact is," recorded Major Hough more bluntly, "that most of the officers had too many camels, too large tents and too much baggage."

So off trudged the Army of the Indus, or at least the Bengal portion of it, with Soojah's levies marching valiantly along and 30,000 camels screaming their rage at the weight of the baggage. The camels turned out to be another mistake. "The country in which operations are about to be conducted is not adapted to wheel-carriages," counselled Fane's warning order, "and you will bear this in mind when making arrangements for the transport of your baggage." Mules and donkeys would have been the answer, and best of all "yaboos", the sturdy ponies of Central Asia, which could carry loads of over three hundredweight for journeys of up to thirty miles a day.[1] But the transport officers, hidebound by the custom of the service, refused to consider anything but camels, although experience had shown that camels

[1] Mackenzie noted with amusement that "the Afghans tie a knot in the middle of the long tails of their horses which, they say, strengthens the animal's backbone!"

from the Indian plains were useless in the mountain country of Afghanistan. They were terrified at the prospect of a steep ascent and would not even go up a hillside to graze; and when they did graze, they had not learnt to distinguish the poisonous herbs of the country. Many died from eating a plant resembling foxglove and all told, in the 1838-39 campaign, more than five thousand of them perished. In fact, as one British General tersely commented, they were purchased apparently only to be buried.

At the start of the march, however, none of this had become apparent. Political Officers had moved in advance of the column, forming depots of grain, fodder and firewood for the army's use, the weather was fine and officers and men were in high spirits. The army had gone to war with intense enthusiasm. It was firmly believed that they would ultimately find themselves up against Russian troops. "To fight with any power which had braved the British flag was agreeable, but to contend at the head of sepoys against the European cohorts of the Czar in the regions beyond the Indus was an honour so rare and unexpected, and fraught with so much promise of distinction and advancement, that not a soldier in the whole length and breadth of India could for a moment tolerate the idea of being left behind."[1]

This enthusiasm was shared by the sepoys, if we can believe a spirited poem of forty stanzas composed by a descendant of Lord Lake, who had led their predecessors to victory over the French thirty-five years before. A Subadar is supposed to be speaking:

But now, my men, the battle-cloud again o'erhangs our head;
They say with murkier gloom then erst it wrapped the valiant dead.
From Ava and Nepaul they come, Afghan and rugged Russ;
All, all unite to swell the battle-torrent's impetus.

Well, let them come; stout hearts and thoughts of bygone fields, my men,
The valour of our sepoy sires lives in us o'er again.
The British banner in our keep has never met with stain,
And as we stood by stout old Lake, hurrah! we'll stand by Fane.

So it was with morale high and hearts cheerful that through that bright December weather ("these," wrote Havelock, "were the halcyon days") the force marched down the line of the Indus, through the state of Bawulpore and on into Scinde, where the Amirs' hash was swiftly and brutally settled. Twenty-five lakhs of rupees—£250,000—was the sum demanded of them, three-fifths of it earmarked for Runjeet Singh, the rest to be paid as tribute to their Afghan overlord, Soojah-ool-Moolk. In vain did

[1] Stocqueler.

87

the Amirs produce two deeds of release, written in the Koran and signed and sealed by Soojah, for which, they protested, they had already paid in full. They were roughly reminded that "neither the ready power to crush and annihilate them, nor the will to call it into action, were wanting if it appeared requisite, however remotely, for the safety or integrity of the Anglo-Indian Empire or frontier". For the moment, might was right and treaty obligations were scraps of paper. When the Indus had been opened for navigation, the Amirs had been specifically assured that no military stores would ever be conveyed along the river. They were now brusquely told that this article of the treaty "must necessarily be suspended during the course of operations undertaken for the permanent establishment of security to all those who are party to the treaty." As if this were not enough, Sir Willoughby Cotton now decided, to the great joy of his loot-hungry troops, to attack and capture the Amirs' capital of Hyderabad. This, he maintained, was for some obscure reason an essential part of his plan for linking up with Sir John Keane's force, of whose whereabouts he was now completely ignorant, as Keane was of his.

The Bombay army had, in fact, already landed on the coast and was consolidating its position. A brigade of troops commanded by a Brigadier with the promising name of Valiant had arrived off the port of Karachi, escorted by H.M.S. *Wellesley*, a 74 flying the flag of Admiral Sir Frederick Maitland. The Admiral, having been informed that the port was garrisoned by 3,000 resolute men under the personal command of one of the Scinde Amirs, called upon it to surrender. He was gallantly answered by the garrison commandant—"I am a Beloochee and I will die first." The *Wellesley* set to work with her broadsides and within an hour the garrison, all twenty of them, had surrendered.

Meanwhile the Bengal contingent was advancing greedily upon Hyderabad. The city was rumoured to contain treasure worth eight million pounds sterling and, as Havelock remarked, "such a prize is not often in a century, even in India, presented to the grasp of a British army. . . . Every soldier, from the general to the private sentinel, was already calculating the amount of his share." But the city was saved, and the avaricious hopes of the troops dashed, by the intervention of Macnaghten, who had become increasingly perturbed by the way in which the lure of Hyderabad loot was distracting Cotton from his primary task of getting across the Indus and moving on Kandahar. "Cotton," wrote the Envoy, "is clearly going on a wild-goose chase. . . . He seems to be travelling by a route which has no road. He will soon, I fear, be in the jungle. If this goes on as it is now doing, what is to become of our Afghan expedition?"

The Envoy intervened with firm decision. Supported by the authority of the Governor-General, he now insisted that the attack on Hyderabad must be abandoned and the advance on Kandahar take priority. There followed some unseemly bickering between the Political and Military heads of the expedition. Cotton was infuriated by Macnaghten's request for 1,000 camels as transport for Soojah's army, which he chose to interpret as interference in his own sphere. He rudely accused the Envoy of wishing to take command of the army and pompously declared that he recognised no superior but Sir John Keane. Macnaghten patched things up by entertaining the General to dinner in his tent and they parted, late at night, "very good friends". The Bengal army, "with light purses and heavy hearts", turned its back on the booty of Hyderabad and marched off to the banks of the Indus.

The river was eleven hundred yards wide and, said James Broadfoot, had "a torrent like a millstream". But with remarkable skill the sappers, in eleven days, had produced an improvised pontoon bridge. They seized about 120 boats and anchored them across the stream, twelve feet apart, with anchors made of small trees joined together and loaded with half a ton of stone. Trees were cut down and sawn into beams and planks; nails were made on the spot; no rope was available, but 500 cables were woven out of "a peculiar kind of grass" fetched from a hundred miles away. The beams were lashed to the boats, the planks were nailed to the beams to make a roadway, and the army marched across. And so, on 10th March, having journeyed hither and thither for three months with very little to show for its efforts, it arrived at the mouth of the Bolan Pass.

4

The Bolan, "a huge chasm, running between precipitous rocks to the length of seventy miles, and rising in that distance to the height of 5,637 feet above the plains below", lay within the domain of Mehrab, Khan of Khelat, a free-booting chieftain who made his living largely by plundering passing travellers. But Sir Alexander Burnes had gone on ahead and purchased the friendship of Mehrab, whose lieutenants did their best to secure an uninterrupted passage for the army. Even so, Baluchi robbers were hovering about, cutting off couriers, murdering stragglers and carrying off baggage and cattle. The Political Officers, however, opposed retaliation and urged appeasement, and an order to use force against marauders produced a complaint from Burnes to Cotton that such instructions "were bloodthirsty and calculated to bring on a blood-feud". Keane, a few months later, wrote bitterly to Auckland that "the political officers led me—and I suppose you—to believe that we should find the country friendly from Shikarpur to Candahar. . . . There was no hint that it was full of robbers, plunderers and murderers, brought up to it from their youth."

Already, although it had yet to set eyes on a single enemy soldier, the Army of the Indus had been brought by its hopelessly inadequate administrative arrangements to within a hairsbreadth of total disaster. Water and forage were scarce, the cattle were suffering terribly and the camels died by scores. Supplies for the army and its unwieldy horde of camp followers were running short, and presently the native troops were put on half-rations, while the size of the British soldier's loaf was reduced. The unfortunate followers fared even worse, being put on a famine allowance of quarter rations. Starvation stared the Army of the Indus in the face.

The British were loud in their complaints that Mehrab Khan was placing every obstacle in the way of their buying grain from the local inhabitants, but the fact was that the peasant farmers of this barren land were working practically on a subsistence basis; to expect them to be able without notice to produce a surplus sufficient for 50,000 men and 30,000 animals was absurd. It was an added discouragement that those who did sell to the British purchasing officers were usually at once relieved of the cash by Baluchi robbers, often within sight of the British camp.

Under these circumstances Cotton decided to push on through the Pass with all possible speed. The huge guns of the siege train were hauled with painful effort over a wretched track, the troops plodded to and fro across the Bolan river as many as eighteen times a day, the sharp flints lamed the camels and cattle. (Cotton, when warned that the Pass was choked with boulders and rough shingle, had naïvely replied that "the stones might be broken".) Each day, the march would begin well before dawn, to the light of flaring torches. Whenever the rough road narrowed, as it frequently did, it soon became a scrum of led horses, camels, followers carrying baskets, stretchers and palanquins, bullocks, mules and asses, troopers and native cavalry, "the quadrupeds roaring, neighing, bellowing and braying, and the bipeds growling, vociferating and abusing each other, and all struggling to get on". Camp would be pitched quite early in the day, and then would begin the laborious task of erecting the officers' tents, while the followers fanned out in all directions in a noisy search for grass, fuel and fodder. The officers, it seems, were still faring pretty well, for on one occasion Havelock, having ridden through the night with a party of cavalry officers, was delighted to find that through the brigadier's "hospitable foresight" a laden camel had been sent on ahead, with the result that at dawn there was found spread on the ground "an ample collation, cold beef, cold mutton, cold game, bread, butter and various other tempting and substantial viands, and wine of several kinds, beer, brandy and cigars". Despite this pleasant picnic fare, even the officers felt relief when, on 26th March, the force won through to the other end of the Bolan and found itself again in open country. The air was clear and crisp, the upland plain was intersected by sparkling streams and dotted with orchards and vineyards, while "the carol of the lark broke with many home associations charmingly on the English ear". All this was some consolation for the fact that on its arrival at Quetta—"a most miserable mud town, with a small castle on a mound, on which there was a small gun on a rickety carriage"—the army had not yet escaped from the threat of starvation.

To Cotton it seemed as impossible to stop where he was as to advance. The camp followers were by now eating sheepskins fried in dry blood, and the troops were being reduced to physical wrecks who gazed with terror at each other's gaunt frames and sunken features. Within a few days Macnaghten would be reporting to the Governor-General that "the fact is, the troops and followers are nearly in a state of mutiny for food". Sir Willoughby reported back for orders to Sir John Keane, now slowly making his way through Scinde with the Bombay force and Soojah's contingent, though how Keane could solve the problem from that distance it was difficult to see. More practically, Cotton sent Burnes posting off to the Khan of Khelat to try by a mixture of bribes and threats to procure extra supplies.

Mehrab Khan, with dignity and good sense, pointed out that there was practically no grain to be had, and that some of his own people had been reduced to feeding on wild herbs and grasses gathered in the jungle. Khelat had never been exactly flowing with milk and honey, and now "the English had come and by their march through his country in different directions destroyed the crops, poor as they were, and helped themselves to water which irrigated the lands, made doubly valuable in this year of scarcity". Macnaghten, though convinced of the enmity of Mehrab and therefore prompt to recommend that his territory be annexed to the kingdom to which Soojah was to be restored, felt constrained to admit that the Khelat ruler "had good cause for dissatisfaction with us". The Envoy was incensed at the army's callous inhumanity and disregard of what would now be called public relations: "a great portion of these evils—the destruction of crops and the taking of irrigation water—was perhaps unavoidable, but little or no effort seems to have been made either to mitigate the calamity or to appease the discontent which has been created by our proceedings."

Under the circumstances Mehrab showed himself a good deal more co-operative than might have been expected. He sent squads off to guard the ripening crops, so that they might be secured for the British; he undertook to guard the lines of communication back to India—an elementary step which the British had apparently ignored—so that any supplies which could be sent up through the Bolan would get through in safety; and he made arrangements to supply anything from ten to eighteen thousand sheep. For good measure, he added a few words of advice, which were duly reported by Burnes to Macnaghten, but which went unheeded. "The Khan, with a good deal of earnestness, enlarged upon the undertaking the British had embarked on—declared it to be one of vast magnitude and difficult accomplishment—that all the Afghans were discontented with the Shah and all Mahomedans alarmed and excited at what was passing—that the Chief of Caubul—Dost Mahomed—was a man of ability and resource, and though we could easily put him down by Shah Soojah even in our present mode of procedure, we could never win over the Afghan nation by it."

For the moment Macnaghten had worries enough of his own, without troubling about such gloomy forecasts. He was with Soojah's army which, with Sir John Keane's Bombay contingent, was making its way through Scinde. Already Keane's force was in straits almost as parlous as Cotton's. He was shrewdly out of beef—"in a wretched plight for want of cattle," said Macnaghten. He therefore pushed on through the Bolan, to be met by Cotton with the depressing news that he had only twelve days' supplies left and the men already on quarter rations. There was also, he thought, every prospect of the army's being opposed at every step as it entered Afghanistan. "Sir W. is a sad croaker," wrote Macnaghten to the Governor-General; "not content with telling me we must all inevitably be starved, he assures me that Shah Soojah is very unpopular in Afghanistan, and that we shall be opposed at every step of our progress."

Macnaghten was more optimistic. He believed—rightly, as it turned out—that the Kandahar Sirdars were at their wits' end, "only thinking how they can make good terms for themselves; or failing that, how they may best contrive to effect their escape". Yet it was no wonder that the Generals were worried about their supplies, or that "Cotton sat still, bemoaning his hard fate, until all ranks from the general to the drummer were discussing but one topic, the miserable outlook for the army and the certain prospect of starvation".[1] The Commissariat was almost unbelievably inefficient; "no language can describe it," said Nott, "nor give any idea of the rascality of its native agents". There were, in fact, two separate Commissariat departments, one for the Bengal army and one for the Shah's force, which frequently bid against each other and pushed to ruinous heights the price of what few local supplies were available. Soojah had a ready answer to the problem but, to his annoyance, the scruples of the British would not let him apply it. He would simply have reaped the growing crops and left the inhabitants to starve. Macnaghten would have none of this; "we are compelled to tell his Majesty's people that they must not touch the green crops of the country. This they think very hard, and so I believe does the King." Soojah indeed remarked that "he never had so much trouble and bother in his lifetime as he has met with during this campaign" and this, from Soojah, with his long record of unsuccessful campaigns, was no mean criticism. "The reason," added Macnaghten, "is obvious; the people on former occasions helped themselves to everything they wanted, and no complaint was permitted to approach the sacred person of his Majesty."

The Envoy was also perturbed by the King's attitude towards his subjects-to-be, the Afghan nation, of whom "his opinion is, I regret to say, extremely low". In fact, Soojah had genially remarked that they were "a pack of dogs, one and all" and Macnaghten could only express the hope that "we must try and bring him gradually round to entertain a more favourable view of his subjects". This was a view which the British officers themselves were already forming. Nott thought them "very fine-looking fellows indeed. . . . I like them very much." He talked to one of them, who had come into camp with a load of fruit to sell. He was "the finest-looking fellow I have ever seen, quite the

[1] Fortescue.

93

gentleman". The Afghan asked Nott why the British were invading his country. "I told him merely for the purpose of putting his rightful King upon his throne. He said '*We* prefer Dost Mahomed.' I said, 'He has no right to the throne.' I shall not forget the expression of his large black eyes: stepping up to me and placing his hand on my shoulder, he said, in a bold yet respectful tone, 'What right have you to Benares and Delhi? Why, the same right that *our* Dost Mahomed has to Caubul, and he will keep it.' " Nott added thoughtfully, "I really believe that the people of Afghanistan will not give up their country without fighting for it, and I know I would not were I in their situation."

Meanwhile, General Keane was taking a grip of the situation. Nott, who disliked him ("the truth is, he is a Queen's officer and I am a Company's; I am decidedly of opinion that a Queen's officer, be he ever so talented, is totally unfit to command the Company's Army"), described him as "bred in rough schools. . . . He had retained all the manners of the Peninsular camp without benefiting by the gloss of courts and the society of cities; his language too frequently reminded his staff and associates of the coarseness of the men who served under Marlborough in Flanders."[1] But at least this rough-tongued general grasped the fact that the only hope lay in pushing on to Kandahar. The decision taken, the task proved surprisingly easy, apart from a shortage of water.[2] Kohun Dil Khan and his brothers, the Kandahar Sirdars, beset by the usual Afghan treachery, fled from the city and the danger of resistance was so slight that it was felt that Soojah's levies could safely take the lead; British gold had purchased a claque of royalist supporters; and on 25th April, 1839, to the cheers of these sycophants—"Welcome to the son of Timur Shah! Kandahar is rescued from the Barukzyes! May your enemies be destroyed!"—Shah Soojah-ool-Moolk triumphantly re-entered Kandahar.

[1] "Sir John Keane's appointment," wrote Nott, "was from the first a dirty job, and has paralyzed and nearly given a death blow to the enterprise."

[2] George Lawrence "saw a trooper of the 16th Lancers, who had a soda-water bottle half full of water, pour the whole contents down the throat of a poor native woman's child, who was just dying of thirst. I could have hugged the fellow for his noble and disinterested act."

5

The apparent delight with which the Kandaharis greeted their returning monarch was much to the liking of Macnaghten, who described their welcome as "feelings nearly amounting to adoration". A fortnight later, however, he was able to see how much this facile enthusiasm for the house of Suddozye was really worth. By now the whole Army of the Indus had arrived and a ceremonial review was held on the plain outside the city. Soojah, seated on a dais under a gorgeous canopy and greeted by a royal salvo of one hundred and one guns, took the salute as the troops marched imposingly past. Space had been reserved for the spectators whose enthusiasm, said the official programme, would be "restrained by the Shah's troops". It was an unnecessary precaution, for the show fell completely flat. "The people of Candahar," said Havelock, "are said to have viewed the whole affair with the most mortifying indifference" and barely a hundred of them turned out to watch. Soojah, however, was delighted with the day's events and grandly declared that their moral influence would be felt from Pekin to Constantinople. Meanwhile, as trimmers, toadies and placemen clamoured for office, he remarked with some humour that since it took God Almighty six days to make heaven and earth, it was very hard they they would not allow him, a poor mortal, even the same time to settle the affairs of a kingdom.

The army now stayed bogged down at Kandahar for two months, waiting for the crops to ripen and replenish supplies. Officers and men were soon thoroughly bored, finding little diversion in a place described by Nott as "a large and very filthy city, containing about 80,000 inhabitants. There is one street, quite through the city, which is some 50 or 60 feet broad; all others are narrow." The sight-seeing possibilities—the white-domed tomb of Ahmed Shah and a fine mosque containing a shirt said to have been worn by the Prophet Mahomed—were soon exhausted. Meanwhile, sickness had broken out. On a diet of mutton and ripe fruit, living under canvas in frightful heat, the British troops were laid low by fever, dysentery and jaundice. It was high time for something to happen. "In truth, my dear Marshman," wrote Havelock to his brother-in-law, "it is time that we should have either a battle, or that which I have grown wise enough to know is a much better thing, a general break up of hostility in the way of timely submission to the Shah."

Of this, however, there was no sign. The only excitement was the despatch of a mobile column under Colonel Robert Sale in pursuit of the Kandahar Sirdars, which returned empty-handed on finding that Kohun Dil and his brothers had taken refuge across the Persian frontier. But already there was ominous evidence of a hardening of national and religious temper against the invaders. The enemies who now lurked round the British camp were of a very different stamp to the Baluchi marauders of the earlier phase, whose motive had been robbery, pure and simple. Now there was bitter hatred too. Two young officers, who thought to lighten the boredom of the long pause at Kandahar by going on a fishing expedition, were savagely attacked and one of them, Lieutenant Inverarity of the 16th Lancers, was murdered. "Remember, gentlemen," warned Soojah, when he heard the tale, "you are not now in Hindustan."

Up in Kabul, Dost Mahomed was mystified by the invading army's prolonged halt at Kandahar. If Keane and Macnaghten really planned to advance upon his capital, he could not understand why they should be wasting their time in utter idleness at Kandahar. He concluded that the British must be planning a move towards Herat and that the Army of the Indus would branch off to the west, deferring operations against Kabul until the following year. He therefore concentrated his attention upon the defence of the eastern approaches, along which the Sikh force was now advancing; to meet this threat he despatched some of his best troops, under command of his favourite son, Akbar Khan.

But at the end of June, after a two months' pause, Keane struck his camp at Kandahar and resumed his ponderous, purposeful march towards Kabul. Directly across his path, two hundred and thirty miles north-east of Kandahar and ninety miles south of the capital, lay the mighty fortress of Ghuznee.

Pride and boast of the Afghan nation—eight hundred years earlier it had been the birthplace of the great empire of Mahmud the Ghaznevid—Ghuznee had not been captured for many a long year and was now confidently believed to be impregnable. During the British delay at Kandahar the defences had been strengthened, six months' provisions laid in and the garrison increased to three thousand men commanded by another of the Dost's sons, Hyder Khan, while another, Afzul Khan, hovered outside with a force of cavalry ready to operate against the invaders' flanks. Once again Dost Mahomed had misjudged the enemy's plans. Crediting Sir John Keane with more skill in generalship than he possessed, he assumed that the British intended to mask Ghuznee and move on past it against Kabul. But Keane had no intention of masking Ghuznee; he proposed to go at it like a bull at a gate.

His own plans were based upon intelligence as erroneous as Dost Mahomed's. Indeed, it was only at Kandahar that Keane had decided to form an intelligence department of his own. "There is no such thing at present," he told Macnaghten. "I have never seen the like in any army." Now his political officers, Major Todd and Lieutenant Leech, assured him that Ghuznee was a place of no great strength and that he would have no trouble in taking it, if in fact the fortress was not abandoned upon the first appearance of his troops. Keane readily swallowed these fatuously optimistic forecasts. He even decided, "with an amount of infatuation which was perhaps unexampled in Indian warfare",[1] to leave behind at Kandahar the massive train of heavy siege artillery. Havelock, who was sure from his own sources of information that Ghuznee *would* be defended, thought it preposterous that, after the labour with which these cumbrous weapons had been dragged up through the mountain passes, they should now be left by the wayside on the first occasion on which they were likely to be needed. He reminded the Commander-in-Chief that Napoleon at Acre, Wellington at Burgos and Lake at Bhurtpore "had each found cause to rue the hour in which they attacked fortifications, unprovided with a sufficient number of guns of breaching calibre", but Keane brushed his arguments aside. Havelock, who detected in the General "a selfishness and self-will that manifested themselves in command in the grossest partiality and a contempt for truth, justice and common honesty", believed that the real reason for this reckless decision lay in the favouritism that Keane always showed to the Bombay Army, while leaving the Bengal contingent "under an indiscriminate ban of exclusion from his confidence". The senior gunner in the force was a Bengal officer; by leaving him with the siege train at Kandahar it could be arranged that a Bombay officer should command the artillery at Ghuznee and reap any honours, rewards or prize money that might be going.

Keane realised his mistake as soon as he came in sight of Ghuznee, on 21st July, 1839, nearly four weeks after leaving Kandahar. It was, he saw, a place "of great strength, both by nature and by art . . . its fortifications rising up, as it were, on the side of a hill, which seemed to form the background to it". It was obviously garrisoned in strength, and it was plain that the massive walls would never be breached by the six-pounder and nine-

[1] Havelock.

pounder pop-guns, which were all that he had with him. Keane was in a fix. To storm the place by escalade would have been ruinously costly in lives, yet with only three days' supplies he could not afford a siege. Soojah suggested pushing on to Kabul and leaving Ghuznee on one side. "If you once breach the place, it is yours," he told Keane, "but I cannot understand how you are to breach it—how you are to get into the fort."

There was, however, a way, and it was presently to be used by the British in reducing many of the mud fortresses with which Afghanistan was dotted. "An Afghan fort," explained Captain Mackenzie, "consists of a square with a tower at each corner, the walls being built of huge masses of mud, some six or eight feet thick at the base and perhaps three at the top, the main building varying in height from twenty to forty feet, and all being pierced with numerous loopholes for wall-pieces and matchlocks. In general, they have only one strong gate, and our mode of taking them is very simple. If a few rounds from a great gun do not do the office of a key, two covering parties keep up a rattling covering fire on the walls while an officer rushes forward with a bag of powder, which he nails to the gate, fires by means of a slow match, and gets out of the way as fast as possible.[1] The gate being shattered, the storming party enters and slays the garrison, if pugnaciously given."

This technique was first tried out at Ghuznee, a very different proposition from the small forts that Mackenzie was describing. But the timely arrival in the British camp of a traitor nephew of Dost Mahomed revealed that one entrance, the Kabul gate, had not been built up, and Captain Thomson, of the Bengal Engineers, volunteered to blow it in by gunpowder under cover of darkness. Keane, rescued from an impasse, took the credit for this "bold and brilliant" plan. He confided it to Macnaghten, who confided it to Soojah, and in consequence it was soon known to every camp-follower. Fortunately it was put into operation so quickly that it hardly had time to reach the ears of the Ghuznee garrison.

On the day before the assault the British had their first taste of the *Ghazis*, dedicated and fearless warriors who fought under the green banner of Islam. The dearest wish of these terrifying fanatics was either to slay the infidel in battle or to meet their

---

[1] But not always fast enough. A hundred forts in the Wuzeran Valley were later destroyed in this way, but at one of them "Lieutenant Pigou was killed by an explosion, the fuse being too short, when blowing in a gateway." (Lawrence).

own death in striving to do so; either way, they believed, they were sure of a place in the Moslem paradise. They preferred close combat and their favourite weapon was the sword.

A cloud of mounted Ghazis now came whooping down upon Soojah's camp, determined to rid their country of a king who had insulted the Moslem faith by returning to power upon the shoulders of infidels. The artillery of the fortress joined in to support them, in particular a brass forty-eight pounder which the Afghans had nicknamed "*Zubur-Zun*", the "Hard-Hitter". One ball from the Hard-Hitter, after a double ricochet across the plain, bounded into the Shah's camp and grazed first the leg of a trooper and then the thigh of a camel. The range was at least two thousand yards and both wounds were trifling, "yet both the soldier and the unlucky quadruped died of them", the camel being presumably as prone to auto-suggestion as the man. Meanwhile a spirited charge by the Shah's cavalry, which had checked the Ghazi onslaught, was followed up by a determined drive by the infantry, under the command of one whose name, like Havelock's, was to become famous in the Mutiny years, Captain James Outram. Some fifty Ghazis were captured and led into the presence of Soojah, whom they incensed by their unrepentant glorying in their deeds and their open reviling of himself. One of them recklessly added point to the argument by stabbing a royal attendant and the exasperated Shah ordered that they should all be taken out and beheaded.

A horrified British officer stumbled by chance upon the butchery as it was being carried out at the back of the Shah's tent. "There were forty or fifty men," he recorded, "young and old. Many were dead; others at their last gasp; others with their hands tied behind them; some sitting, others standing, awaiting their doom; and the King's executioners and other servants amusing themselves (for actually they were laughing and joking, and seemed to look upon the work as good fun) with hacking and maiming the poor wretches indiscriminately with their long swords and knives." The slaughter of these Ghazi prisoners was chalked up in Afghan memories against Soojah and his British allies. "The day of reckoning came at last," wrote Kaye grimly: "and when our unholy policy sunk unburied in blood and ashes, the shrill cry of the Ghazi sounded as its funeral wail."

But for the moment the "fearfully bloody sight", as the British eye-witness described it, was forgotten in the excitement of the forthcoming night attack. The night of 22nd July was dark and stormy and a boisterous wind drowned the noise of the advance as

Thomson and his sappers moved cautiously round to the Kabul gate. Here they stacked up nine hundred pounds of gunpowder, in seventy-five pound bags, and by three o'clock in the morning all was ready. Keane's light artillery created a diversion by opening a harmless fire upon the walls (it did no damage except "carrying away the head of a brave Afghan, who stood upon the parapet waving a flag and calling upon us to advance"[1]) and a row of blue lights flickered up along the ramparts as the Afghans, manning the walls in anticipation of an escalade attack, obligingly looked in the wrong direction. The sappers, crouching in the rain by the Kabul gate, touched off the hose, a sausage-shaped cloth tube full of powder. It failed to ignite on the first application of the port-fire but after Lieutenant Durand had scraped at it with his finger-nails it spluttered into life. The sappers scampered to safety, there was a terrific explosion, and a cloud of black smoke rose skywards as the masonry and beams of the gate came crashing down. A bugle shrilled the "Charge!" and the forlorn hope, the light infantry companies of the four European regiments, under Colonel Dennie of the 13th Light Infantry, rushed into the breach. British bayonet and Afghan scimitar clashed in the narrow entrance as the storming column advanced into the breach by sections, each discharging its volley point-blank and then making way for the next. At such a range and with such a close-packed target even the musket could not fail to do deadly execution. The defenders began to give ground, and above their heads the leading assailants could now glimpse the morning sky and a twinkling star or two. They pushed on into the fortress, and soon three resounding cheers told those outside that Dennie and his men were in Ghuznee.

In close support came the main storming column under Brigadier Sale, only to be checked briefly at the gate as one of Thomson's sapper officers, dazed by the explosion, reported that the entrance was choked by rubble and that he had been unable to see daylight. Sale overheard him and precipitately ordered his bugler to sound the retreat. The call was taken up by the whole column, which halted in confusion. Fortunately Captain Thomson was at hand to correct Sale; Dennie was indeed inside the fortress; his men were already up on the walls firing down upon the garrison as they swarmed to meet Sale's men in the breach. The bugles again sounded the advance and the storming column surged forward. Before long the colours of the British regiments were flapping from the ramparts in the morning breeze and

[1] Lawrence.

nothing remained but some warm work in the way of mopping up. In the main square—"a scene of blood and confusion"— riderless and hysterical horses, many of them wounded, "were running about in all directions, fighting with each other, kicking and biting, and running quite furious at any one they saw";[1] eventually the troops had to be ordered in self-defence to shoot the unhappy animals. Meanwhile in a fury of despair the Afghans rushed out from their lairs upon the attackers, only to be shot down by the muskets of the British or spitted on their bayonets. Some, trying to escape by the ruined Kabul gate, stumbled, wounded and exhausted, over the burning timbers and were slowly roasted to death by the smouldering fire of their thick sheepskin jerkins. Some were bayoneted as they lay, others hunted into corners and shot down like mad dogs, a curse and a prayer upon their lips. By midday all was over. The impregnable fortress of Ghuznee had been captured at a total cost to the victors of seventeen killed and a hundred and sixty-five wounded. The Afghans had lost about 1,200 killed and 300 wounded, while 1,500 prisoners were taken.

It was remarkable that no Afghan who dropped his arms was refused quarter, even at the height of the assault, nor was there any attempt by the victorious troops to rape any of the women found within the walls. Havelock unhesitatingly attributed this "self-denial, mercy and generosity of the hour" to the fact that the rum had given out a fortnight earlier and that no liquor had been found among the loot of Ghuznee. "The character of the scene in the fortress and the citadel would have been far different if individual soldiers had entered the town primed with arrack, or if spirituous liquors had been discovered in the Afghan depots." Ghuznee proved to Havelock's satisfaction that troops could make forced marches of forty miles and storm a fortress in a little over an hour without the aid of rum, behaving afterwards "with a forbearance and humanity unparalleled in history". What was more, the army medical officers definitely attributed the rapid recovery of the Ghuznee wounded to their previous, and enforced, abstinence from strong drink. "All the sword cuts," recorded James Atkinson,[2] "united in the most satisfactory manner, which we decidedly attributed to the men having been without rum for the previous six weeks." And so, concluded Havelock triumphantly, "let it not henceforth be argued that distilled spirits are an indispensable portion of the soldier's ration".

Major Hough, Deputy Judge Advocate General of the Bengal

[1] Hough.   [2] *The Expedition Into Afghanistan.*

column, who wrote a rival history of the campaign, was not so sure. He noted that the rum ran out at a time when the European troops "owing to eating the fat Doomba mutton, which is rich, and drinking the water of the country possessing an aperient quality, suffered much from bowel complaints", and he added tartly that "whatever may be the opinion of the '*Abstinence Societies*', all sound medical men declare the sudden deprivation of spirits to be injurious". Havelock would no doubt have retorted that for those who had never drunk rum in the first place, there would have been no deprivation. But then Havelock held extreme views on the subject. He attributed two slight attacks of fever to having consented, at the suggestion of friends, "to drink a few glasses of wine daily, instead of restricting myself as I had done for many months to pure water". After a quick recovery he again became a teetotaller and "from the time that the pure element became once more my only drink, I enjoyed a total exemption from the evils of any serious ailment". He was thus strengthened in his conviction "that water-drinking is the best regimen for a soldier".

6

Not long before the storming of Ghuznee, Captain Lawrence, returning from a reconnaissance of the fortress, had fallen in with a solitary enemy horseman who engaged him in conversation. The Afghan told Lawrence that he had visited the British camp and seen the troops. "You are an enemy of tents and camels," he said scornfully; "*our* army is one of men and horses." With the capture of Ghuznee this contemptuous attitude vanished. Although the British did not immediately realise it, the whole campaign had to all intents and purposes been decided by this single stroke.

Soojah, watching the assault from close in, had shown an icy courage under fire. Although dismissed by Lawrence's Afghan acquaintance as a *kumbukht* (unlucky person) "who, the moment you turn your backs, will be upset by Dost Mahomed, our *own* king", he sat his horse "as firm as a rock, not showing the slightest alarm either by word or gesture, and seeming to think it derogatory to his kingly character to move an inch whilst the firing lasted". Keane and Macnaghten now joined him, and together they rode down into the captured fortress.

Hyder Khan, the young commander of the garrison, was found lurking in a house and brought before the monarch. Soojah, who had been warned by his British mentors that there must be no repetition of the disgraceful massacre of the Ghazi prisoners, received him with kindness, declaring courteously that the past was forgiven and that the young Sirdar might go in peace.

The Dost's other son, Afzul Khan, who had been waiting to loose his cavalry upon the British when they fell back baffled from Ghuznee, was awe-struck to see their colours flying from the citadel. He promptly abandoned his elephants and baggage and fled to Kabul, where his father angrily refused to receive him. But the Afghans, shaken to the depths of their being by the capture of their impregnable fortress, had little stomach for a further trial of strength with these formidable invaders and Dost Mahomed's brother, Jubbar Khan—Burnes' host at breakfast years before— arrived at Ghuznee under flag of truce to negotiate. He tendered Dost Mahomed's submission to Soojah, but claimed for him the hereditary office of Vizir, so long held by the Barukzye family. Soojah refused, doubtless remembering Futteh Khan's dubious record of loyalty, and Dost Mahomed was offered instead an "honourable asylum" in British India. Jubbar Khan indignantly rejected the offer and declared that he and his brother would fight to the last. On this heroic note he rode back to Kabul.

Meanwhile Keane had issued a sonorous General Order to celebrate the capture of Ghuznee. Having begun by remarking that he felt that he could hardly do justice to the gallantry of the troops, he did his best to do so in twelve long paragraphs (more words than Wellington took to describe Waterloo), thanked over twenty officers by name, and concluded by stating that "no army that has ever been engaged in a campaign deserves more credit than that which he has the honour to command, for patient, orderly and cool conduct under all circumstances, and Sir John Keane is proud to have the opportunity of thus publicly acknowledging it". Under the influence of this resounding tribute Sir Robert Peel was presently to describe the capture of Ghuznee as "the most brilliant achievement of our arms in Asia", a eulogy which, as Fortescue says, is "quite ridiculous".

Shrewder critics noted that Keane, who had a grudge against Colonel Dennie, the leader of the forlorn hope, was careful to give all the credit to Colonel—now Brigadier—Robert Sale, whose precipitate action in sounding the retreat had nearly wrecked everything. Sale—"Fighting Bob"—was quite undeservedly to become *the* hero of the Afghan war. He had commanded the Queen's 13th Light Infantry, a regiment described by Mackenzie as being in "a very bad state". Its ranks having been decimated by disease in Burma, it had been reinforced by recruits who were the sweepings of the gaols of London. It was in a "frightful state of insubordination".[1] One officer and several N.C.Os were shot and Sale himself often received anonymous threats of murder. Each time that this happened he would come on parade next day with the letter in his pocket and give the order to load with blank cartridge, an open challenge to any malcontent to slip a ball down his barrel. Sale, sitting like a ramrod astride his charger in front of his mutinous battalion, would then give the order "Present-fire!" But the bluff was never called, and after the noise of the harmless volley had died away, Sale would shout triumphantly "Ah, its not my fault if you don't shoot me!"

Mixed with this jovial paternalism were sterner measures. Four culprits each morning, and another four each evening, would be tied up to the triangles to receive up to eight hundred lashes for such spirited crimes as attempting to stab an officer. When they came out of hospital the smallest sign of insubordination, such as an impertinent reply, brought an immediate sentence of three hundred lashes. This Draconian discipline achieved its purpose and the men, as one of the officers said, became "mere babies, you could do anything with them".

Despite these ferocious punishments, Sale's men worshipped him, largely because "nothing could induce him to behave himself as a General should do. Despite his staff's protests, he used to ride about two miles ahead of his troops, and in action would fight like a private." As a result, he invariably got wounded, and this added to his popularity. Ghuznee had been no exception. Havelock had found him rolling on the ground, locked in conflict with a burly Afghan who had felled him with a blow in the face from his scimitar. Sale kept a tight grip of his adversary's weapon hand as he grappled with him. Captain Kershaw of the 13th happened to come along at this moment and Sale, with what may be considered remarkably courteous aplomb considering his position, politely suggested that he "do him the favour to pass his sword through the body of the infidel". Kershaw, with equal courtesy, obliged but apparently passed on his way without waiting to see how effective his intervention had been. The Afghan continued to struggle with desperate violence until Sale, momentarily uppermost in this deadly wrestling bout, managed to deal him a blow with his sabre which cleft his skull from crown to eyebrows. The Moslem gave one loud lamentable cry of "Ne Ullah!" (Oh, God!)", after which, it is hardly surprising to hear, "he never spoke or moved again".

[1] Mackenzie.

Dost Mahomed would have staked all on a last stand in front of Kabul, but Afghans could never see much sense in dying in the last ditch and, as the British advanced from Ghuznee towards the capital, his troops began to melt away. The Kuzzilbash mercenaries were deserting in droves and now one of his chief supporters, Hadjee Khan Khaukur—"a man of mean extraction and the son of a goatherd"—went over to the enemy. Dost Mahomed made a last appeal to his men. "You have eaten my salt these thirteen years," he cried; "grant me but one favour in requital for that long period of maintenance and kindness—enable me to die with honour. Stand by the brother of Futteh Khan while he executes one last charge against the cavalry of these Feringhee dogs; in that onset he will fall; then go and make your own terms with Shah Soojah."

There was no response. The Dost, mastering his despair with quiet dignity, discharged the Kuzzilbash mercenaries from their allegiance and dismissed all those who wished to purchase safety by submitting to Soojah. Then, with a handful of devoted followers, he rode off northwards towards the Hindu Kush mountains.

Within twenty-four hours a mounted column under Outram set off in pursuit. They should have had no difficulty in overtaking the Amir, whose party included women and children and was further slowed down by having to carry Akbar Khan, who had fallen sick and been withdrawn from the defence of the Khyber line against the Sikh force. But the guide who rode with the British column was that same goatherd's son, Hadjee Khan Khaukur, who, though he had deserted Dost Mahomed, firmly believed in hedging his bet and had no intention of seeing the Amir captured. By finding every pretext for delay he so slowed down Outram's little column that Dost Mahomed was able to get across the northern frontier and find refuge with the independent Uzbeg tribes beyond the Hindu Kush. Outram's party returned empty-handed to face the mocking cackles of their friends, who told them that they were mad to have gone on such a wild goose chase, while Keane himself jeered that "he had not supposed that there were thirteen such asses in his whole force".[1]

On 6th August, 1839, Shah Soojah and the British army arrived before the walls of Kabul and next day the old King re-entered his capital. There were no signs of welcome and the inhabitants looked on with "the most complete indifference"[1] as the Shah rode in, Macnaghten and Burnes riding alongside in the full rig of the diplomatic service. This impressive uniform

[1] Lawrence.

consisted of "a cocked hat fringed with ostrich feathers, a blue frock coat with raised buttons, richly embroidered on the collar and cuffs, epaulettes not yielding in splendour to those of a field marshal, and trowsers edged with very broad gold lace". The British in their finery quite outshone the Shah, and to judge by the reception of the citizens of Kabul, it would be long before Soojah would be safe without the support of British bayonets.

The Simla Manifesto had proclaimed that when once Soojah had been restored "and the independence and integrity of Afghanistan established" the British army would be withdrawn, This was still Lord Auckland's wish. On 20th August he minuted that, "I am anxiously desirous that the forces which compose the Army of the Indus should be once more stationed within our own provinces." Plainly a force of some kind must be left to prop up the Shah, and it was at first thought that five or six regiments would suffice and that the whole of the Bombay contingent could be withdrawn, together with part of the Bengal army. But by the beginning of October the British were having second thoughts. They were haunted by the notion of Dost Mahomed hovering somewhere beyond the Hindu Kush and rousing the Uzbeg tribes to come sweeping down upon the hated Soojah, and it was decided that a much larger garrison than they had originally intended must be left in Afghanistan. The whole of the Bengal contingent—a division of infantry, a regiment of cavalry, gunners and ancillary units—was now earmarked to winter in the country. Sir John Keane handed over command to Sir Willoughby Cotton and, having uttered the gloomy and well-founded prophecy that there would soon be a signal catastrophe, marched the remainder off to India.

7

There was still some fighting to be done, for it had been enthusiastically decided that Mehrab Khan, the ruler of Khelat, must be chastised for his offences, though no one was very clear just what those offences were. There was, however, a general impression that he had been guilty of acts of indescribable treachery, and that during the advance of the Army of the Indus through Baluchistan he had continually molested the British columns. All the hardships endured by the army, the near-starvation suffered by man and beast, were now confidently attributed to the wickedness of the Khan. No one now remembered that there had been a famine in his land before ever the army arrived in it, and that the wanton damage done by the troops had made the famine worse. No one remembered that it was only Mehrab Khan's help that had enabled the army to make a safe passage of the Bolan Pass. Burnes had advised that he should be humbled, and that was enough for Macnaghten.

It was enough for the Governor-General too. Auckland confirmed that Macnaghten had his authority to annexe Khelat to the kingdom of Afghanistan, adding that "it is my strong opinion that no power should be left in the hands of Mehrab Khan, who has shown himself our bitter and deceitful enemy, wholly unworthy of our confidence". At least Auckland remembered, though nobody else did, that after the abject failure of Soojah's 1834 expedition it was the Khan of Khelat who had given aid and comfort to the Shah. This, thought Auckland, entitled Mehrab to generous treatment as an individual. "Mr. Macnaghten," opined the Governor-General, "will naturally not fail to second any proposition of a liberal personal support to the chief which the Shah may be disposed to make, in generous acknowledgement of those services."

Neither Mr. Macnaghten nor the Shah wasted much thought over such sentimental weakness. In mid-November General Willshire, with the 2nd and 17th Queen's, the 31st Bengal Native Infantry, two howitzers, four of the Shah's six-pounders and a detachment of cavalry, arrived at the gates of Khelat, where Mehrab Khan, hardly able to believe that those whom he had so recently escorted through the Bolan would now turn and rend him, had been slow to adopt defensive measures. When at last he realised that the British were in earnest he flung a brave defiance at them, and glowered down upon them from the fortress of Khelat, a stronghold nearly as formidable as Ghuznee.

The citadel of Khelat rose high over the town itself, and to the north-west lay three hills on which the Khan had posted infantry with three supporting guns. Willshire, decided that these heights must be carried before the town itself could be attacked, planned to drive the enemy down from the hills to the gates of Khelat and send the British storming column rushing in alongside them. The first phase went perfectly. The hills were carried, the guns captured, and then, with the shrapnel playing on them with deadly effect, the Baluchi infantry broke and ran for the gates. The British chased in hot pursuit, but they were just too late; the gates were slammed in their faces.

The storming column took cover behind some ruined buildings while Willshire brought his guns into play upon the gates from a range of only two hundred yards. The gates collapsed, the storming columns rose from their cover and rushed forward with a cheer. There followed a fierce hand-to-hand struggle, with every inch of ground disputed. In one courtyard Lieutenant Loveday saw "a heap of their dead, some forty or fifty—some very fine handsome fellows—their shields shot through, and broken swords and matchlocks lying about in every direction, telling of the fierce fight". The assailants at length forced their way into the inner heart of the citadel where, sword in hand, Mehrab Khan and his principal chiefs stood at bay. The Khan fell dead, a musket ball through his heart, and eight of his chief ministers and generals were slain at his side. As at Ghuznee, so at Khelat; another reputedly impregnable stronghold had fallen to the British in a matter of hours.

Next day Loveday saw the corpse of Mehrab Khan being carried past on its way to burial—"a fine-looking man. There was one little hole in his breast, which told of a musket ball having passed through. He had no clothes on, except his silk *pyjammahs*". One of the slaves whispered a request to the British subaltern for a shawl to serve as a shroud. Loveday had no shawl, but luckily remembered that he possessed a brocade bed-cover, "which I had bought in the days of my folly and extravagance at Delhi". This he generously presented to the burial party, "who were delighted with this last mark of respect". As things turned out, he might have kept it as a shroud for himself.

It had all been very successful and chivalrous, and when the news reached Macnaghten as he was being entertained to dinner by the hospitable Avitabile, Runjeet Singh's Italian governor of Peshawar, the health of the victors was drunk with enthusiasm and the "three times three" of a hearty British cheer. Those who felt that Mehrab Khan might have been hardly used discreetly kept their misgivings to themselves, and all agreed that it was a great feat of arms, worthy to rank with the taking of Ghuznee. Indeed, the Indian regiments rated it higher, for at Ghuznee Keane had composed the storming column exclusively of European troops, whereas the 31st Bengal Native Infantry had acquitted themselves manfully at the assault on Khelat. So the sepoys were happy, the British were happy, Macnaghten was happy, and presumably Shah Soojah, to whose kingdom the territory of the dead Khan was now annexed, was happy too. But the Baluchi and the Afghans nursed in their hearts a bitter and growing hatred of these English invaders who were making their Naboth's vineyard a wilderness, and calling it a peace.

8

Before the British could feel secure there remained one military task, and it would prove more difficult and protracted than the brutally swift destruction of the Khan of Khelat. The thought of Dost Mahomed, up to God only knew what mischief beyond the Hindu Kush, sent shivers down Soojah's spine and even disturbed Macnaghten's normal outlook of fatuous optimism. "You rightly conjecture," he wrote to Colvin, back in India, "that the Barukzyes have most inflammable material to work upon. Of all moral qualities avarice, credulity and bigotry are the most inflammable, and the Afghans have all these three in perfection."

Dost Mahomed, however, had decided that he had no chance of rousing enough support among the petty Uzbeg chiefs to attempt a counter-attack, and early in 1840 he sought asylum at the court of Nasrullah Khan, Amir of Bokhara. Nasrullah was a savage tyrant, and barely sane. He had come to the throne fourteen years before, having first murdered his father, his elder brother, and, as an added precaution, his three younger brothers. After this bloodthirsty start he had, at the beginning of his reign, shown signs of moderation. "Before he came to the throne," wrote a young Indian visitor to Bokhara approvingly, "he loved boys, but now religion." But soon he had reverted to his normal mood of dark suspicion and truculent ferocity. He had also ostentatiously given himself the same title that Dost Mahomed had taken for his war against the Sikhs a few years earlier, "Commander of the Faithful". Macnaghten correctly forecast that "it is very unlikely that the two Ameers-ool-Moomuneen will ever act cordially together." And so it turned out. Nasrullah welcomed the Dost effusively and urged him to send for his family who would, he promised, receive every kindness. Dost Mahomed, who knew his host's character very well, was not deceived. He wrote to his brother, Jubbar Khan, an open letter which Nasrullah was carefully allowed to see, requesting him to send his family to the friendly court of Bokhara. Secretly, however, he enjoined Jubbar to put them to death rather than let them set foot in Bokhara. Nasrullah, whose chief interest lay in the royal family's jewels of which he had planned to relieve them on arrival, was full of wrath when he discovered the deception. Laying his heavy hand upon Dost Mahomed, he cast him into prison with the threat that "there shalt thou remain until thy family is brought to Bokhara".

The Dost was not the only distinguished prisoner in Nasrullah's dungeons at this time. Colonel Charles Stoddart, who was last heard of successfully delivering an ultimatum to Mahomed Shah of Persia at Herat, had been despatched from that city to Bokhara at the end of 1838, with instructions from M'Neill to negotiate a treaty of friendship and to secure the release of some Russians whom Nasrullah was holding prisoner. Between British and Russians, rivals though they might be, there was no personal enmity, but rather a feeling of friendly mutual respect appropriate to civilised men alone among the barbarians of Central Asia. There was also the practical motive for Stoddart's mission that to free the Russian prisoners would remove an obvious pretext for Russian interference.

Stoddart was given a reasonably courteous reception by the unpredictable tyrant, but unwisely conducted himself with an arrogance that moved the Amir to wrath, a wrath heightened by the discovery that the visitor had brought no presents and that his credentials had not been signed by Queen Victoria in person. Before long, one dark night, Stoddart was roughly arrested and hurried off to the Black Well, vilest of all Nasrullah's dungeons. This was "a noisome pit, twenty-one feet deep, full of men's bones, decomposed animal matter and other indescribable filth, and swarming with a mass of specially bred vermin and reptiles, kept by the Amir in order the better to torment his victims, and including enormous sheep ticks that burrowed deep into the flesh, producing terrible sores".

Stoddart's resistance having been worn down by two months of this horrible treatment, his grave was dug before his eyes and he was threatened with burial alive unless he consented to become a Moslem. Sensibly enough, he agreed to be converted, and was thereupon released from the Black Well. But his position remained precarious and Nasrullah played with him like a cat with a mouse, the treatment varying in accordance with reports of British progress in Afghanistan.

Macnaghten now had a double motive for moving against Bokhara. Dost Mahomed was there, and the Envoy would have preferred him in some safer place, where he could do no harm. But "the first thing to be gained", wrote Macnaghten to Burnes early in 1840, "is the punishment of the Shah of Bokhara for his frequent and outrageous violation of the law of nations, and the release of our agent Colonel Stoddart, who without some exertion on our part will, it is likely, be doomed to incarceration for life."

It was a true forecast, for Stoddart was never to leave Bokhara alive. In the summer of 1842 his long martyrdom came to an end.

By this time he had been joined by Captain Arthur Conolly, who had come to negotiate his release and had been promptly cast into gaol with him. A mission of Russian officers, then at Nasrullah's court, strove long and honourably to secure the safety of their British rivals but eventually had to take their leave and Stoddart and Conolly were left alone, at the mercy of the merciless Nasrullah. At first, wrote Conolly in a letter that survived him, he had viewed the tyrant's conduct "as perhaps dictated by mad caprice; but now, looking back upon the whole, we saw instead that it had just been the deliberate malice of a demon, questioning and raising our hopes, and ascertaining our condition, only to see how our hearts were going on, in the process of breaking".

By June, 1842, the ruler of Bokhara, tired of his game of cat and mouse, decided to end it. Flushed with victory over the neighbouring petty state of Khokund, he celebrated his success by putting his English captives to death. Stoddart and Conolly were brought from their miserable dungeon and led to an open square in Bokhara, where a large crowd had gathered to witness the execution. Their hands tied, the two officers were made to stand for some time, watching their graves being made ready. Stoddart was then called forth to die. Crying aloud against the tyranny of Nasrullah, he knelt down and his head was lopped off with a huge knife. It was now Conolly's turn. He was offered his life if he would renounce Christianity and turn Mahomedan. With brave indignation he replied, "Stoddart became a Mussulman, and yet you have killed him. I am prepared to die." He then knelt down and stretched forth his neck for the executioner.

By the time the heads of Stoddart and Conolly fell beneath the headsman's knife in Bokhara, Macnaghten himself would be dead. But for the moment it is still 1840, with the Envoy determined to despatch a force against Bokhara. It need not be a great one; "a brigade of ours, with a due proportion of artillery, would, I think, from all I have heard, be fully competent to overcome any opposition that could be offered to us between this and Bokhara". This reckless proposal shocked some of the military. "Where is your reserve?" wrote Nott to a friend; "why, truly, on the left bank of the Sutlej, with a warlike and not very friendly nation (the Sikhs) having an army of 100,000 men, besides four or five deep and rapid rivers, between you and these supports. . . . Yet some senseless unthinking people talk of pushing a weak brigade as far as Balkh; whereas, unless you get large reinforcements, it is possible that you will find some difficulty in holding your ground at Caubul and in the Khyber Pass."

Macnaghten, however, felt certain that the petty states between the Hindu Kush and the River Oxus must be annexed to Soojah's dominions so that they might be saved from the tyranny of Bokhara. Moreover, this step seemed to him urgently necessary to forestall a more powerful adversary than Nasrullah, for the troops of the Czar had occupied Khiva and Macnaghten was determined "if possible, to frustrate the knavish tricks of the *Russe log* in that quarter".

It occurred to him that there might be some security risk in thus openly discussing his plans in letters to India, and he waxed enthusiastic about a new precaution of which he had recently learned. "Are you in possession," he wrote to the Governor of Agra, "of the *hikmut* of concealed writing, by means of conjee-water and a solution of iodine? This is much better than any cypher. The paper is to all appearances blank, but when rubbed over with the solution, the words written with conjee-water start into life, as it were, most miraculously. Something unimportant is generally written with common ink, and what is intended as secret is interlined with conjee water. Try this some day. Any medical man in your neighbourhood will give the solution. . . . When there is any writing of this kind on my paper, I shall put the day of the month in letters instead of figures. Perhaps you would adopt the same sign."

At the same time, without bothering to mess about with conjee-water and iodine, Macnaghten was expressing himself *en clair* and with vigour on the need for urgent action to counter the influence not only of the Russians but of the French, who had begun again to fish in the muddy waters of Persian politics. A hint of impatience with the Governor-General's indecision was allowed to appear. "Unless Lord Auckland act with vigour and promptitude to secure and open our rear," wrote the Envoy sharply, "we shall soon be between two fires—if not under them. We are supine, whilst our inactivity will probably be the cause of our ruin." He went on to complain that while the French had gratuitously supplied the Persians with 300,000 muskets, he himself, despite urgent and repeated requests, had been unable to secure a single one.

Muskets, indeed, seemed urgently necessary, for in the summer of 1840 Dost Mahomed, disguising himself by dyeing his beard black with ink, had escaped from Bokharas and the Uzbeg fighting men had flocked to his standard. By now his wives and children had surrendered to the British, but when reminded that they were in the enemy's power he replied with sad determination, "I have no family; I have buried my wives and children." Early in September an agitated Macnaghten was reporting to Auckland that the whole country between Kabul and the Oxus was up in favour of the Dost, while the Kohistan was ripe for revolt and Kabul itself seemed to be on the eve of an insurrection.

On top of this, he was menaced by the treacherous intrigues of the Sikhs on the east and the Heratis on the west. Macnaghten, always ready to bite off more than he could chew, would have countered by seizing both Peshawar and Herat, but the Governor-General would not hear of it. "Oh! for a Wellesley or a Hastings at this juncture," lamented the Envoy. Auckland, he declared, had got things back to front. "He says, so long as we are continually agitating the question of taking possession of Peshawar and Herat, we cannot expect honest co-operation from the powers owning these places; thus overlooking the fact that but for the dishonesty of those powers the question would never have been contemplated by us." In petulant impatience he added, "This drivelling is beneath contempt."

To Auckland himself he wrote more respectfully but very pessimistically: "My Lord; I am much fatigued, having been severely worked the whole day; but I write these few lines just to apprise your Lordship that affairs in this quarter have the worst possible appearance." He went on to quote Willoughby Cotton, who had written that, "I really think the time has come for you and I to tell Lord Auckland, *totidem verbis*, that circumstances have proved incontestably that there is no Afghan army, and that unless the Bengal troops are instantly strengthened, we cannot hold the country."

By an Afghan army Cotton meant an army loyal to Soojah. To emphasise his point a report now came in that up in the Hindu Kush region a newly-raised regiment of the Shah's infantry, headed by their commandant, Saleh Mahomed, had deserted *en bloc* to Dost Mahomed.[1] A little earlier the blunt-spoken Nott, having inspected the Shah's 2nd Cavalry at Kandahar, had reported that, "I think it my duty to acquaint you that the regiment is quite inefficient. The majority of the men are of that description which assures me they never can be brought to any serviceable state."

Macnaghten, a centralising bureaucrat if ever there was one, felt harassed beyond endurance and wrote peevishly that "these

[1] Saleh Mahomed, who reappears later in the story, told Captain Johnson, Paymaster of Soojah's forces, that his men deserted in disgust at the behaviour of their British N.C.O.s.

matters of course engross my serious attention, and I have about fifty chits to answer every half hour". Suddenly, however, there was a turn for the better. Dennie, marching from Kabul with a regiment of Native Infantry to reinforce the tiny British garrison in Bameean, unexpectedly bumped up against the main body of Dost Mahomed's Uzbeg warriors. Though vastly outnumbered, neither Dennie nor his troops hesitated for a moment. His two guns opened up with shrapnel upon the close-packed Uzbeg ranks until the enemy broke, the four hundred Afghan cavalry who had been attached to Dennie's command were loosed in pursuit and the Uzbeg retreat became a rout. The Dost himself only escaped capture through the fleetness of his horse.

At the news of what he described as "this glorious success", Macnaghten's mercurial spirits soared from the depths of gloom to the heights of optimism, but his joy was short-lived. "I am like a wooden spoon," said Dost Mahomed grimly; "you may throw me hither and thither but I shall not be hurt." Defeated on the Hindu Kush, he now bobbed up in the Kohistan, and the Kohistanis, exasperated by the efficiency with which taxes were being collected under British supervision, flocked to his support. "There never was such a set of villains," commented Macnaghten angrily. Having intercepted several letters from the Dost "from all of which it appears that he meditates fighting with us so long as the breath is in his body", he was moved to talk of "showing no mercy to the man who was the author of all the evil now distracting the country" and to ask "whether it would be justifiable to set a price on this fellow's head". This was a line of talk much to the liking of Soojah, who had long been anxious to "hang the dog", and who now taunted Macnaghten with his mistaken leniency. "I suppose you would even now," said the King, "if I were to catch the dog, prevent me from hanging him." "It will be time enough to talk about that when your Majesty has caught him," replied Macnaghten, and to Auckland, while recommending that no mercy should be shown, he added that "should he be so fortunate as to secure the person of Dost Mahomed, I shall request his Majesty not to execute him till I can ascertain your Lordship's sentiments".

Meanwhile a force under Sir Robert Sale (the hero of Ghuznee had been made a Knight Commander of the Bath) had pushed up into Kohistan to meet the menace of the Dost, who had gathered around him a considerable body of supporters. In some preliminary skirmishing Edward Conolly, a young relative of Macnaghten and the brother of Arthur Conolly, was shot through the heart. Then, on the clear, bright autumn morning of 2nd November, 1840, the two little armies bumped unexpectedly up against each other in the valley of Purwandurrah. Dost Mahomed, unprepared for battle, was starting to withdraw when he observed that Sale's native cavalry were moving round to his flank. He promptly abandoned all thought of retreat and, at the head of a small body of Afghan horse, began a slow and steady advance towards the enemy.

"Front! Draw swords!" shouted Captain Fraser, who commanded Sale's two squadrons. Then, taking post well in front of his men, he ordered the charge. The British officers rode furiously at the enemy, assuming that their men would follow but the troopers, with no stomach for the encounter, were moving only at a slow trot, which soon dropped to a walk. "Cavalry waiting to receive a charge are lost," said George Lawrence, "and our men, after feebly crossing swords with the enemy, turned and fled, leaving their officers to their fate." Lieutenant Crispin was cut to pieces; Dr. Lord, the Political Officer, was first brought down by a bullet and then despatched with a dagger. James Broadfoot, one of three brothers all of whose lives would be forfeit to Asia in the space of a few years, was seen cutting his way through the Afghans until the sapper cap, by which his friends had kept him in view, disappeared in the middle of a group of Afghans. Fraser's charger carried him right through the enemy and he rode slowly back to the infantry, bleeding profusely from a number of wounds and with his right hand nearly severed at the wrist.

Dost Mahomed was deeply impressed by the bravery of these five British cavalry officers who had charged home into the Afghan horse while their own troopers galloped headlong from the field. Indeed, some said that it was this episode that made him despair of ever beating such an enemy and decide that surrender was the only course. Meanwhile, however, while small clusters of Douranee horsemen chased Sale's cavalry for a mile or more, the main body of the Dost's cavalry pushed home their charge almost within range of the British guns which, with the infantry, had been drawn up to receive them. "The gallant old Ameer," as Lawrence called him (he was exactly fifty years old), "had been foremost in the fight, encouraging his men with his turban in his hand." But the Dost had more sense than to order his cavalry to charge massed infantry and artillery, and after the Afghans had stood for some time masters of the field, with Dost Mahomed's blue standard waving in triumph, they quietly withdrew.

Burnes, who had witnessed the ignominious defeat of the

British, wrote post-haste to Macnaghten, urging that the force should retire on Kabul and that all the British forces be concentrated at the Capital. Two days after the battle Macnaghten, "rather indignant at this very desponding letter from Sir A. Burnes", was returning with George Lawrence from his evening ride in the suburbs of Kabul when an Afghan rode up and asked Lawrence "if that was the Lord Sahib". He then seized Macnaghten's bridle, exclaiming "The Amir! The Amir!" "Who? Who? Where? Where?" cried Macnaghten, "surprised and agitated". And up rode a second horseman, who threw himself off his horse, seized the Envoy's stirrup leather and then his hand, which he pressed to his forehead and his lips in token of submission.

It was indeed the unpredictable Dost Mahomed, who had ridden straight from the field of victory at Purwandurrah to surrender in person to Macnaghten. He had decided that there was no point in pursuing the struggle against the slow-moving but overpowering might of the British. He had at last met them face to face in the field and, at the head of his little force, had emerged victorious; now, therefore, with his honour untarnished, he could surrender. All this was explained to Macnaghten as they rode towards the British lines, and the Envoy's generous nature was touched. "You are welcome, you are welcome," he told the Dost, and when the latter surrendered his sword, saying "he had now no more use for it," it was at once returned. There was to be no more talk of setting a price on the fellow's head, or hanging the dog. Macnaghten's only thought was to console a gallant adversary in the hour of defeat, and he succeeded so well that a few days later he was reporting that Dost Mahomed had said that there was no need to place a guard over him "as he would not go were I even to attempt his expulsion with blows of a stick". In a burst of enthusiasm the Envoy added that "he is certainly a wonderful fellow". Lawrence, however, thought his appearance rather disappointing, "quite different from what I had imagined. He was a robust, powerful man, with a sharp aquiline nose, highly arched eyebrows, and a grey beard and moustache, which evidently had not been trimmed for a long time."

Shah Soojah refused to see the wonderful fellow, alleging that he would not be able to show common civility to such a villain. "This is well," commented Macnaghten, "as the Dost must have suffered much humiliation in being subjected to such an ordeal." The Dost was greatly distressed by a rumour that he was to be exiled to London, but Macnaghten reassured him. His destination was to be Ludhiana. And within ten days of his surrender he was on his way, under strong escort. "I trust that the Dost will be treated with liberality," wrote Macnaghten, urging that he deserved more generous treatment than Soojah in his exile had received. "The Shah had no claim upon us. We had no hand in depriving him of his Kingdom, whereas we ejected the Dost, who never offended us, in support of our policy, of which he was the victim." This was candour indeed from one of the principal authors of that policy and of the notorious Simla Manifesto.

Auckland too may have thought that Dost Mahomed was perhaps the victim of injustice. He received him with courtesy and respect before establishing him in Ludhiana (in that very same residence once occupied by Soojah) and charging the revenues of India with a pension in his favour of two lakhs of rupees. The final seal of success now seemed to have been set upon the British gambit. The two pawns, Amir and Shah, who at the start of the game had been respectively located in Kabul and Ludhiana, had been neatly transposed. Moreover, the Dost, apparently resigned to his lot, was urging his sons to follow his example and surrender to these chivalrous captors. Only Akbar Khan refused to obey his father's command. He preferred to live the life of an outlaw, lurking out beyond the Hindu Kush, irreconcilable, implacable, biding his time.

PART III

THE RISING

I

IT had been August, 1839, when Soojah and his British protectors had made their triumphant entry into Kabul. From then until the surrender of Dost Mahomed, fifteen months later, the Army of Occupation, Macnaghten, the Shah and, indeed, the latter's Afghan subjects had each to contend with many vexations, and before long most of them, each for his own reasons, were in a state of ill-tempered discontent.

The first problem had been to get the troops housed in something more substantial than tents before the bitter Afghan winter set in. Alexander Burnes optimistically reported that he knew the very place or, rather, places—three diminutive forts several miles west of Kabul, but Durand found them quite unsuitable, having neither cover, space, water nor anything else to commend them. The obvious solution to the problem was the Balla Hissar, the great citadel that dominated Kabul and was, in fact, a city within a city, and a reluctant consent was extracted from Shah Soojah to its occupation. Durand at once set his pioneers to work on repairing the dilapidated fortifications, only to excite a wail of protest from the Shah, who complained that as the citadel overlooked his own palace as well as the town, its occupation by a foreign garrison would weaken his dignity and hurt Afghan feelings. Macnaghten bowed to Soojah's objection and Durand was sharply ordered to discontinue his operations. He could have made the Balla Hissar a stronghold which a thousand men, with a few guns and properly provisioned, could have held against all Afghanistan. As it was, he was left only with the consolation that at least the troops would be under cover for the winter, some in the citadel itself, but most of them in makeshift accommodation hastily knocked together at its base.

Soojah accepted their presence with an ill grace, for already his triumph was turning to dust and ashes in his mouth. On first entering his palace after an exile of thirty years he had run with childish eagerness from one well-remembered room to another, only to burst into tears when he saw the dilapidations of years of neglect under the Barukzye rule. And somehow everything seemed to have got much smaller. He would sit for hours gazing lugubriously out of a window of the palace and once, after a long silence, remarked that "everything appeared to him shrunk small and miserable; and that the Kabul of his old age in no respect corresponded with the recollections of the Kabul of his youth". Underlying his disappointment was the unwelcome realisation that he must continue to be fettered by his British paymasters, since he was in no position to do without either their gold or the protection of their bayonets.

He was unpopular from the start with his Afghan subjects who, if they had not disliked him for himself, would have hated him for the government which he had established. "Bad ministers," commented Alexander Burnes, "are in every government solid grounds for unpopularity, and I doubt if ever a king had a worse set than Shah Soojah." One of the most detested was the aged Mullah Shikore, whom Soojah had brought with him out of exile in Ludhiana. This ancient's memory had gone, along with his ears, which had been cropped for some offence against the Shah in years gone by. He was now totally incapable of recognising a face, even if he had seen it only the day before, and the simplest business required the laborious taking of copious notes. The Mullah's spite and incompetence soon created a vicious circle. He oppressed the people. The people complained to the British—for whom the Mullah nursed an abiding hatred; the British remonstrated with the Mullah; and the Mullah then punished the people for having complained to the British.

The Afghans had other grievances besides those directly created by the tyrannical behaviour of this unpleasant old man. For one thing, the tax collectors, backed by British bayonets, were carrying out their duties with an unwelcome and unprecedented efficiency, and these exactions came at a time when the cost of living had soared, a phenomenon rightly attributed to the presence of the Army of Occupation. The Commissariat was buying up all available commodities at preposterous prices, with the obvious consequence that the purveyors held back their supplies in order to force prices higher still. The Kabul housewives sharply commented that the English had enriched only the grain-sellers, grass-sellers and provision merchants, while reducing the chiefs to poverty and killing the poor by starvation.

The only compensation for the wives of Kabul was one calculated to make their husbands still more bitter in their hatred of the invaders. Afghan women were proud of their beauty and "owing to other peculiar circumstances" (a delicate hint at the homosexual

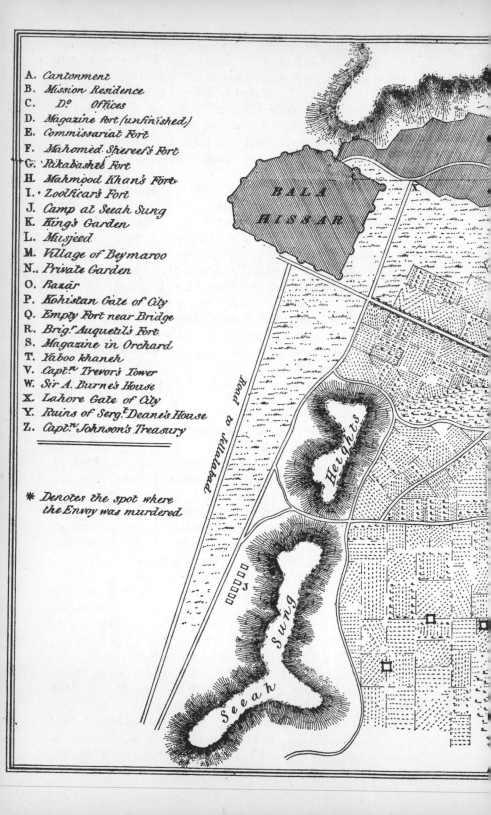

A. Cantonment
B. Mission Residence
C.   Do   Offices
D. Magazine Fort (unfinished)
E. Commissariat Fort
F. Mahomed Shereef's Fort
G. Rikabashee Fort
H. Mahmood Khan's Fort
I. Zoolficar's Fort
J. Camp at Seeah Sung
K. King's Garden
L. Musjeed
M. Village of Beymaroo
N. Private Garden
O. Bazar
P. Kohistan Gate of City
Q. Empty Fort near Bridge
R. Brig.r Anquetil's Fort
S. Magazine in Orchard
T. Yaboo khaneh
V. Capt.n Trevor's Tower
W. Sir A. Burne's House
X. Lahore Gate of City
Y. Ruins of Serg.t Deane's House
Z. Capt.n Johnson's Treasury

* Denotes the spot where
    the Envoy was murdered

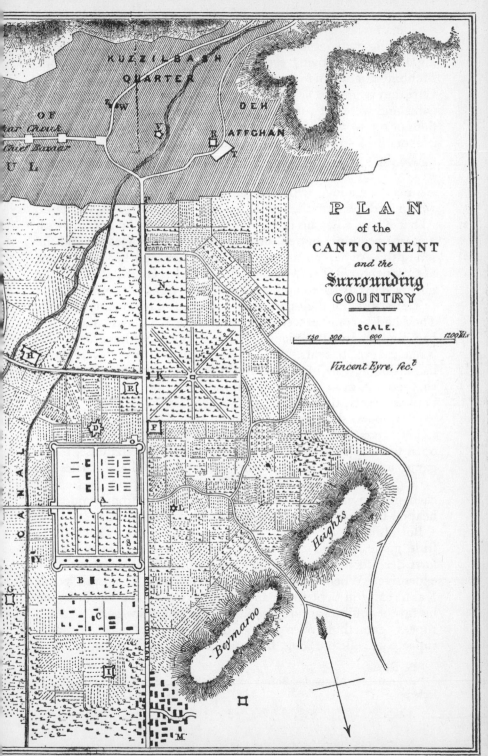

PLAN
of the
CANTONMENT
and the
Surrounding
COUNTRY

SCALE.

150   300   600   1200 Yds

Vincent Eyre, Sec.ᵗ

KUZZILBASH QUARTER

New   DEH

AFFCHAN

OF

ar Chowk

Chief Burdur

U L

CANAL

Heights

Beymaroo

J & C. Walker, Lith: 9 Castle St

preferences of many Afghan men, who proverbially believed that a woman was a duty, but a boy a pleasure) "were very far from being inexorable to the strangers".[1] The British officers had a gallant and a roving eye and, says Kaye, "the inmate of the Mahomedan Sanana was not unwilling to visit the quarters of the Christian stranger . . . the temptations which are most difficult to withstand were not withstood by our English officers. The attractions of the women of Caubul they did not know how to resist. It is enough to state broadly this painful fact."[2] At least let it be added that there was one British officer whose intentions were strictly honourable. Captain Warburton of the Bengal Artillery fell deeply in love with a niece of the exiled Dost Mahomed, whom he duly married, with Macnaghten and Burnes as witnesses. Akbar Khan, when his time came, presently pursued the lady with a most uncousinly hatred, but she escaped his vengeance and the son of this Afghan mother and British father later became famous as Colonel Sir Robert Warburton, K.C.I.E., C.S.I., and kept the unruly Khyber tribes under his discipline from 1879 until 1898.

The British, for their part, were at the outset reasonably content. They had become exceedingly bored with Kandahar but Kabul had many more attractions. "It is well built and handsome, and is one mass of bazaars," wrote Lieutenant Rattray; "every street has a double row of houses of different heights, flat-roofed and composed of mud in wooden frames . . . the houses overhang the narrow streets; their windows have no glass but consist of lattice-work wooden shutters, which push up and down and are often richly carved and otherwise ornamented. The shop windows are open to the sun, and the immense display of merchandise, fruits, game, armour and cutlery defies description. These articles are arranged in prodigious piles from floor to ceiling; in the front of each sits the artificer engaged in his calling, or from amidst the heaped-up profusion peeps out the trader at his visitors."

But although the British, if they wished, could buy their fill of fruit, game, armour and cutlery, there were other creature comforts dear to their hearts that were at first scarce and ruinously expensive. When Colonel Arnold of the 16th Lancers died at Kabul early in September and his effects were auctioned among his brother officers according to army custom, his wine fetched 300 rupees—something over £20—a dozen, and his cigars sold at a rupee each. Before long, however, private enterprise stepped in

[1] Fortescue.

[2] Regrettably, Alexander Burnes seems to have been one of the leaders in lechery.

to remedy the deficiency and less than two years later Alexander Burnes could write from his residence in Kabul that those officers who chose to drop in could "discuss a rare Scotch breakfast of smoked fish, salmon grills, devils and jellies, and puff away at their cigars till ten". At his weekly dinner parties, "as the good river Indus is a channel for luxuries as well as commerce, I can place before my friends at one-third in excess of the Bombay price my champagne, hock, madeira, sherry, port, claret, sauterne, not forgetting a glass of curaçao and maraschino, and the hermetically sealed salmon and hotch-potch (veritable hotch-potch, all the way frae Aberdeen), for deuced good it is, the peas as big as if they had been soaked for *bristling*."

Even before the channels of trade began to flow and provide them with the food and drink so lovingly described by Burnes, the British were basking in a pleasant glow of contentment. On the face of it their campaign had been a triumphant success, achieved at little cost.[1] All told, from 1st November, 1838, until 1840, only thirty-four British officers had lost their lives, and of these not more than four or five had been killed in action. Of the rest, a return painstakingly compiled by Major Hough shows that there were two suicides, three accidentally burnt to death, all on the same day, (presumably a tent caught fire), three murdered by marauders and several fatal cases of heat stroke; as a pathetic postscript there was poor Captain Timings of the Bengal Horse Artillery, who died at Kabul and whose cause of death was laconically recorded as "worn out".

Now, for their greater comfort, a fountain of honours began to spray distinctions upon the heads of the British. Soojah grandly instituted an Order of Merit of the Douranee Empire, of which the insignia were a star and a ribbon of green and crimson silk, and which was lavishly distributed. Of more lasting worth were the honours now beginning to flow from Downing Street. The London Gazette of 11th December, 1839, announced an earldom for Auckland and a barony for Keane, while Macnaghten became a Baronet and Colonel Wade a Knight. Eleven days later another shower flowed from the cornucopia. Generals Willshire, Thackwell and Sale were made Knight Commanders of the Bath, Sir Willoughby Cotton was advanced to G.C.B. and fourteen less

---

[1] But General Nott saw little cause for pride. "By heavens," he wrote angrily, "200 disciplined troops would have sent this army back in disgrace; but good fortune, backed by Jack Company's rupees, paves the way . . . I have never seen, heard or read of such a shameful and entirely unnecessary waste of public money." (Stocqueler.)

senior officers, including Eldred Pottinger of Herat, were made Companions of the same Order. A host of brevet promotions were announced and the only surprising omission from the honours list was the name of Colonel Dennie, who had led the forlorn hope at the storming of Ghuznee and who moreover had thirty-eight years' service to his credit. Evidently, in his case, Keane's "malignant personal animosities" were still at work.

Gratified by this official recognition of their success, the British officers were not slow to introduce into Afghanistan their own peculiar sports and pastimes. The 16th Lancers, whose stay in the country was short (they returned to India with Keane in November, 1839), had taken with them their pack of foxhounds. As Emily Eden tartly commented, "that does not look like having undergone great privation", and she noted that the returning heroes, all of whom insisted that the only distress suffered by the army had been a shortage of wine and cigars, "are all looking uncommonly fat". Meanwhile, those who remained with the army of occupation in Kabul began to organise horse-racing, the first meeting being held within a few days of their arrival at the capital. This was much to the liking of the Afghans, who were inveterate gamblers, and several of them entered their own horses for the various events. They also welcomed British participation in their own cock-fighting and wrestling matches and, when winter gripped the land, watched in astonished admiration as the English on their skates skimmed gracefully over the frozen lakes. The one British sport which left them baffled was cricket, and "they looked on with astonishment at the bowling, batting and fagging out of the English players; but it does not appear that they were ever tempted to lay aside their flowing robes and huge turbans and enter the field as competitors".[1]

Horse-racing, skating, even cricket and amateur theatricals—all these the Afghans were ready to tolerate and even welcome. They hated the British collectively as fiercely as ever, but for their Feringhi conquerors as individuals they were beginning to feel an affectionate admiration. At this point, however, the British introduced a new feature which, with its implications of a permanent occupation, aroused alarm and resentment. They sent for their wives and families to join them.

[1] Havelock.

2

The new Baronet started the fashion. Before the year 1839 was out, Macnaghten had so firmly convinced himself that Afghanistan was settling down in peace under the restored dynasty that he sent his young kinsman, Edward Conolly,[1] to escort Lady Macnaghten up from India. Presently the newly-knighted Sale's formidable lady, Florentia, arrived with her daughter, Mrs. Sturt, whose husband was a gunner subaltern in charge of the engineers and public works department at Kabul. At last they came in droves, not only the wives and children of the British officers and other ranks, but of the Sepoys too, for the Company's Indian troops were encouraged to send for their families the better to reconcile them to a long exile in this harsh and barren land. The Afghans, drawing their own conclusions, were filled with dismay and resentment at the prospect of the Feringhi invaders and their Hindoo mercenaries sitting on their necks indefinitely.

Soojah, seeing everyone else's wife coming to Kabul, decided that his might as well come too. But so numerous were the royal harem that it seemed to him that they could only be housed in the Balla Hissar, with the corollary that the citadel must be evacuated by its British garrison. He made urgent representations to Macnaghten, and the Envoy yielded. It was decided to leave only a handful of troops in the Balla Hissar and to build cantonments on the plain outside Kabul for the bulk of the army.

In the siting and design of these cantonments the British made every conceivable mistake, but it would never be ascertained with certainty upon whom lay the responsibility for these enormous errors. Sturt, Sale's son-in-law, was in charge of the work, but by the time a scapegoat was sought, Sturt was dead. In any case his contemporaries thought him "a talented and sensible officer" and believed that if he had made mistakes it was because he "was often obliged to yield his better judgment to the spirit of false economy which characterised our Afghan policy". And with Sturt dead, as Eyre commented, "the credit of having selected a site for the cantonments, or controlled the execution of its works, is not a distinction now likely to be *claimed* exclusively by *any one*".

The chosen site was a piece of low swampy ground a mile or so north-east of the city. A quarter of a mile to the east ran the Kabul River, and between river and cantonments, a mere 150 yards from the latter, was a wide irrigation canal. On every side the site was commanded by hills or forts, not one of which was

[1] Killed in the following autumn. See page 114.

occupied by the British. Away to the south-west loomed the Balla Hissar and a mile or so distant, beyond the Kabul River, rose the long low ridge of the Seeah Sung Hills. The ground between Kabul and the cantonments was a mass of orchards and gardens, intersected everywhere by deep watercuts and hopeless for the quick movement of artillery or cavalry. As Eyre said, "it must always remain a wonder that any government, or any officer or set of officers, who had either science or experience in the field, should in a half-conquered country fix their forces in so extraordinary and injudicious a military position".

Having chosen the worst possible site, the British went on to lay out the camp to the worst possible design. It was a rectangle, 1,000 yards long and 600 yards broad, surrounded by a low rampart and a narrow ditch, with a round flanking bastion at each corner. The perimeter, nearly two miles round, was far too long to be manned effectively by the garrison and, to make matters worse, there was added at the northern end a space half as large again, known as the "Mission Compound". Half of this compound was allocated for a residence for the Envoy and the remainder was crowded higgledy-piggledy with the houses of his bodyguard and the Mission staff. This compound "rendered the whole face of the cantonment to which it was annexed nugatory for purposes of defence".[1] Finally, by a truly stupendous act of folly, the commissariat stores were carefully sited a quarter of a mile *outside* the cantonment. The Chief Commissariat Officer, Captain Skinner, pleaded in vain for space inside the perimeter. He received from Willoughby Cotton the extraordinary answer that "no such place could be given him, as they were far too busy in erecting barracks for the men to think of commissariat stores". Inevitably, within a few days of trouble starting, the garrison, cut off from its supplies, would be brought to its knees by the threat of starvation. Eyre might well comment that "our cantonment at Caubul, whether we look to its situation or its construction, must ever be spoken of as a disgrace to our military skill and judgement".

Lieutenant Sturt was outspoken in his criticism of the folly that he had been ordered to execute. "But the warnings were not attended to," said his mother-in-law, Lady Sale; "and as when he gave his advice it was seldom adhered to, he became disgusted, and contented himself with zealously performing his duties and making himself generally useful, acting the part of an artillery officer as well as that of an engineer". But Sturt himself, perhaps with the despair of Cassandra, had snapped back impatiently and

[1] Eyre.

almost with insubordination at another trenchant critic, Brigadier Abraham Roberts, [1] who was now in command of Soojah's levies and who had returned from leave in India to be shocked by the sight of these indefensible cantonments.

Roberts also freely criticised the general dispositions of the army throughout Afghanistan. The plan adopted was, in modern idiom, one of "penny packets". Garrisons, a battalion or two of infantry and a handful of cavalry, were stationed at Kabul, Jalalabad, Ghuznee and Kandahar, with even smaller detachments of Soojah's unreliable levies at other outlying spots. The lines of communication between the different posts were vulnerable in the extreme and were wholly dependent on the goodwill of the local tribes, a goodwill only to be purchased by generous cash subsidies. The road from Kabul down through Ghuznee to Kandahar was passable only by permission of the Western Ghilzyes, while the Eastern Ghilzyes held the route from the capital to Jalalabad in the hollow of their hand. So long as the Danegeld performed its service all might be well, but if once the lines of communication were cut and one garrison were attacked by a concentration of the enemy, no other could come to its aid without having to fight its way through some of the worst country in the world.

Macnaghten, always ready to denounce as "croakers" those who inconveniently drew attention to real dangers and difficulties, was much annoyed by the blunt criticisms of Brigadier Roberts, the more so as it appeared that Roberts was receiving altogether too much support for his views from Calcutta. Macnaghten wrote petulantly to Colvin, complaining that "I do not receive that support to which the overwhelming difficulties of my position entitle me. In deciding upon a controversy thrust upon me by Brigadier Roberts, the government convey to me an implied censure for not supporting his military position, though the justice of my views is admitted; and take that occasion of conveying a compliment to Brigadier Roberts, though he had written to me a most disrespectful letter."

The Envoy hinted strongly that he might feel obliged to resign. "I have never yet served in an office where I had not the confidence of my superiors, and my inclination to do so is by no means strengthened after a laborious public life of thirty-one years." The threat was effective and the irritating Roberts was presently replaced by a more amenable Brigadier named Anquetil.

Even Macnaghten, with his incorrigible habit of seeing only

[1] Roberts had an eight-year-old son, Frederick, who would one day become Lord Roberts of Kandahar.

what he wished to see, could hardly have believed that all was well in Afghanistan in the year 1840. The army of occupation, merrily engaged in cricket, horse-racing, amateur theatricals and skating, according to the season, appeared on the face of it to be firmly in the saddle, but in fact its situation was extremely perilous. It was not only its internal lines of communication but those back to its main base in India that were of gossamer strength. On the southern route, through the Bolan, there was added to the danger of marauders the terrible factor of heat. One of the staging posts on this route, reached after a march across 150 miles of burning desert, was Dadhar, a furnace of a place of which the saying ran, "Oh, Allah! Wherefore make hell when thou hast made Dadhar?" Here, in their tents, inside which the temperature rose to 120° and more, two British officers died of the heat, "their bodies turning as black as charcoal".[1] Another convoy lost six out of fourteen British officers, dead from heat, while a hundred sepoys and at least three hundred followers also perished. Cholera as well as heat and thirst attacked this unhappy contingent, and the memory of the sun "turned to a ball of red-hot copper" by the dust of the desert long haunted the survivors. When another party, this time fifty European troops under an officer, started out along the Sind route, the officer and nine of the men were dead within two days, while many others collapsed under the sun. Such were some of the perils of the southern road to Afghanistan.

The northern route not only included the dangerous Khyber and other passes, but traversed the Punjab and so was dependent upon Sikh goodwill. But with the death of Runjeet Singh at the end of 1839, an event celebrated by *suttee* on a memorable scale ("those poor dear ranees," wrote Emily Eden, "whom we visited and thought so beautiful and merry, have actually burnt themselves") the British had lost their only true ally among the Sikhs. By now, the Sikh contingent supplied under the tripartite treaty was more inclined to fight against the British than for them, and behaved outrageously towards British officers passing through Sikh territory on their way to or from Afghanistan. Only the presence of Avitabile as Governor of Peshawar saved the situation, and the terror which this tough Neapolitan inspired in Sikh and Afghan alike was all that prevented the two from uniting against the British and cutting off all access to or from the Khyber.

Colin Mackenzie, who was posted to Afghanistan in the autumn of 1840, stayed some days with Avitabile on his way through Peshawar, and was considerably impressed by one who for many

[1] Stocqueler.

years would be "spoken of by the Afghan population with the admiration of a troop of jackals for a tiger". The Governor's appearance, thought Mackenzie, was "rather *outré*: a tall burly man, ordinarily apparelled in a magnificently laced Horse-Artillery jacket, wide crimson Turkish trousers drawn in at the ankle, a golden girdle and a very handsome sabre; his large Jewish features and bronzed countenance adorned with fierce mustachios, which look like twisted bayonets, with a thick gray beard; the whole surmounted by a gold-laced forage cap which he never takes off".

Avitabile, who feared neither God nor man, "hangs a dozen unhappy culprits, looks to the payment of his troops, inspects his domestic concerns (especially his poultry yard, in which he takes much pride), sets a-going a number of musical snuff-boxes, etc., all by way of recreation before dinner. He seems withal to be a good soldier and a just man, that is, impartially stern to Sikhs and Mahomedans."

Upon this formidable character, "a famous man in his way, who certainly keeps his province in better order than any other Sikh governor",[1] the safety of the British in Afghanistan now largely depended. Macnaghten, for some reason, perversely chose to resent the way in which Avitabile cowed the Khyber tribes into docility with a strong hand, and thought it a course "calculated to do us infinite mischief. . . . Why should he seek to exasperate us?"

The situation was no better in the far west where, at Herat, "the insolent ingratitude of Yar Mahomed had reached a pitch of sublime daring". The debauched Kamran having retired from active life, the sinister Vizir was now *de facto* ruler of Herat, and had made a treaty with the British under which Herat was bound not to enter into negotiations with any other state without the knowledge and consent of the British Resident. In return, lakh upon lakh of rupees from India were showered upon Yar Mahomed. But "nothing seemed to satisfy the cormorant appetite of the Heratees, and at length even the rupees of India ceased to possess a charm".[2] Within weeks of the signing of the treaty it was discovered that Yar Mahomed was secretly negotiating with the Persians, expressing his hatred of the English and offering to place Herat under Persian protection. Sir John Kaye, almost apoplectic with indignation at such treachery, fulminates that "in the history of human infamy there is nothing more infamous than the conduct of this man".

Macnaghten had to contend with other and more violent

[1] Mackenzie.   [2] Stocqueler.

I   129

troubles closer at hand. Khelat had been summarily annexed to Soojah's realm, but the Baluchi subjects of the late Mehrab Khan were far from accepting this decision willingly. Rebellion would be easy, for the British had no troops to spare to garrison this "poor but vast country", as Burnes described it, and worked mostly through solitary Political Officers who "sate themselves down, with only a handful of fighting men at their command, as though all their paths were pleasantness and peace and all their homes bowers of repose". At Khelat itself Lieutenant Loveday, who had generously given his brocade bedspread to serve as a shroud for Mehrab Khan, had been installed as Political Officer, and early in 1840 the Baluchi tribes came swarming down upon him like angry hornets. After a few days' siege, Khelat surrendered to the rebels. "The Belooch," wrote Nott of this episode, "is a very different fellow to the Afghan—he is *obstinately brave*. They are undoubtedly the best swordsmen in the world. In an affair where the reckless Hammersley got wounded the other day, he declares that he saw one of these fellows keep sixteen or twenty of our cavalry at a distance for a considerable time, and cut some of them down. The dethroning of Mehrab Khan was a most shameful affair, and retribution has come."

It had certainly come for the hapless young Loveday. Taken prisoner by the Baluchi, he was fettered by the ankles and hurried from one village to another to be put on show in the bazaars, "buffeted by newcomers of their tribes and beaten if he attempted to remonstrate".[1] A few months later a British punitive force took the field from Kandahar and defeated the rebels. But they were too late to save Loveday, for when they reached the enemy's deserted camp they found the young Political Officer chained to a camel-pannier, naked except for a pair of thin drawers, emaciated and dead. His servant, a native boy who had faithfully followed his master into captivity, was weeping over the body and two farewell messages, one to his sister and an unfinished letter to a friend, were lying beside it. His throat had just been cut by the sabre of his Baluchi gaoler, who subsequently explained that he had been compelled to take this extreme course to forestall a rescue. The murderer, who was duly hanged at Quetta, had apparently debated the cruel necessity with his victim, for he naïvely explained, at his trial, that at Loveday's urgent entreaty he had endeavoured to refer the matter to the Khan, Mehrab's young son, for his sanction; failing to find the Khan, he had decided to act on his own responsibility.

[1] Stocqueler.

Khelat was not the only part of the country to give trouble. No sooner had the British begun to relax after the surrender of Dost Mahomed in the late autumn of 1840 than the Douranee tribes north-west of Kandahar were up in arms against Shah Soojah. The Douranees, the tribe that had produced Ahmed Shah, founder of the empire, had enjoyed exceptional privileges under the earlier Suddozye kings, but Dost Mahomed, the Barukzye, had cut them down to size. With the restoration of Soojah the Douranees had looked for great things and when Soojah was slow to fulfil their hopes, their angry disappointment soon turned to active rebellion. Macnaghten affected to regard their conduct with a patronising superiority. "These people are perfect children, and should be treated as such. If we put one naughty boy in the corner, the rest will be terrified. We have taken their plaything, power, out of the hand of the Douranee chiefs, and they are pouting a good deal in consequence."

The task of putting the naughty boys in the corner fell to General Nott, now in command at Kandahar. Enough has already been heard of William Nott to justify Kaye's description of him as "a capable officer of rather irritable temperament . . . a man of some talents but blunt address—an honest plain-spoken soldier, not always right, but always believing himself to be right—hearty, genuine and sincere". He had enraged Macnaghten by his hearty, genuine and sincere contempt for Soojah and the rest of the royal family, and the Envoy had gone to the length of complaining officially to Auckland over Willoughby Cotton's refusal to support him in bringing the contumacious Nott to heel. "If such an outrage as that committed by General Nott is to be tolerated and justified, there must be an end of our efforts to make it be believed that Shah Soojah is the King of this country." The outrage, it seems, was that Nott "refused to pay the Prince the common compliment of calling upon him, although told that such a civility was expected". Nott, who in a letter to his daughters had described Soojah as "most certainly as great a scoundrel as ever lived!", typified the attitude of many British officers towards Soojah, a view which Macnaghten thought originated from their belief that the Shah was the cause of their detention in a land "not overflowing with beer and cheroots".

For the moment, however, the blunt and irritable Sepoy General at Kandahar did all that was asked of him quickly and well. A detachment of his garrison moved out against the rebels and on 3rd January, 1841, broke and routed them after a brisk little battle. The military task having been thus accomplished, it

131

was left to the Political Officer at Kandahar, Major Rawlinson, he who had had the chance meeting in the desert with Captain Vickovich, to find out exactly what had driven the Douranees to revolt.

Rawlinson, clear-sighted and pessimistic, agreed in effect with Burnes, who had written that "we shall never settle Afghanistan at the point of the bayonet". He reported to Macnaghten that "the state of the country causes me many an anxious thought— we may thresh the Douranees over and over again, but this rather aggravates than obviates the difficulty of overcoming the national feeling against us". Macnaghten took him severely to task for "taking an unwarrantably gloomy view of our position, and entertaining and disseminating rumours favourable to that view. We have enough of difficulties and enough of croakers without adding to the number needlessly." He added sharply that "these idle statements may cause much mischief... I know them to be utterly false as regards Caubul and I have no reason to believe them true as regards the country about Candahar".

Rawlinson hastened to excuse himself and Sir William graciously replied that "I am not going to read you a lecture, because when you indited your letter of the 28th ult. you pleaded guilty to the influence of bile ... but I must pen a few remarks in the hope of inducing you to regard matters as little more '*couleur de rose*'." Macnaghten himself was certainly taking a most determinedly rosy view, and the only fly that he could see in the ointment was Calcutta's unreasonable attitude on the question of finance. "His Majesty's revenue," he wrote, "is little more than fifteen lakhs per annum, hardly enough for the maintenance of his personal state, and yet the government below are perpetually writing to me that this charge and that charge is 'to be defrayed out of his Majesty's resources'. God help the poor man and his resources!!!"

Warnings of more serious trouble were obstinately ignored. "All things considered," wrote the Envoy happily, "the perfect tranquillity of the country is to my mind perfectly miraculous. Already our presence has been infinitely beneficial in allaying animosities and pointing out abuses. .... We are gradually placing matters on a firm and satisfactory basis."

There were those who thought differently. To Colin Mackenzie, though he agreed that troubles seemed temporarily lulled after Dost Mahomed's surrender, "the idea of withdrawing our troops for the next ten years, *if ever*, is perfectly chimerical". And he had seen very plainly the perilous situation of the army of occupation. "Our gallant fellows in Afghanistan," he wrote, a year before the revolt, "must be reinforced or *they will all perish.*" As for Nott, that harbinger of doom, he had written to his daughters that "all goes wrong here". And Nott knew why. "The authorities are never right, even by chance, and although most of them are stupid in the extreme, they fancy themselves great men, and even possessed of abilities and talents. They drink their claret, draw large salaries, go about with a numerous rabble at their heels—all well paid by John Bull—or rather by the oppressed cultivators of the land in Hindostan. . . . We are become hated by the people, and the English name and character, which two years ago stood so high and fair, has become a byeword. Thus it is to employ men selected by intrigue and patronage! The conduct of the *one thousand and one* politicals has ruined our cause, and bared the throat of every European in this country to the sword and knife of the revengeful Afghan and the bloody Belooch, and unless several regiments be quickly sent, not a man will be left to note the fall of his comrades."

Macnaghten, however, cared for none of these things. With the Douranees, the Kohistanis and the Ghilzyes all simmering with unrest, he was still writing blithely that "the country is perfectly quiet from Dan to Beersheba". The Envoy penned these words on 20th August, 1841; the rebellion would burst upon him in less than ten weeks' time, and he himself had less than five months to live.

3

A few months earlier, in the spring of 1841, it had become known that Willoughby Cotton was about to retire and that the Army in Afghanistan was to have a new commander-in-chief. There was keen speculation as to Cotton's successor and public opinion favoured General Nott, who of the available officers was unquestionably best fitted for the post. His appointment would have been popular with officers and men, and was backed by the Commander-in-Chief in India, Sir Jasper Nicolls. But Nott himself had no illusions about his chances. He had trodden too often on too many toes to have any hope of securing an appointment which he felt sure would be settled by the usual jobbery of the Auckland administration and with the usual favouritism being shown to Queen's officers over Company's.

For one thing, Nott had never tried to hide his contempt for the politicals, and the politicals, with their direct access to Macnaghten, were powers in the land. "Unthinking and inexperienced people" had been one of Nott's politer descriptions of them, and as for the "high authorities at Kabul"—in other words the Envoy and his staff, they were like "small birds I have seen frightened in a storm, ready to perch upon anything, and to fly into the arms of the first man they meet for protection. Poor men! what will they do when *real* danger comes?" These freely uttered strictures attracted official reproof on an occasion when "it appears that a *private* letter of mine, freely commenting on the proceedings of the Politicals in this country was *kindly* sent to Government and I am called upon to state my reasons for having written it".

By this time Nott had grown fairly hardened to "laudatory wigs". He had once gloomily described himself, in a letter to his son, as "the beast who annoyed and defied Sir John Keane and Lord Auckland, and ruined himself and his prospects. Never mind—the grave will soon cover me." Normally, however, he professed indifference to admonitions from on high. On an occasion when he had threatened to place "a silly political" under close arrest, he wrote that no doubt Macnaghten "will inform the Governor-General that he is horrified at my conduct to a public functionary, and I shall in due course hear something *very wise* from his Lordship, which I shall not care so much about as my old grandmother would for a brass farthing". Of the Envoy he held the lowest of opinions. "The system of government in this country is, and has always been wrong, *very* wrong, and never will be right until Macnaghten is withdrawn. . . . It would take many years to *undo* what that man Macnaghten has done. How could Lord Auckland allow such a man to remain in authority here, bringing into contempt everything connected with the name of Englishmen? It is horrible!"

Nor was it only the civilians in uniform with whom Nott had come in conflict. Early in the campaign the well-known chip on his shoulder as to the merits of Queen's officers and Company's[1]

---

[1] Nott was not alone in his grievance. In *The Choice of a Profession*, published (ironically enough in the year the Mutiny broke out), by Chapman and Hall, Mr. H. Byerley Thomson, Barrister-at-law, has this to say:

"This splendid army, great in emoluments, and eminent in services, though looked down upon by the Queen's officer, can afford to hold its own, both on the ground of the magnificent empire it has won and keeps for Britain, and the high character and military talents of its officers. . . . The supercilious Queen's officer, whilst affecting to despise the *servant* of the Company, is forgetting his early training in London drawing rooms, and has few opportunities of showing his superiority to his fighting brother of the Company, except in blackballing him at his club. At the same time the Company's officer is winning empires in the East, and enjoying a hearty had caused a furious quarrel with Keane, who had ordered him to place himself under command of General Willshire for the attack on Khelat. "I must distinctly state to you," wrote Nott in reply, "that I conceive myself to be senior to *local* Major-General Willshire, and therefore can obey no orders originating with that officer, nor can I serve under him." This piece of contumacy was reported to Auckland who was understandably shocked by Nott's conduct and asked Keane to be "pleased to convey to him, in such terms as may seem to you to be sufficient, the expression of my displeasure". Nott was compelled to submit, a humiliation exasperated by his receiving at the same time a demand from the Auditor-General for the refund of 9,000 rupees of command pay that he had drawn during his short time in charge of the 1st Division. "The officers of the Indian army," he exploded to his daughters, "are a set of helots, and bear kicks like asses."

There had been an extraordinary scene between two very angry generals at which, according to Nott, the conversation went as follows:

"Keane to Nott: Your conduct for an officer of your rank is very extraordinary, the most extraordinary I have ever heard of.
Nott, at last: Well, your Excellency, I trust that I have left no ill impression upon your mind. I see the whole affair; I am to be sacrificed because I happen to be senior to the Queen's officers.
Keane: Ill impression, sir! I will never forget your conduct as long as I live.
Nott: Oh! your Excellency, since that is the case, I have only to wish you a very good evening."

With all these black marks against his name, Nott can have felt little surprise when he was now left to growl in his corner, down at Kandahar, and the appointment of commander-in-chief, Afghanistan, went, as he had predicted, to a Queen's officer. The Indian

grumble that an ancient professional jealousy excludes him from general command. It is hoped that the days of so unfair a distinction are numbered. . . . With the exception of this invidious distinction, the Company's officer is far better off than the royal soldier. His pay is better, his pension more liberal, his promotion more certain, his opportunities of great employment more numerous, and the appreciation of his abilities and zeal more certain to be rewarded. . . . He can afford to marry early, and if a man of talent, can often accumulate a fortune. He is from the first a person of importance, and with proper conduct is certain to obtain fair success."

Government's disastrous choice was Major-General William George Keith Elphinstone, briefly but not unfairly dismissed by Nott as "the most incompetent soldier that was to be found among the officers of the requisite rank".

Elphinstone's qualifications for the post were slender indeed, and amounted to little more than being "of good repute, gentlemanly manners and aristocratic connexions". (He was a grandson of the 10th Lord Elphinstone, and therefore a cousin of Mountstuart, who was a son of the 11th Baron.) He had last seen active service on the field of Waterloo, a quarter of a century before, where he had commanded the 33rd Foot with sufficient distinction to be made a Companion of the Bath and a knight of the Orders of William of Holland and St. Anne of Austria. After many years on half pay he had returned to the active list as a Major-General in 1837, and since 1839 had been in command of the Benares division of the Bengal army. He was now elderly, nearly sixty years old, and far from well. Not long before his posting to Kabul Emily Eden had seen "Elphy Bey", as she nicknamed him, being carried along in a palanquin at Futtehpore and "in a shocking state of gout, poor man. One arm in a sling and very lame, but otherwise is a young-looking general for India. He cannot, of course, speak a word of Hindoostanee."

Elphinstone at least had no illusions about his own capacity, and did his best to refuse the Afghan command, protesting that his very indifferent state of health made him quite unfit for it. The Governor-General, however, had pressed the appointment upon him. His great merit in Auckland's eyes was that he would get on with Macnaghten, which was more than Nott would ever have done. Elphinstone, with his gentle courtesy and kindly nature, could get on with almost anyone. But even Elphinstone drew the line somewhere and, as ill luck would have it, his line was drawn at his own second-in-command, Brigadier John Shelton.

Shelton, the Colonel of the 44th Regiment, had only two qualifications for his post, long service in India and a good measure of physical bulldog courage. Years before, at the storming of St. Sebastian in the Peninsular War, he had lost his right arm, and was said to have stood outside his tent, unmoved and uncomplaining, while the surgeons removed the shattered limb from its socket. Fortescue generously surmises that it may have been "incessant physical pain, due to the rough surgery of those days" that had embittered his character. By now he was assuredly a morose, obstinate and cantankerous man. He had brought a relief brigade up to Afghanistan at the end of 1840 and Colin Mackenzie, joining him *en route*, had seen something of his quality. "Found Shelton's brigade near Lalpura," he wrote in his journal, "as I expected, Shelton has marched the brigade off its legs, and has brought the troops into the field the next thing to being wholly inefficient. A bad feeling exists between the Queen's 44th and the native troops. Swords and bayonets have been drawn between them. . . . Beasts of burden, camels, etc., have died in great numbers and will continue to die from overwork. . . . Shelton's gross want of arrangement and the unnecessary hardship he has exposed the men to, especially during their passage through the Khyber, have caused much discontent. Part of the horse artillery on one occasion mutinied and refused to mount their horses."

This was the man with whom Elphinstone, on his arrival at Kabul in April of '41, found himself saddled as second-in-command. From the outset Shelton made no attempt to conceal his contempt for his commanding officer while Elphy Bey, in so far as it was within his gentle nature to dislike anyone, disliked and distrusted Shelton. The inability of Major-General and Brigadier to co-operate with each other was all that was needed to set the final seal of doom upon the Kabul force.

Cotton, when he handed over his command to Elphinstone, had confidently assured him that "you will have *nothing to do here, all is peace*". Elphinstone, however, like others before and after him,[1] saw at once how vulnerable were the cantonments, and generously offered to buy some of the surrounding land at his own expense so that the orchards and gardens that encroached so closely on the perimeter could be levelled and a field of fire cleared. When this offer was declined he joined with Macnaghten (who had repeatedly asked Auckland's permission to buy in the neighbouring forts and raze them to the ground, but had always been refused on grounds of expense) in a plan to build a small "citadel" to overawe Kabul. Elphinstone's proposal was that ground to the south of the cantonments should be acquired and a small fort built, in which all the garrison's guns and stores could be concentrated, thus freeing the bulk of his force for mobile operations. Macnaghten readily gave his support to this eminently sound suggestion and the work was put in hand. But when Calcutta heard that the cost would be no less than £2,400 a peremptory

[1] Major Abbott, for example, the Chief Engineer to General Pollock's army the following year, reported on "the extreme faultiness of the position. The cantonment appears to have been purposely surrounded by difficulties." (Mackenzie.)

veto was applied and thereby another nail was hammered into the coffin that was being made ready for the Army of Afghanistan.

The fact was that not only Government in Calcutta but, behind them, the Court of Directors and the Board of Control back in London had become increasingly perturbed at the cost of maintaining Shah Soojah on his throne. Even before the end of 1840 the Secret Committee had written that it was plain that Soojah had no hold upon the affections of his people and that they could see nothing in his continued support that would compensate for an annual drain on the Treasury of India of over a million sterling a year. The Board of Control recommended a frank confession of failure and the abandonment of the country, but the Supreme Council in Calcutta, in March, 1841, had reluctantly decided to continue with the occupation and to accept the fact that this must cost at least a million and a quarter pounds per annum.

Sir Jasper Nicolls, the Commander-in-Chief, who had not been consulted, disapproved strongly. "I would record my opinion," he wrote in his journal in May, '41, "that the whole thing will break down. We cannot afford the heavy yet increasing drain upon us. Nine thousand troops between Quettah and Karachi; at least 16,000 of our army and the Shah's to the north of Quettah. The King's expenses to bear in part—twenty eight political officers to pay, besides Macnaghten—Dost Mahomed's allowance-barracks—a fort or two to build—loss by exchange, etc., etc. To me it is alarming." A few days later he added that "it will never do to have India drained of a million and a quarter annually for a rocky frontier, requiring about 25,000 men and expensive establishments to hold it, even by threats as at present". But as Auckland had re-affirmed the policy of continuing the occupation, those who hoped for a withdrawal could now only await the imminent downfall of the Whig government in England and the return to power of the Tories, who were believed to be opposed to the whole policy of the expedition across the Indus.

To Macnaghten this was an appalling thought. "If they—the Tories—deprive the Shah altogether of our support . . . they will commit an unparalleled political atrocity." It would be, he said, not only a breach of treaty but "a cheat of the first magnitude". He had insisted upon Soojah's conducting himself according to European notions of civilised behaviour, with the result that all his enemies were alive and unblinded, whereas had he been left to his own devices, "he would have adopted the Afghan method of securing his sovereignty". In any case, argued the Envoy, the task of pacification was all but complete and "the whole country is as quiet as one of our Indian chiefships—and more so". Macnaghten would admit that "a million and a quarter per annum is certainly an awful outlay", but this, he thought, could be greatly reduced. There was no need to keep so many troops in Afghanistan, for "barring Herat, I am quite certain that the Shah's force would be ample, with the addition of one European regiment at Caubul and another at Candahar, to keep the entire country in order". What was more, he wrote in September, 1941, "I am, too, making great reductions in our political expenditure." The reductions that he made were precisely those that now precipitated the rising in rebellion of the whole Afghan nation.

4

From immemorial times the Ghilzye tribes who held the mountain passes through which the main trade routes ran had assumed the right to exact tribute from all those that passed by. Being reasonable men, according to their lights, they had always been ready to accept in lieu an annual subsidy from the Government of the day, in return for which they guaranteed safe-conduct for all travellers. "To the politics of Afghanistan," said Havelock, "they were magnanimously indifferent. They cared not which of their rulers, whether Barukzye or Suddozye, lorded it in the Balla Hissar, provided they were left in the undisturbed enjoyment of their ancient privileges of levying tribute from caravans, or of mercilessly plundering all who resisted the exaction; or received from the existing Government a handsome annual stipend, in commutation of the sums raised in virtue of their prescriptive rights."

The rulers of Kabul had always found it better to subsidise the Ghilzyes rather than to attempt to subdue them, and this policy had been maintained when Soojah had been re-established on the throne. The annual payment to the Eastern Ghilzyes, who controlled the most direct route to India, through Jalalabad and the Khyber, had been fixed at the equivalent of £8,000, and the Ghilzyes had scrupulously observed their side of the bargain. "They had prevented even a finger from being raised against our posts, couriers and weak detachments. Convoys of all descriptions had passed through these terrific defiles, the strongest barriers of mountains in the world, with little or no interruption from these predatory tribes. The transmission of letters to our own provinces was as regular as between Calcutta and any station in Bengal."[1]

[1] Havelock.

Macnaghten, determined to show that the cost of the occupation of Afghanistan could be reduced, now decided to halve the Ghilzyes' annual stipend. Their chiefs were summoned to Kabul to be told the unwelcome news. They received it with an apparently impassive indifference and, after a silent and courteous salaam to the Envoy, withdrew to their own country, some ten miles east of Kabul, where they showed their real feelings by instantly blocking the passes. The next caravan that came through from India was beaten up and plundered in the old traditional style and, so far as the northern route was concerned, the Army of Occupation had been effectively cut off from its base.

Macnaghten had a personal reason to be annoyed at the Ghilzyes' action, which was, he said, "very provoking to me at this juncture" (the beginning of October, 1841). For his long exile in Afghanistan was about to be ended with the reward of the Governorship of Bombay, the sweetest plum that the Honourable East India Company had to offer, short of the Governor-Generalship itself. He was planning to leave Kabul before the end of October and anything that threatened the peace of the country in the interim was liable to upset this programme. Burnes, living a life of idleness as Resident in Kabul and eagerly waiting to inherit the post of Envoy, made common cause with Macnaghten for once, and each reassured the other that all was very well. Only two months earlier Macnaghten had written to Auckland recommending that five additional regiments be sent up to Afghanistan, two of them to be European. In reply, letter after horrified letter came from Calcutta demanding retrenchment, and in an evil hour Macnaghten let himself be over-persuaded by Burnes that the outlook was so peaceful that not only could the request for additional troops be cancelled but that part of the existing Army of Occupation might safely be withdrawn. It had therefore been arranged that the 1st Brigade, commanded by Sale, should be withdrawn by way of Jalalabad to India. "The general impression," wrote Lady Sale, wise before the event and writing in October, "is that the Envoy is trying to deceive himself into an assurance that the country is in a quiescent state. He had a difficult part to play, without sufficient moral courage to stem the current singly."

So now the luckless Macnaghten, the tantalising prize of peaceful and civilised Bombay so nearly within his grasp, proceeded to make light of the Ghilzyes' rising. He described them airily as "kicking up a row about some deductions which have been made from their pay", adding "the rascals will be well trounced for their pains". He did not, he said, "apprehend any open opposition", and hoped to be off to Bombay within the next ten days. He would leave a paper of instructions with Burnes. "The country, I trust, will be left in a state of tranquillity, with the exception of the Ghilzyes between this and Jalalabad, and I hope to settle their hash on the road down, if not before." But Macnaghten would never set foot on the road down; the hash to be settled was his own, not the Ghilzyes'.

Humza Khan, the governor of the Ghilzyes, was now sent down from Kabul by Soojah to bring the rebels back to their allegiance, a mission that surprised no one by its failure since, as even Macnaghten knew, "Humza Khan is at the bottom of the whole conspiracy." It was decided to try sterner measures. Sale's Brigade, now on the point of returning to India, would take the rebels in its stride and Colonel Monteith was sent ahead with an advance guard to clear the way. Monteith was promptly attacked at night while camping at Boothak, the first staging post out of Kabul on the Jalalabad road. "Only imagine the impudence of the rascals," said Macnaghten wrathfully, "in having taken up a position with four or five hundred men in the Khoord-Caubul Pass, not fifteen miles from the capital."

In the fighting in which Monteith and, in due course, the main body of Sale's force were engaged, it became apparent that the Afghans had some considerable advantages. Artillery apart, they were better armed than the British and Sepoy infantry, whose smooth-bore flintlock muskets were mostly old, often missed fire and had barrels so worn that the weapons had lost what little accuracy they had ever possessed. Lieutenant Eyre recorded one occasion when the Afghans "unflinchingly received the discharge of our musketry which, strange to say, even at the short range of ten or twelve yards did little or no execution". The Afghan jezail, with its long rifled barrel, far outranged the British musket and was much more accurate. Some, so heavy that they were fired from rests, could throw their bullets nearly half a mile.[1] Moreover, the Afghans fought intelligently. Not for them the thin red line or the British square, standing in full view of the enemy weapons and firing from the upright position. They took advantage of natural cover and "until they commenced firing not a man was known to be there. They were concealed behind rocks and stones", which provided not only concealment but aiming

[1] Sir Charles Napier, however, claimed a few years later to have proved that the musket, if kept in good order, was on balance the better weapon (Fortescue).

rests. They were "marksmen who seldom missed their aim" and, what was more, "they appeared to pick off the officers in particular". Eyre shrewdly commented that "our infantry soldiers, both European and Native, might have taken a salutary lesson from the Afghans in the use of their fire-arms; the latter invariably taking steady deliberate aim, and seldom throwing away a single shot; whereas our men seemed to fire entirely at random, without any aim at all". Another Afghan tactic that impressed the British, though they made no attempt to copy it, "consists in dropping their men fresh for combat; each horseman takes a foot soldier up behind him, and drops him when he is arrived at the spot he is required to fire from".[1]

Macnaghten was so impressed that towards the end of October he recommended that a force of jezailchis be recruited locally to keep the passes clear. The suggestion reached London three months later and drew a snort of contempt from the Duke of Wellington. "Mr. Macnaghten," he wrote, either unaware of or deliberately ignoring the baronetcy, "has discovered that the Company's troops are not sufficiently active personally, nor are they sufficiently well armed for the warfare in Afghanistan. Very possibly an Afghan will run over his native hills faster than an Englishman or a Hindoo. But we have carried on war in hill countries, as well in Hindostan and the Deccan as in the Spanish Peninsula; and I never heard that our troops were not equal, as well in personal activities as by their arms, to contend with any natives of any hills whatever. Mr. Macnaghten ought to have learnt by this time that hill countries are not conquered, and their inhabitants kept in subjection, solely by running up the hills and firing at long distances. The whole of a hill country . . . should be occupied by sufficient bodies of troops, well supplied, and capable of maintaining themselves; and not only a Ghilzye or insurgent should be able to run up and down hills, but not a cat or a goat, except under the fire of those occupying the hills. This is the mode of carrying on the war, and not by hiring Afghans with long matchlocks to protect and defend the communications of the British army. . . . It will not do to raise, pay and discipline matchlock-men, in order to protect the British troops and their communications, discovered by Mr. Macnaghten to be no longer able to protect themselves."

Wellington's caustic memorandum had opened with the percipient remark that "it is impossible to read the letter from Mr. Macnaghten to the Secretary to the Government in India, with-

[1] Eyre.

out being sensible of the precarious and dangerous position of our affairs in Central Asia". When the Duke wrote these words he could not know that the Kabul force had already been destroyed to the last man but one, and that Macnaghten had been dead a month, his corpse hacked in pieces and its portions displayed in triumph in the bazaar. This last consideration might not have modified the Duke's contempt for "the gentleman employed to command the army", as he sarcastically described Macnaghten, yet it is arguable that on the particular issue the Envoy was right and the great Duke wrong. Macnaghten was ahead of his time, and it would be another generation before the British would turn the poachers into gamekeepers by raising the Khyber Rifles and other famous corps to keep the peace on the north-west frontier.

Wellington apparently also overlooked the fact that "the gentleman employed to command the army" was Elphinstone, not Macnaghten. The latter was responsible only in the political and diplomatic sphere, and if he expressed views on military matters it was largely because neither his commander-in-chief nor the second-in-command, Shelton, seemed capable of doing so. The experience of Captain George Broadfoot at this time reveals the depths of pusillanimity to which the army command had sunk.

George Broadfoot, thirty-four years old, red-haired and bespectacled, was the eldest of three brothers, the sons of a clergyman who had been minister at Kirkwall, in the Orkneys. The youngest brother, James, had been killed at Purwandurrah the previous autumn and William's life was about to be forfeit to Afghanistan. George himself had first appeared on the Afghan scene at the end of 1840, as the officer commanding the escort that accompanied the blind ex-king, Zemaun Shah, and the enormous harems of Soojah and Zemaun on their return to Kabul. The escort, a mixed force of Sikhs and Gurkhas, had turned mutinous, but they reckoned without Broadfoot. When the first man refused an order to ground arms, Broadfoot promptly floored him with a blow over the head from the butt end of his pistol; the next man also refused, and Broadfoot broke the pistol butt on his skull, felling him with his second pistol when the man tried to use his musket. He then seized one of the ringleaders and gave him five hundred lashes on the spot. "The effect," said Mackenzie admiringly, "was wonderful."

This formidable young officer had brought with him two hundred Hindustani recruits, the nucleus of a regiment of Sappers and Miners that he now raised for Soojah's levies. In his local recruitment he was advised by a shrewd Afghan named Gul Sha, soon nicknamed "the Murderer" because he once refused to enlist men from a certain village on the grounds that he had killed three men there and had not yet paid the blood fine. The Murderer advised Broadfoot not to take "respectable men, well-to-do in the world, but men of broken clans, ruined, houseless, and with no other resources, like those who joined David in the cave Adullam".[1] The result was what Havelock's biographer called "one of the most extraordinary regiments that ever was arrayed on a battlefield", and Broadfoot himself wrote with pride that:

> "My corps, Sappers, 600, is:
> 300 Hindostanees . . . . . brave;
> 200 Ghoorkhas . . . . . . braver;
> 100 Afghans and Hazaras . . . heroes."

The "desperate and intractable characters" that made up the ranks of the Shah's Sappers and Miners had been "instructed in all the duties of entrenching and siege operations, and were encouraged to become superior light troops".[1] Broadfoot had imposed upon them an iron discipline, "punishing their faults with a severity which many would have deemed ferocious".[1] At the same time he was "like a father to these men in attention to their real wants"[1] and in return his desperadoes worshipped their hot-tempered young commanding officer with an almost religious devotion. There was such competition to join his corps that he would only accept would-be recruits on probation, leading them personally into the thickest of the enemy fire, where "the slightest disposition to shrink from it was fatal to their hope of enlistment".[1]

Early in October, 1841, Broadfoot got a note from Brigadier Anquetil, now in command of all Soojah's troops, directing him that a hundred of his sappers, with himself in command, were to accompany Monteith's force, the vanguard for Sale's Brigade, on the march back to India. To Broadfoot, who liked to know where he stood (the slapdash Burnes, he said, regarded him as "a sort of professional pedant"), these orders seemed much too vague; in particular, he wanted to know whether the march was likely to be opposed and what tools of their trade, such as picks, shovels and axes, his sappers ought to carry. The quest for this information took him first to Monteith, who simply answered that he could give Broadfoot no orders as he had received none himself; he had not even been told that Broadfoot was to come with him, but said amiably that he would be glad of his company. As for orders, Broadfoot might apply to Elphinstone, Macnaghten or anyone

[1] Mackenzie.

else he liked. He, Monteith, had no intention of doing so. "He knew these people (the Envoy and his staff) too well, admitted all the dangers of going on service in the dark, but said it was not the custom here to consult, or even to *instruct*, the commanders of expeditions. He spoke bitterly of sending officers and troops on wild-goose chases, bringing them into scrapes and letting them get out, if they could, for the Envoy's credit, but if his politicals failed, to their own discredit."[1]

Taking his leave of the fatalistic Monteith, Broadfoot now alerted Lieutenant Eyre, in charge of the Ordnance stores, to prepare the sort of equipment that he thought he might need; he also sent some of his own men down to the bazaar artificers to bespeak such tools as the Ordnance could not provide. After these wise precautions he reported to General Elphinstone himself and there followed a series of interviews so extraordinary as to be almost unbelievable if we had not Broadfoot's own detailed account. They give an accurate foretaste of vacillations of the kind that would shortly bring the Kabul force to complete disaster.

Broadfoot found the General "very ill", but "he received me with his usual cheerful kindness; insisted on getting up and was supported to his visiting room. This so exhausted him that it was half an hour before he could attend to business, indeed several ineffectual efforts to do so had excited him so much that I was sorry I had come at all." Elphinstone apologetically explained that he was as ignorant as Monteith as to the nature of the expedition, having merely been ordered by Macnaghten to send Monteith with a given number of men; whether this was a measure of precaution or hostility he had no idea.

Elphinstone readily agreed that Broadfoot was entitled to be given the information for which he had asked, but said that he himself could give him no orders and was unwilling to refer to the Envoy on a point which ought to have been left to himself to arrange; though how he could have arranged it is difficult to see, for he was admittedly totally ignorant of the situation. After some further talk he gave the persistent Broadfoot a note to Macnaghten, "begging him to listen to me, and saying he considered what I wanted was reasonable; viz. to know whether there were to be hostilities or not, with whom, and the strength and position of the enemy". This ended Broadfoot's first interview with Elphinstone, and off he went with his note to Macnaghten.

[1] Broadfoot.

"The Envoy seemed to be annoyed, said the General expected him to turn prophet; how could he predict whether there would be hostilities or not? and finally, he desired me to state all my wants to the General, and promised to sanction whatever the latter proposed."

So back to Elphinstone went Broadfoot, with a note from Macnaghten, which the General read aloud. It provocatively included the sneer about being asked to turn prophet, and added that the Envoy could not say whether there would be hostilities at all. Elphinstone was "much hurt and agitated on reading this note, and complained bitterly of the way he was deprived of all authority and reduced to a mere cipher". Broadfoot thought him far too weak and excitable for business, changed the subject, and soon afterwards tried to take his leave. He was, however, immediately called back, Elphinstone having suddenly remembered the business in hand. The General bravely said that as Broadfoot had been thrown on his hands, he would not shirk the job. Broadfoot was therefore asked to repeat his reasons for declining to estimate the tools and stores required, so long as he was left in ignorance of the nature and extent of the work to be done. Broadfoot recapitulated his reasons, and they were solemnly taken down in writing, Elphinstone explaining that he would not otherwise be able to remember them. But, after all his brave talk, the answer as before was to send Broadfoot back to Macnaghten.

On Broadfoot's second visit to the Envoy, "the latter was peevish and spoke of Gen. Elphinstone's being fidgety". He said that the only person who could give the required information was Captain Macgregor, the Political Officer for the region, and until Macgregor returned, nothing could be done. Broadfoot therefore returned to Elphinstone's Headquarters to wait until Macgregor's information might be supposed to have arrived. He then returned for the third time to Macnaghten, and found him "apparently irritated at something". The Envoy's information indicated that a force ought to be sent to Tezeen, but that the rebels were about to quit. "As to their forts, they were very weak." Broadfoot at once said that information so vague was useless, and a heated argument ensued, with Macnaghten angrily saying that the enemy were contemptible, "the Eastern Ghilzyes the most cowardly of Afghans (a foolish notion he and Burnes had); that as for me and my sappers, twenty men with pickaxes were enough; it was a peaceable march to Jalalabad, and all that we were wanted for was to pick stones from under the gun-wheels". Broadfoot at once asked whether they were the Envoy's orders; no, said Macnaghten impatiently, only his opinion, given at the request of Broadfoot and Elphinstone; the General was responsible, and must decide on what sappers and tools must go.

Broadfoot now returned for the fourth time to Elphinstone's headquarters, where he found the General "lost and perplexed". At this point they were joined by the Adjutant-General, Captain Grant, the man who, as Broadfoot later heard, was "the poor General's evil genius during the subsequent troubles". Elphinstone eagerly asked Grant's opinion, and the Adjutant-General replied with a boorish discourtesy that surprised Broadfoot, who by now could hardly have been surprised at anything. Grant, "after abusing the Envoy, spoke to the General with an imperiousness and disrespect, and to me, a stranger, with an insolence it was painful to see the effects of on the General, who yet tried only to soothe him. He advised the General not to have anything to say to Macnaghten, to me, or to the sappers, saying Monteith had men enough, and needed neither sappers nor tools. At last he took a newspaper, went to a window, and would no longer speak to the General on the subject, saying 'You know best.'"

After this demonstration of the staff's regard for Elphinstone, Broadfoot was sent back, for the fourth time, to Macnaghten. The Envoy impatiently repeated that he had given his opinion and that Elphinstone was responsible. When Broadfoot again remarked that the Eastern Ghilzyes could be formidable foes, Macnaghten lost his temper and, unpardonably, snapped that if Broadfoot was afraid that Monteith's march might bring on an attack, he need not go, he was not wanted; there were others. Broadfoot at once rose, saying that he declined to listen to such language and made a low bow. Macnaghten "seemed very angry, though half sorry, but said nothing. As I was mounting my horse, however, he came out, and held out his hand in evident kindness, though still ruffled; and so we parted, never to meet again."

For the last time Broadfoot returned to Elphinstone, whom he found in bed "and quite worn out". But the General kept him at his bedside, "and told me once more how he had been tormented by Macnaghten from the start"; reduced, to use his own words, from a General to the Lord Lieutenant's head constable. At last, with a dreadful urgency, Elphinstone said: "If anything occurs, and in case you have to go out, for God's sake clear the passes quickly, that I may get away. For, if anything were to turn up, I am unfit for it, done up body and mind, and I have told Lord Auckland so." Elphinstone repeated this exhortation two or three times, adding gloomily that he doubted very much if ever he would see home, even if he did get away. Broadfoot took his leave, feeling that there could be little hope for a force commanded by a general in such a frame of mind and infirmity of body.

5

"Unfit for it, done up body and mind" had been poor old Elphinstone's cry from the heart to Broadfoot. To his kinsman, Lord Elphinstone, he had gone into greater detail in a letter written from Kabul about three months earlier:

"My dear Elphinstone,

"I have been prevented writing to you by almost incessant severe illness since I came here. I arrived on 30th April and on that day had an attack of fever followed by rheumatic gout, which laid me up till the 24th May, when I got about for 14 days; but on 6th June I was again ill with fever, followed as before with gout and rheumatism, by which I have been confined frequently to bed ever since, and with little prospect of recovery. I am worse to-day than a month ago. My right wrist is so painful I cannot move it [the letter was written in trembling characters with the left hand] ... I have it now in wrist, knee and ankle, and if ordered by the medical committee I shall apply to Lord Auckland to be relieved. ... My stay would be useless to the public service and distressing to myself."

At long last Auckland had listened to the pleadings of the invalid, who had been told that he might return to India with the Macnaghtens, while Nott was ordered up from Kandahar to take over the command. Had these orders arrived a few weeks, even perhaps a few days, sooner, all might yet have been well, for both Mackenzie and Broadfoot firmly believed that, despite the defective position of the cantonments, "if we had had a single General fit to command, no disaster would have happened at Caubul". But an evil star shone on the British. It was just too late and, before either Nott or Elphinstone could move, the storm had broken.

Monteith, who had been joined by Sale, was still endeavouring to clear the passes between Kabul and Jalalabad and news now came back to the capital that they had been briskly engaged with the Ghilzyes in the Khoord-Kabul region. The troops had fought well and, on the whole, had had the better of the exchange. George Lawrence found it "very interesting and exciting to see the gallant bearing of the European and native soldiers emulating

148

each other in ascending and driving the enemy from heights hitherto deemed inaccessible". Broadfoot's tough irregulars "nobly justified my hopes and rewarded all the trouble I have taken; they have literally borne the brunt of every action of importance, being first in every assault and last in the retreat".

Casualties, however, were fairly heavy. Among those wounded, almost inevitably, was General Sale himself, who thus maintained his record and his popularity. "I could not help admiring old Sale's coolness," said his brigade major, when the general had his leg fractured by a ball. "He turned to me and said, 'Wade, I have got it,' and then remained on horseback directing the skirmishers until compelled from loss of blood to make over command to Dennie." Lieutenant Mein had a particularly nasty wound in the head and lost part of his brain; the ball split in two, one part entering the brain and the other running along under the skin of his scalp to the back of his head. Surprisingly, he recovered and later told Lawrence that he had distinctly heard him say, "Poor fellow, it is all up with you." Those who fell wounded during tactical retreats were doomed. "They were of course abandoned," wrote Broadfoot, "the enemy as they came up falling upon them in heaps like hounds on a fox."

The heaviest losses were suffered in a night attack on the British encampment, an attack generally believed to have been helped by the treachery of Soojah's cavalry, who had admitted the Ghilzyes within the lines. Macnaghten was much annoyed by Monteith's reporting officially to this effect. "If Monteith had clear proof against the party," he wrote, "he should have summarily executed the whole of them. If his accusation rests on suspicion alone, he has acted most unwisely and most unjustly. It is a very convenient and very common process to ascribe to our Afghan allies every calamity that befalls us." But Macnaghten was about the only person who had any doubts about the matter.

The October fighting had indeed been, as Broadfoot said, "far more serious than was expected", and had demonstrated that "even against Afghans no rules of military science can be neglected with impunity". Yet the British had had sufficient success to enable Macgregor, the Political Officer attached to Sale's brigade, to start negotiations and Macgregor "half frightened, half cajoled the refractory Ghilzye chiefs into what the sequel proved to have been a most hollow truce; for the term *treaty* can scarcely be applied to any agreement made with men so proverbially treacherous as the whole race of Afghans have proved themselves to be".[1] Macnaghten considered that "we are well out of the scrape, as we are positively unable to compete with these mountaineers and their jezails". Yet the success of Macgregor's negotiations was a misfortune. It enabled Sale's brigade to resume its march towards India, so that when Kabul rose in rebellion and the eastern passes were again promptly blocked, Sale was on the wrong side of them and the Kabul garrison effectively cut off from hope of rescue or reinforcement.

Macnaghten had convinced himself that the Ghilzye rising was an isolated outbreak, believing that the various Afghan tribes were incapable of co-operating and could therefore be dealt with separately. "One down, t'other come one, is the principle with these vagabonds," he wrote cheerfully, "and lucky for us that it is so." Others were not so sure. Sturt, who employed a good deal of local labour in the public works department, was repeatedly warned by his Afghan contacts that a widespread plot was afoot, while Eldred Pottinger, now Political Officer out in the Kohistan north west of Kabul, was reporting that in that region every hour "brought rumours of the formation of an extensive conspiracy". Pottinger later concluded that Ghilzyes, Kohistanees and Douranees had all been in league together from the beginning of September. But when the Ghilzyes rose in October, the Kohistanees remained quiet, and Burnes and Macnaghten decided that Pottinger was an alarmist.

Yet for those who had eyes to see, there was abundant evidence that the Ghilzyes had friends within the gates. The officers on piquet duty with Sale's brigade, reported the brigade major, "distinctly saw the enemy moving off towards Caubul, which proved the chiefs there to be in league with them; but the Politicals consider this 'quite a mistake'." On the evening of the night attack upon Monteith large parties of armed retainers of the great men of Kabul had been seen riding out from the city to the scene of action and returning in the small hours next morning. It was obvious what they had been doing, but already a kind of paralysed inertia was beginning to descend upon the British commanders and although these belligerent horsemen rode back through the heart of the British camp at Seeah Sung, it apparently did not occur to Brigadier Shelton "even to question them, still less to detain them".

By now British officers and men were being openly insulted in Kabul, even by the shopkeepers, "and the whole demeanour of the people was that of anticipated triumph in the destruction of the

[1] Eyre.

English".[1] Captain Waller was wounded by an assassin's pistol, Dr. Metcalfe would have been cut down but for the speed of his horse, a private soldier was found on the main road with his throat cut. When Shelton for some reason refused to post the usual night guard of Sepoys over the Horse Artillery lines, an Afghan calmly walked into one of the tents, pistolled a sleeping trooper and escaped. A recruit on sentry duty was murdered at his post by killers who crept up to him in the dark and shot him. In this last instance there was little doubt about the identity of the murderers, for the sentry had been shot close to a house belonging to a group of fakirs and his belt and accoutrements were found there next day. Even Elphinstone was angry, and urged that the chief fakir should be publicly hanged but Macnaghten thought that this would be "highly impolitic". Fate overtook the holy man a few months later when he went a-begging to Jalalabad and had the ill luck to present his alms bowl to Private Collins of the 13th Light Infantry, "an Irishman of extraordinary gallantry but a great ruffian". Collins, who thought that there was something familiar about the beggar, twitched aside his cloak and there, on his shoulders, were the badges of the sentry murdered those many months before. Without hesitation the Irishman seized the man by the scruff of his neck, held him face downward in a pool and "quietly drowned him like a dog". There was some disturbance and the guard was called out. There, sure enough, was the body of the drowned fakir. "How did this happen?" Major Wade asked the guard. "We don't know, sir," they replied woodenly, "we didn't see anything."[1]

Back in October, when Broadfoot ordered entrenching tools from the smiths of Kabul, the surly artificers at first refused to execute any orders for the Feringhis; they muttered that they were too busy forging weapons, thus giving another clue as to what was about to happen. Burnes, however, optimistically surmised that the arms were being manufactured "for the wandering tribes about to migrate".[2] Their true purpose would soon become apparent, and meanwhile Broadfoot was not the man to stand any nonsense from the craftsmen of Kabul. Over each recalcitrant he posted one of his own ferocious irregulars who stood with his hand on his dagger until the quota of implements had been reluctantly completed. These tools would in due course prove to be the salvation of the garrison of Jalalabad.

The fact was that by the middle of October, 1841, the chiefs in Kabul, finally exasperated by the cutting of their subsidies, had

[1] Mackenzie.   [2] Broadfoot.

made up their minds that the time had come for a night of the long knives. The lead was taken by Abdoollah Khan, a great Achukzye landowner from the Pisheen valley, whose ruthless nature is best illustrated by the popular belief that to rid himself of an elder brother, who stood between him and an inheritance, he had buried him up to his chin in earth, with a rope round his neck. The other end of the rope was haltered to a wild horse, which was then driven round in circles until the victim's head was twisted from his shoulders. The other ringleader was Amenoolah Khan, a camel-driver's son who by his talent, courage and cunning had risen to be one of the most powerful of Afghan noblemen. Though by now he was old, palsied and almost speechless, he was yet a force to reckon with, for he owned the whole Logar valley and could put 10,000 fighting men into the field. Until he threw off the mask, Amenoolah was believed to be one of Soojah's staunchest supporters.

The two Khans now industriously spread abroad a rumour among the Kabul chiefs that Macnaghten was planning to seize them all and send them prisoner to London. They also forged a document in Soojah's name, in which he was purported to exhort all good Afghans to rise and put the Feringhis to the sword. The excitable Afghans were quickly worked up into a state of un-reasoning fury and hatred. But the Khans did not yet feel strong enough to attempt an attack upon the cantonments, contemptible as these might be. There was an easier victim, closer to their hand. In the city of Kabul itself, alone and almost defenceless, lived the now-hated British Resident, Alexander Burnes. "Here is my advice," muttered old Amenoolah to the conspirators; "everything we do is made known to Burnes; take courage, therefore, and *lose no time*; attack the kafir at once in his house, before he can know our plans". The savage Abdoollah readily agreed; he had an insult to avenge, for Burnes had caught him out in intrigue with the Ghilzye insurgents and had called him a dog, threatening to have his ears cropped. The Resident's doom was sealed.

The Residency at Kabul was a large court-yarded mansion in the heart of the city. Two other British officers had houses in the same street, Captain Warburton, who had married Dost Maho-med's niece and was the Commander of Soojah's artillery, and Captain Johnson, who was the Paymaster of Soojah's army. Moreover, Johnson's house contained a prize that appealed to the Afghans' cupidity as much as their hatred of the British thirsted for the blood of Burnes next door. For the Paymaster had found it a personal inconvenience to keep the cash for the Shah's troops in the cantonments and had asked Macnaghten's permission to have it transferred to his own house. "Captain Johnson," Macnaghten had gaily replied, "may keep his cash where he pleases," and it now reposed next door to the Residency, protected by a small guard of Sepoys and constituting a standing temptation to the needy and avaricious Afghans.

Burnes, in the Residency, was in what he described as "the most nondescript of situations", his job in life being apparently to draw a large salary every month and to give advice that was never taken. "I am now a highly paid idler," he wrote to a brother at home, "having no less than 3,500 rupees a month as Resident at Caubul and being, as the lawyers call it, only counsel and that, too, a dumb one—by which I mean that I give paper opinions, but I do not work them out." Of his breakfast parties, his dinners and his cellar of excellent wines and liqueurs something has already been said. "I lead," he said, "a very pleasant life, and if rotundity and heartiness be proofs of health, I have them." Staying with him at this time were his brother, Lieutenant Charles Burnes—"little Charley" whom he had picked out so long ago as a lad made for Indian service—and his assistant, George Broadfoot's brother William.

Burnes was waiting eagerly to hear whether he had been selected to succeed Macnaghten as Envoy. "Ay! What will this day bring forth?" he wrote in his journal on the morning of 31st October, 1841. "It will make or mar me, I suppose. Before the sun sets I shall know whether I go to Europe or succeed Macnaghten." But the sun set, and still the news had not come. The 1st of November dawned, and Burnes wrote in the journal, "I grow very tired of praise, and I suppose I shall get tired of censure in time." It was his last entry. There would be no more, either of praise or censure, to worry him in this world.

Nothing in Kabul could ever be kept secret for long, and by the evening of 1st November Burnes' Afghan servants were warning him that there was a plot against his life and urging him to withdraw to the safety of the cantonments. All through the night similar warnings were being brought to the Residency by friendly Afghans. Burnes' reaction was mixed. In one of the last letters he wrote he is said to have stated that he was a marked man, and would inevitably be the first victim of the outbreak that he now saw approaching, but that he would not flinch from doing what he believed to be his duty, although all his warnings had been disregarded. So, too, on the night of the 1st, when his Hindu secretary warned him that the conspiracy was about to erupt, "he rose from his chair, sighed, and said he knows nothing but the time has arrived that we should leave this country". Yet on the same evening, at what would be his last meeting with Macnaghten he was congratulating Sir William on his departure "at a period of such profound tranquillity". And he reassured his anxious servants that he had done the Afghans no injury; why, then, should they harm him?

Before dawn on the 2nd Osman Khan, Soojah's Vizir, came in person to urge Burnes to seek safety in the cantonments. Again Burnes refused. Paymaster Johnson, his neighbour (who fortunately for himself had slept the night in cantonments), later wrote that "Sir Alexander scorned the idea of quitting his house, as he had every hope of quelling the disturbance; and let the worst come to the worst, he felt too well assured that neither the Envoy nor the General would permit him to be sacrificed whilst in the performance of his public duty, so long as there were 6,000 men within two miles of him." But even had Burnes been minded to seek safety in flight, it was now too late. As dawn broke on 2nd November Abdoollah Khan's murder gang arrived at the gates of the residency.

At the outset there were, perhaps, not more than thirty of them, but the word ran round and they were quickly reinforced. "The plunder of my treasury," said Captain Johnson, "my private property and that of Sir Alexander . . . was too great a temptation to the inhabitants of Caubul, and when 300 men would have been sufficient in the morning to have quelled the disturbance, 3,000 would not have been adequate in the afternoon." At first Burnes, trusting in the power of his silver tongue to quell the tumult, would not let the Residency guard open fire. He managed to get a message off to the cantonments warning Macnaghten that the Residency was under siege, and asking for troops to be sent. But it would be several hours before any troops could arrive and meanwhile the screaming mob was every minute growing larger, bolder and more furious. Burnes, with his brother and Broadfoot standing beside him on a balcony, endeavoured to address them, but he might as well have spoken to a pack of wolves. All he could see below was a sea of implacable furious faces, all he could hear was voices yelling for the blood of the Englishmen. Shots rang out and at long last the officers on the balcony above, the guard in the house below, opened fire. Broadfoot picked off six of the enemy before falling dead with a bullet through his heart. "In him," said Eyre, "was lost to the state not only one of its bravest and most intelligent officers, but a man who for honesty of purpose and soundness of judgment, I may boldly aver, could not be surpassed." It was a year to the day since his brother had been killed at Purwandurrah.

The mob had now forced its way into the Residency garden and had fired the stables, which were blazing furiously. Burnes was reduced to appealing to the avarice of his assailants, offering them large sums of money to spare his own and his brother's life. He was answered by angry shouts, bidding him come down into the garden. And now a mysterious figure joined him on the balcony, a Kashmiri Mussulman who had somehow managed to get into the house. This man swore to Burnes by the Koran that if the brothers would stop firing on the mob and come down into the garden, he would lead them to safety. Since it was now plain that no help from the cantonments could arrive in time, the two Burnes threw on native dresses and followed their guide down into the garden. But before they had gone more than a few yards from the house the Kashmiri Judas shouted at the top of his voice: "See, friends! This is Sekundur Burnes." It took the mob less than a minute to finish off its victims. Naib Sherif, an old bon viveur who had spent many jolly evenings with Burnes, later collected the pieces and buried them before morning.

6

The mob now cut the throats of such of the Residency guard as were still alive and sacked the Residency itself before turning gleefully to the even richer plunder of Captain Johnson's house next door. Here, as at the Residency, the Sepoy guard—a subadar and twenty-eight privates—fought magnificently, without thought of flight or surrender, until every man had been killed. The Afghans, never merciful in victory, then slaughtered all Johnson's servants and every woman and child whom they found in his house. The loot was rich indeed, £17,000 of government money and the Paymaster's private property to the value of ten thousand rupees. What was more, the rioters burnt the office records for the past three years "which," said Johnson, with the indignation of the true paymaster, "comprise unadjusted accounts to nearly one million sterling".

Yelling with excitement the mob now swept off through the city, gutting shops, burning houses, and murdering men, women and children, apparently at random. But already some of the rioters, and all the more law-abiding citizens, were beginning to feel appalled at the thought of what had been done and at the prospect of the vengeance that would surely be exacted when the disciplined troops from the cantonments marched in. "They are coming—they are coming," ran the rumour, with anxious glances cast in the direction of the camp, until at last it was realised that, incredibly, "they" were not coming at all. The British Resident, his brother and his assistant had been brutally done to death, a Sepoy detachment slaughtered to the last man, and the Treasury looted; yet a mere two miles away six thousand troops of the Army of Occupation remained inactive within their lines.

About seven o'clock on the same morning George Lawrence, who had returned to the cantonments after helping Sale's Brigade to clear the eastern passes, was just settling to his desk when an excited messenger rushed in with the news that the shops were closed, the streets of Kabul filled with armed men, and the Residency surrounded. Lawrence hurried to report to Macnaghten, whom he found already in conference with Elphinstone. With them were Elphinstone's *a.d.c.* Major Thain, and two of his staff officers, the mannerless Captain Grant and Captain Bellew. They were discussing Burnes' note with its urgent appeal for assistance. Lawrence was asked for his opinion and without hesitation suggested that a regiment should at once march straight from cantonments to the Residency, and should then send strong detachments to arrest the ringleaders, Abdoollah and Amenoolah. This bold proposal "was at once set down as one of pure insanity and under the circumstances utterly unfeasible".[1] While the conference continued its debate, Lawrence was ordered to ride to the Balla Hissar. He was attacked on the way by an Afghan, who sprang from a ditch and lunged furiously at him with a huge two-handed sword. Lawrence hurled his stick at the assailant, drew his sword and rode him down, before continuing to the citadel. Here he found Soojah walking up and down in great agitation, exclaiming, "Is it not just what I always told Macloten Sahib would happen, if he would not follow my advice?" This evidently referred to Soojah's urgent requests to the Envoy to be allowed to arrest and execute a number of the disaffected chiefs before they could strike. It now seemed as if there might have been much to be said for this course.

Back in the cantonments neither Elphinstone nor his staff could suggest a plan, and it was left to Macnaghten to do so. The Envoy bethought him of Brigadier Shelton, who had been stationed with a small force out on the Seeah Sung hills, where he had been preoccupied with composing official complaints to

[1] Lawrence.

Elphinstone at his being kept out in bivouac when, as second-in-command, he should have been given the quarters vacated by Sale. Lady Sale, who was still living there, waiting to travel down to India with Elphinstone and the Macnaghtens, was much annoyed by what she considered Shelton's indecent haste and commented sharply that "as long as Brig. Shelton's duty keeps him at Seeah Sung, he has no business in cantonments". At any rate, there he still was, and Macnaghten now suggested that part of his force should be withdrawn to the cantonments and that Shelton himself should lead the remainder to the Balla Hissar, "there to operate as might seem expedient . . . and assistance, if possible, sent to Sir A. Burnes".

Rumours of some kind of upheaval in the city had already reached Shelton when, between nine and ten o'clock in the morning, he received Elphinstone's order to march on the Balla Hissar, followed immediately by a counter-order to stand fast, as Soojah had objected. Shelton irritably replied "that if there was an insurrection in the city it was not a moment for indecision, and recommended him (Elphinstone) at once to decide upon what measures he would adopt". Back, presently, came Elphinstone's answer: march at once to the Balla Hissar and get further orders from Captain Lawrence, who was already there. This too was at once overtaken by a further message, this time from Lawrence, telling him to stop where he was and await further instructions. The Brigadier, now understandably enraged, sent Sturt, Lady Sale's son-in-law, to find out exactly what was happening up in the citadel. Almost at once, however, Lawrence himself arrived at Seeah Sung with the message that Shelton should march at once to the Balla Hissar.

The Brigadier seemed to Lawrence "almost beside himself, not knowing how to act, and with incapacity stamped on every feature of his face". Lawrence, who knew Shelton as a man "dissatisfied with his position, a great croaker and anxious to return to India", had always suspected that in a crisis he would be found wanting. Even so, "Brig. Shelton's conduct at this crisis astonished me beyond expression". He asked Lawrence what he ought to do. "Enter the city at once," replied Lawrence promptly, only to be sharply rebuked with the retort that "my force is inadequate, and you don't appear to know what street firing is". "You asked my opinion," snapped Lawrence, "and I have given it; it is what I would do myself." This bickering was resolved when Shelton, with three companies of the 54th Native Infantry, the Shah's 6th Infantry, four guns and a detachment of the Queen's 44th, marched unopposed into the Balla Hissar, to be further irritated on arrival at being asked by Soojah "as well as I could understand, who sent me and what I came there for". He had misunderstood the Shah's question. What Soojah was in fact asking was why the troops did not take action, and to Lawrence he "seemed to be, as well he might, deeply annoyed that they did nothing".

Down in the cantonments the wildest rumours were now flying about. It was said that Burnes had gone off to consult with the Vizir and, except for a bullet in the leg, was safe; it was said that Soojah had sent word to Macnaghten "that Burnes was all right" but that a few hours later he had confessed that he had no idea what had happened to the Resident. There were other British officers living in the city whose lives were in peril, such as Captain Trevor, commander of the Shah's Lifeguards, who with his wife and seven children lived in a tower in Kabul. Already there were gloomy rumours about the fate of the Trevor family. One was to the effect that only Trevor, his wife and one child had escaped, while the other six little Trevors had all been murdered; another version was that the entire family had been wiped out except for Trevor himself. In fact the Afghan lifeguards had defended the tower manfully and the whole family had managed to make their way to the cantonments. It had not been a pleasant journey. As they walked along an Afghan struck at Mrs. Trevor with his sabre, but an Indian trooper beside her "saved her by stretching out his bare arm. The hand was cut off by the blow, yet he continued to walk by her with the blood flowing from the stump until they reached cantonments, an act of true heroism."[1] Among all the rumours that were busily flying about the one thing certain was that there was incessant firing from Kabul city and that from the Balla Hissar the Shah's guns were booming out in reply.

For, in truth, the only person who on this calamitous November morning took prompt and direct action in an attempt to save Burnes was Shah Soojah himself, who had immediately ordered one of his own regiments, under his Prime Minister's personal command, to go down into the city and crush the tumult. His troops plunged down into Kabul with more spirit than judgment and were quickly entangled with their guns in the narrow winding streets.[2] They were brought to a standstill by heavy sniping from

[1] Mackenzie.
[2] Havelock, a year before, had foreseen this danger. The Balla Hissar, he wrote, "is the key of Cabool", but its garrison would have to overawe the

158

rooftops and doorways and before long had to abandon their guns and scurry back in disorderly rout to the Balla Hissar. Shelton's force arrived from Seeah Sung in time to cover their retreat and retrieve the abandoned guns.

George Lawrence, who had ridden ahead of Shelton to the Balla Hissar, had been attacked on the way by an Afghan who, "grinding his teeth and grinning with rage and hatred of the Feringhees, aimed a blow at him with a sword". Lawrence spurred his horse out of harm's way and Lady Sale recorded with satisfaction that the attack was revenged by a trooper's "shooting the fellow". Lawrence still had to run the gauntlet of a fusillade of shots from about fifty assailants but managed to reach Soojah's presence in safety.

His conference with the King was suddenly and dramatically interrupted by the ghastly appearance in the doorway of Lieutenant Sturt, who staggered towards them streaming with blood. On the very threshold of the audience chamber he had been set on by an Afghan, "a young man well dressed", who stabbed him again and again, in the face, the shoulder and the side. His wounds, though horrible to see, were fortunately not mortal and Lawrence had him carried back to the cantonments in Soojah's own palanquin. By the time he was got to bed, the blood had clotted and the wound in his face had affected his tongue and the nerves of his throat, so that he could neither swallow nor articulate. By the constant application of warm wet cloths his wife eventually managed to free his mouth of the clotted blood and late that night she and her mother, Lady Sale, were overjoyed to hear him whisper the one word "*bet-ter*". So Sturt lived to die another day.

By now Shelton's force had arrived in the Balla Hissar, to find Soojah in a state of high excitement and boldly declaring that if the rebellion was not all over by the following morning, he would burn Kabul to the ground. "By no means an easy task," commented Lady Sale, "the houses are all flat-roofed and mud-roofed. . . . By throwing shells into the houses you may fire them; and the individual house, being ceiled with wood, blazes fiercely until the roof falls in, and the mud and dust smother the fire without danger to the adjacent buildings." No doubt it appeared to

citizens "with their mortars and howitzers; for in a land where every male has in his house, or about his person, a musket and long bayonet . . . a sword and shield, a dagger, a pistol or a musketoon, a contest in crooked lanes of flat-roofed houses with a population estimated at sixty thousand souls would be unequal, excepting for very numerous forces indeed; in any case injudicious".

Soojah, as it did to Lady Sale, "a very strange circumstance that troops were not immediately sent into the city to quell the affair in the commencement; but we seem to sit quietly with our hands folded, and look on". She had no doubt of the reason. "The state of supineness and fancied security of those in power in cantonments is the result of deference to the opinions of Lord Auckland, whose sovereign will and pleasure it is that tranquillity do reign in Afghanistan; in fact, it is reported at Government House, Calcutta, that the lawless Afghans are as peaceable as London citizens; and this being decided by the powers that be, why should we be on the alert? Most dutifully do we appear to shut our eyes to our probable fate."

Soojah was truculently declaring that if Sturt's assailant was not at once surrendered by the Meer Aker, the official in whose house he had sought sanctuary, the Meer Aker would himself be hanged. But inwardly the poor old King was quaking with terror, for he had already sensed that the probable outcome would be that the British would withdraw from the country and leave him to his fate; nor had he much doubt what that fate would be. When Shelton arrived, the King, in his anxiety to please, abandoned his usual hauteur and insisted on entertaining the British officers to dinner. His guests, apparently because they were unable to change into mess kit, boorishly received the invitation with "extreme disgust . . . neither men or officers having an article of any kind besides what they wore".[1] Over dinner the Shah, pathetically trying to ingratiate himself, earnestly asked the opinion of his guests, particularly, says Lady Sale, "that of ——, whose conduct was represented on the emergency as pitiful and childish in the extreme, not having a word to say nor an opinion to offer". The pitiful and childish ——, as she hardly bothers to conceal, was in fact Brigadier Shelton.

Meanwhile, down in the cantonments, the British had been spending the 2nd November in futile debate. Elphinstone, although the Envoy was only a few hundred yards away from him, seemed to think it necessary to conduct communications with him in writing, and already the note of pathetic helplessness that was to be the hallmark of the General's behaviour throughout had become plainly apparent.

"My dear Sir William [he wrote],
    "Since you left me, I have been considering what can be done to-morrow. Our dilemma is a difficult one. Shelton, if rein-

[1] Lady Sale.

forced to-morrow, might no doubt force in two columns on his way towards the Lahore gate, and we might from here force that gate and meet them. But if this were accomplished, what shall we gain? . . . Where is the point you said they were to fortify near Burnes' house? . . . To march into the town, it seems, we should only have to come back again; and as to setting the city on fire, I fear from its construction that is almost impossible." There was no thought of taking the initiative in Elphinstone's mind. "We must see what the morning brings" he concluded helplessly "and then think what can be done."

During the night the 37th Native Infantry, recalled from Khoord-Kabul, came marching in, in good order, over the Seeah Sungh hills and thus reinforced, Elphinstone decided on action. It was, however, too little and too late. A mere three companies of infantry, with two guns of the Horse Artillery, were ordered to advance upon the Lahore gate of Kabul, with no very clearly defined object and with no coordination of any kind with Shelton in the Balla Hissar. The commander of this sortie soon had to order a hasty retreat in the face of heavy and increasing opposition. Already, as a direct result of the British failure to crush the rising in the first few hours, thousands were joining the rebel cause. Mohun Lal, Burnes' secretary, put it in a nutshell. "As soon as the murder of Sir Alexander (whose name was awfully respected) and the pillage of treasure was known in the adjacent villages, it brought next day thousands of men under the standard of the rebels." By noon on the 3rd November, said Macnaghten, "the road between the cantonments and the city was hardly passable".

That morning Macnaghten and his household moved from the Mission Compound into the cantonments proper, which rather belatedly were ordered to be put into a state of defence. The nakedness of the land was now plainly revealed, for the Army of Afghanistan had been kept woefully short of artillery, and of its few guns some had already gone with Sale's brigade, while others were in the Balla Hissar. Lieutenant Eyre found that to defend the enormous camp perimeter he had only six 9-pounder iron guns, four howitzers and three 5¼-inch mortars, a mere thirteen pieces in all. To make matters worse, the only artillerymen available to man this meagre ordnance were eighty of the Shah's Punjabees "very insufficiently instructed, and of doubtful fidelity".[1]

[1] Eyre. Captain Nicholls and his Horse Artillery were at this time still in the Balla Hissar.

The only other positive step taken on the 3rd November was to increase the garrison of the commissariat fort, four hundred yards from the cantonments, to a subaltern's guard of eighty men. This command was entrusted to Ensign Warren of the 5th Native Infantry, "a man of cool determined courage, who said little and always went about with a couple of bull-dogs at his heels".[1] Between this fort and the cantonments was another small tower, known as Mahomed Sheriff's fort, and Elphinstone half-heartedly suggested that this too might be garrisoned. Macnaghten, however, declared that it would not be politic to do so, and the General did not press the point. Twenty-four hours later it was in the hands of the Afghans, who came swarming through the gardens and orchards that lay between it and the cantonments. The insurgents promptly laid siege to the commissariat fort, and the taciturn Warren reported that unless reinforced he would be compelled to abandon it. Elphinstone thereupon ordered two companies of the Queen's 44th to reinforce Warren, but had so little appreciated that the fort, with almost the entire supplies for the army inside it, was the key to the cantonments that he allowed the 44th the alternative of enabling Warren to evacuate it in safety. The operation quickly petered out in failure, both company commanders being shot dead and the troops driven back by a fierce fire opened upon them from Mahomed Sheriff's fort. In the afternoon a second attempt was made to relieve Warren, mainly with cavalry, who were likewise repulsed, as "from the loopholes of Mahomed Sheriff's fort—from every tree in the Shah's garden—from whatever cover of wood or masonry was to be found—the Afghan marksmen poured, with unerring aim, their deadly fire upon our advancing troops".

Captain Boyd, the Chief Commissariat Officer, had been appalled to hear that the General was contemplating the evacuation of the commissariat fort, with the loss of all the stores. Lady Sale too had perceived the vital importance of the post. "We have only three days' provisions in cantonments," she wrote in her journal on 3rd November; "should the Commissariat Fort—an old crazy one undermined with rats—be captured, we shall

[1] Mackenzie. Bulldogs were an additional peril to the occupying troops. Not long before, Mackenzie had called to Captain Troup's bulldog "Nettle, Nettle!" Next instant Nettle was clinging like a leech to his right arm, having gone mad. He managed to hold it at arm's length and throttle it with his left hand. "I never saw anything so hideous as that dog's head, his jaws reeking with blood and foam, his mouth wide open, his tongue swollen and hanging out, and his eyes flashing a sort of lurid fire." Mackenzie escaped rabies by applying caustic, which left a circular scar nearly two inches in diameter.

not only lose all our provisions but our communications with the city will be cut off. . . . No military steps have been taken to suppress the insurrection, nor even to protect our only means of subsistence (the godowns) in the event of a siege. The King, Envoy and General appear perfectly paralysed by this sudden outbreak."

Boyd was doing his best to impress upon Elphinstone the necessity of holding the commissariat fort and the General, "ever ready to listen to advice and sometimes to take it", promised reinforcements. By nightfall no steps had been taken to implement this promise and Boyd, now accompanied by Paymaster Johnson, returned to urge upon the General the vital need to hold the fort. Temporarily convinced, Elphinstone sent an order to Warren bidding him hold the fort to the last—an order which Warren later denied having received. The futile debate at headquarters continued throughout the night. Boyd, Macnaghten and others were pressing for immediate action, but Elphinstone, still racked by indecision, was canvassing the views of all and sundry, and even subalterns were asked for their opinions. He took Eyre into his private room and anxiously asked him what he ought to do, saying that "he could not bear to contemplate such a frightful loss of life". Major Thain and Captain Grant were then called in, but the meeting was obviously getting nowhere, since "the General had an unfortunate habit of flying from one subject to another, it being impossible to keep his attention fixed to an argument for any length of time". Eyre eventually suggested that he should be guided by the opinion of the sorely wounded Lieutenant Sturt and Elphinstone "eagerly jumped at the idea, as releasing him from the burden of responsibility. . . . The whole night was lost by indecision."

About all that emerged was that the General had "an insuperable repugnance" to night operations, and was ready to quote innumerable instances of their failure in Europe. "It was an inconceivable trial to one's patience," recalled Mackenzie, "to be doomed to listen to such stories at this serious crisis, when every moment was of infinite value. No one could tell an anecdote better, and unfortunately for us he had one always ready, even at the most unseasonable time."

At last opinion began to crystallise that as a necessary preliminary to relieving the Commissariat fort the enemy must first be dislodged from Mahomed Sheriff's tower. While this was being further discussed another message came in from Warren, reporting that the enemy were now mining under the walls of the Commissariat fort and the more faint-hearted Sepoys escaping over them to make their way back to cantonments; unless immediately relieved, he wrote, he would be forced to abandon his position. In reply he was assured that reinforcements would reach him by 2 a.m. at the latest. The task should have presented little difficulty for a scout sent to reconnoitre Mahomed Sheriff's fort had now returned with the news that there were only about twenty Afghans sitting outside it, smoking and gossiping, and that the garrison inside seemed very small. Cautiously, a second scout was sent off to corroborate the first, which he duly did, only for another hour or two to be wasted in argument. Finally a detachment was ordered to be ready to move by 4 a.m., two hours later than the latest hour by which Warren had been promised relief, but even then the troops were not ready, and the sun was in the sky before they had formed up to move off. At that instant, however, Warren and what was left of his garrison, having despaired of reinforcement, came marching in to cantonments. To the Assistant Adjutant General's pompous order to state in writing his reasons for abandoning his post, Warren dourly replied that he would give them to the Court of Inquiry which he requested might be convened to investigate his conduct. "It was not, however, deemed expedient to comply with his request."

The loss of the stores in the Commissariat fort was now to be enhanced by the loss of the only alternative supply, a large quantity of grain and meal collected by Captain Johnson for Shah Soojah's troops. This depot had originally been sited within the Balla Hissar but, typically, Soojah had raised objections and it had therefore been moved to a godown fort on the outskirts of the city. It was now guarded by a garrison commanded by Colin Mackenzie, who had under him twenty sepoys of the Shah's infantry, fifty of Broadfoot's sappers and ninety of his own Afghan jezailchis, cheerful ruffians who adored their Scottish commander and would come and lean on his shoulder or put their arms round his neck, while speaking to him, as if he had been one of their own countrymen.

On the morning of 2nd November Mackenzie was startled by the apparition of "a naked man, covered with blood, from two deep sabre cuts in the head and five musket shots in the arm and body".[1] He turned out to be a trooper who had been sent with a message from Macnaghten to Trevor, but had been intercepted by the insurgents. "This being a rather strong hint as to how things were going," wrote Mackenzie, "I immediately ordered all the gates to be secured, etc." It was not a moment too soon, and

[1] Mackenzie.

before long he found himself under furious attack from hundreds of the insurgents. For two days Mackenzie's garrison held out manfully, while the enemy threw in all they had, including a large wall-piece, "a long gun too heavy to hold, made to rest on the wall".[1] Mackenzie's jezailchis, far from feeling any qualms at firing on their own countrymen, seemed to relish the contest and in any lull, "whenever the Jezailchis could snatch five minutes to refresh themselves with a pipe, one of them would twang a sort of rude guitar as an accompaniment to some martial song which, mingling with the notes of war, sounded very strangely".[1] Tempting offers to betray their Feringhi officer, shouted to them by the assailants, were treated with amused contempt and Hasan Khan, the Jezailchis' subadar, "more than once pretended to listen to the overtures of the enemy in order to lure them from under cover, and then sent his answer in the shape of a rifle ball".[1] All this time Mackenzie had been expecting relief from the cantonments, but he had looked in vain for "the glittering bayonets through the trees". His ammunition was almost exhausted and, without ammunition, there was little more that could be done. "I think we have done our duty," Hasan Khan told him; "if you consider it necessary that we should die here, we will die, but *I* think we have done enough." Mackenzie accepted this sensible view. He ordered a sortie and his splendid little garrison, not a European except himself among them, made a fighting retreat to the cantonments. "For two days Colin Mackenzie fought," wrote George Broadfoot later, "and then cut his way to the large force, who did not seem able to cut their way to him, bringing in all his men and the crowd of women and children safe. A more heroic action never was performed. The unhappy women and children have *since* perished or gone into slavery, because five thousand men could not do what he did."

In three days, therefore, the British had managed to lose nearly all their supplies. Even more serious than the threat of starvation —which was in fact quickly remedied by the energetic efforts of the commissariat officers—was the moral effect of this exposure of British imbecility. The sight of a rabble gutting the commissariat fort while the British troops looked passively on from the cantonment walls was enough to decide many waverers. The scene, according to Captain Johnson, "was this day something similar to a large ants' nest", with thousands of Afghans swarming to and fro, each busily taking off all that he could carry. Elphinstone's troops were furious—particularly furious, perhaps, as they

[1] Mackenzie.

saw the rum ration vanish into Afghan hands—and clamoured so loudly to be led out against the enemy that the General was momentarily roused to contemplate once more the possibility of launching an attack upon Mahomed Sheriff's fort. This thought was duly communicated to the Envoy, now living within a few yards of him, in a letter which courteously began, "My Dear Sir William: After due consideration we have determined on attacking the fort this morning, with fifty men of the 44th and 200 Native Infantry." But Elphinstone's heart was not in the matter and he was dubious of success. "It behoves us," he added, "to look to the consequences of failure: in this case I know not how we are to subsist or, from want of provisions, to retreat. You should, therefore, consider what chance there is of making terms, if we are driven to this extremity." Thus, already, within three days of the unavenged murder of Burnes, the British commander-in-chief was thinking and writing of "making terms".

7

It was not really Elphinstone's fault and the officers who served under him, with few exceptions, recognised the fact. Despite his imbecile vacillations, they nearly always spoke of him with affection and respect. The plain fact was that disease had ruined his physique and crippled his mental powers. "He had almost lost the use of his limbs. He could not walk; he could hardly ride. The gout had crippled him in a manner that it was painful to contemplate." The responsibility for letting such a man, in the moment of crisis, be found in command of the Army of Afghanistan rests firmly upon the shoulders of the Governor-General. Against the advice of the Commander-in-Chief and in the face of Elphinstone's own protests, Auckland had insisted on putting him in charge of the only part of the army that was likely to be actively employed. "Among the general officers of the Indian army were many able and energetic men, with active limbs and clear understandings. There was one—a cripple, whose mental vigour much suffering had enfeebled; and *he* was selected by the Governor-General to command the army of Afghanistan." Eyre, who was genuinely fond of Elphinstone and was with him to the day of his death, described him as having "a mind and talents of no ordinary stamp", but criticised him for "the fatal error of transporting himself suddenly from a state of prolonged luxurious repose, at an advanced age, to undertake the fatigues and cares inseparable from high military command, in a foreign uncongenial climate. . . .

His fate ought to serve as a warning to others of his class who, priding themselves on a *Peninsular* fame of some thirty years' standing, are too apt to forget the inroads that time may have meanwhile made on mind and body."

From the moment of his arrival at Kabul in the spring the General had been, in his own words, "unlucky in his state of health", suffering almost continuously from fever and rheumatic gout. One of the very brief intervals when he felt well enough to mount a horse occurred on the fatal 2nd November and he decided to ride forth and inspect the troops, but instantly "had a very severe fall—the horse falling upon him". From then on it was painfully obvious to everyone that the Kabul army was leaderless. Elphinstone, ignorant of Afghanistan, of the feelings of its people and of the language they spoke, sought every man's advice—captains, subalterns, anyone who had a plan to propose or any kind of advice to offer, and as he was at the mercy of the last speaker, he was "in a constant state of oscillation; now inclining to one opinion, now to another; now determining upon a course of action, now abandoning it; the resolutions of one hour giving way before the doubts of its successor until, in the midst of these vacillations, the time to strike passed away for ever, and the loss was not to be retrieved".

Yet, in this first week of November, the situation was still by no means hopeless. The energetic efforts of the commissariat officers had practically made good, in a matter of days, the supplies lost when the commissariat fort and the godowns had been looted by the insurgents. They had found the inhabitants of the neighbouring villages still willing to sell grain to the Army of Occupation at reasonable prices, a clear indication that many Afghans even now believed that before long the British must surely shake off their unaccountable inertia and in their customary irresistible fashion crush the revolt. But Elphinstone, to whom every bush had become a bear, now discovered another danger—"a very serious and indeed awful one", as he told Macnaghten, carefully putting it in writing as usual. Ammunition, said the General, was running short, and therefore there must be no delay in making terms, not indeed "humiliating terms, or such as would reflect disgrace on us; but this fact of ammunition must not be lost sight of". In a melancholy postscript he added: "Our case is not yet desperate; I do not mean to impress that; but it must be borne in mind that it goes very fast."

What gave Elphinstone this obsession about a shortage of ammunition is a mystery, but the wholly imaginary danger had been preying on his mind from the outset and when, on 6th November, Sturt, who had made a surprising recovery from his wounds, had with considerable effort got three nine-pounders and two howitzers into action, Major Thain was at once sent to warn him to be careful not to expend ammunition, as powder was scarce. "There being at that time," commented Lady Sale, "a sufficiency for a twelve months' siege!" And with another expressive exclamation mark she added in her journal for 6th November—"This day Gen. Elphinstone wrote to the Envoy to state that we were in want of ammunition, requesting him to endeavour to make arrangements with the enemy!"

Macnaghten might well reflect that the British case was indeed "going very fast", not because of an imaginary shortage of ammunition but because of the hopeless quality of his military commander. Since it was now clear that General Nott would not be able to get through from Kandahar to take over the command, Macnaghten sent message after imploring message to Sale, entreating him to bring his brigade back to Kabul. It seemed odd that the message should go to Sale as an appeal from the political head rather than as an order from the army commander in Afghanistan, whose area of responsibility Sale had not yet left, but that was the way that things were done in Kabul in 1841. Eventually Elphinstone was persuaded to endorse Macnaghten's request, but the message was worded so carefully that, as Lady Sale saw, it was very doubtful whether Sale could or would take the responsibility of complying. He was told that he was to return to Kabul provided that he could return without endangering the force under his command. "Now," commented Lady Sale, who in the Victorian manner always referred in her diary to her husband by his surname alone, "in obeying an order of this kind, if Sale succeeds, and all is right, he will doubtless be a very fine fellow; but if he meets with a reverse, he will be told, 'You were not to come up unless you could do so safely!'"

In the event, as will be seen, Sale refused to bring his brigade back to Kabul and Macnaghten, with neither Nott nor Sale available, could think of only one other step that might conceivably stiffen the military backbone. It was decided to recall Brigadier Shelton and his troops to the cantonments. He seemed to be serving no useful purpose in the Balla Hissar and was believed at least to be in better health and more energetic than Elphinstone. Accordingly, on the 9th, the one-armed Brigadier marched back from the citadel to the camp, nor was any attempt made by the enemy to bar his passage.

Although Shelton's churlish and cantankerous nature made him unpopular with officers and men alike, he had the reputation of a sturdy fighter, and now he was welcomed almost as a saviour. Morale was low, and he later reported that he had been "sorry to find desponding conversations and remarks too generally indulged, and was more grieved to find the troops were dispirited". His own behaviour, and desponding conversations, would soon drive their morale to new depths. He had not hitherto spent much time in cantonments—it will be remembered that he had just been bitterly complaining at being kept out of his house in the compound—and now, with thunderous looks, he stalked round the camp in purposeful reconnaissance. It was, he found, "of frightful extent —with a rampart and ditch an Afghan could run over with the facility of a cat, with many other serious defects", and he quickly concluded that so many troops would be required for the defence of the perimeter that few, if any, could be spared to make up the mobile columns that would be needed if the British were to do anything other than stand on a rather hopeless defensive. Having as he thought, been put in command of the cantonments, he now began to give orders, only to find that he could not even site a gun without being overridden by Elphinstone, and that whenever he gave an order, "Elphinstone soon corrected it, by reminding me that he commanded, not I."

The unfortunate truth was that the courteous and gentle Elphinstone found his tough, stupid and bad-tempered Brigadier quite insufferable. "I regret to be obliged to disclose," wrote the General, "that I did not receive from Brigadier Shelton that cordial co-operation and advice I had a right to expect; on the contrary, his manner was most contumacious; from the day of his arrival he never gave me information or advice, but invariably found fault with all that was done, and canvassed and condemned all orders before officers, frequently preventing and delaying carrying them into effect." In a plaintive afterthought Elphinstone added—"He appeared to be actuated by an ill feeling towards me. I did everything in my power to remain on terms with him. I was unlucky also in not understanding the state of things, and being wholly dependent on the Envoy and others for information."

Shelton's presence in the cantonments had therefore had an effect precisely the opposite of that intended by Macnaghten. The Brigadier had but one object in view, said Lady Sale, and that was to get back, at all hazards, to Hindostan. From the very first, said Eyre, he had seemed to despair of the force being able to hold out the winter at Kabul, and was strenuously advocating an immediate retreat to Jalalabad. He made no attempt to conceal his views, and despondency soon spread among officers and men. "The number of *croakers* in garrison," said Eyre, using one of Macnaghten's favourite expressions, "became perfectly frightful, lugubrious looks and dismal prophecies being encountered everywhere . . . and it is a lamentable fact that some of those European soldiers, who were naturally expected to exhibit to their native brethren in arms an example of endurance and fortitude, were among the first to lose confidence and give vent to feelings of discontent at the duties imposed on them."

Elphinstone was indeed now conducting matters in a fashion so extraordinary that any soldiers, British or Indian, might have been forgiven for losing heart. He was perpetually convening conferences misleadingly called "Councils of War"—making war being about the last thing that anyone contemplated—at which it seemed that any officer, however junior his rank, was welcome to participate. "Numbers of young men gave much gratuitous advice," wrote Lady Sale, "in fact, the greater part of the night was spent in confusing the General's ideas." The result was what could have been expected. Elphinstone's own judgement appeared to Lady Sale to be good, "but he is swayed by the last speaker, and Capt. Grant's cold cautiousness and Capt. Bellew's doubts on every subject induce our chief to alter his opinions and plans every moment".

Those officers who were ready to advise resolute action were usually junior in rank and were invariably overridden. Sturt, for example, urged from the outset that the cantonments should be abandoned and the whole force flung into the Balla Hissar, there to stick it out until reinforcements arrived, but "the cry is, how can we abandon the cantonments that have cost us so much money?"[1] Later, when affairs were still more desperate, the same course was again urged upon the General, but Shelton loudly proclaimed that a retreat to the citadel was impossible, as the force would have to fight its way there. "For one mile and a half!" commented Lady Sale scornfully, "if we could not accomplish that, how were we to get through a week's march to Jalalabad?"

She had hoped with the rest that Shelton's arrival in the cantonments would bring some improvement, but she had never shared the optimism of the majority, who "expect wonders from his prowess and military judgment". Although conceding that "he possesses much personal bravery", she had accurately divined

[1] Lady Sale.

that his arrival was "a dark cloud overshadowing us". His behaviour at the Councils of War was abominable. Openly despising the unhappy Elphinstone, he would bring his bedding roll to the conference and immediately curl up on the floor in apparent slumber, any request for his views being met by snores, genuine or feigned. Elphinstone meekly tolerated this dumb insolence without demur. Shelton's open contempt for his superior officer was only exceeded by his violent dislike of Macnaghten, whom he continually criticised in the rudest terms until it became too much for Mackenzie, who rounded on the Council of War and told them that they were behaving like a pack of troublesome schoolboys and that this constant carping at the Envoy behind his back was disgraceful. "Damn it, Mackenzie," snarled Shelton, unabashed, "I *will* sneer at him! I *like* to sneer at him!"

This cantankerous officer was now to be given an opportunity to demonstrate his own skill in command, and the result was disastrous.

8

A few hundred yards from the north-west corner of the cantonments lay a low range of hills known as the Beymaroo and, below them, a village of the same name, from whose inhabitants Paymaster Johnson had been successfully buying fresh supplies of food for the troops. Incensed by the villagers' collaboration with the Feringhis, the Afghan insurgents now began to appear daily upon the Beymaroo hills whence, said Johnson, "they repeatedly visited the village of Beymaroo, destroyed the houses and plundered the inhabitants and have expelled them from their homes on account of their aid to us in bringing in grain". Moreover, from the high ground, where they had installed two small cannon, they were able to keep up a continuous dropping fire upon the cantonments.

Macnaghten, who by now was displaying more resolution than any of the military commanders, urged that a force be sent to dislodge the enemy from the hills and bring this intolerable state of affairs to an end. At once Shelton objected and procrastinated until at last the Envoy rounded on him sharply. "Brigadier Shelton," he said peremptorily, "if you will allow yourself to be thus bearded by the enemy, and will not advance and take these two guns by this evening, you must be prepared for any disgrace that may befall us."

Stung to action at last, Shelton marched out on 13th November at the head of a strong force, three or four squadrons of cavalry, seventeen companies of infantry and two guns. Those left behind in cantonments, watching in painful anxiety the column wind its way up the slope of the Beymaroo, saw to their horror a cloud of Afghan cavalry charge straight down upon it. The 44th, who led the column, waited till the horsemen were within ten yards and then fired a volley. When the smoke had cleared, it was seen that not a man nor a horse had been touched, and the 44th, not surprisingly "having no confidence in their weapons",[1] broke and fled. "My very heart," said Lady Sale, "felt as if it leapt to my teeth when I saw the Afghans ride clean through them. The onset was fearful. They looked like a great cluster of bees."

It was only a momentary check, but it did no good to the morale of the 44th. The British re-formed and again advanced, under cover of the two guns, which Eyre was now working to good effect. The heights were carried, the enemy withdrew and the two Afghan guns were abandoned. The British removed one and spiked the other. Then, claiming victory, they withdrew to the cantonments. A few days later the Afghans had reoccupied the Beymaroo heights and the task had to be done all over again.

On the 22nd a feeble and ineffective attempt was made by a small force under a Major Swayne to drive the Afghans from the high ground, and when this failed, it was decided that Shelton must once more take the field. He objected strongly. The troops, he said, were exhausted and the move would only increase the number of sick and wounded, without producing any solid gain. Somehow, he was overruled, and early on the morning of the 23rd he moved out under cover of darkness to storm the heights and occupy Beymaroo village. He took with him seventeen companies of infantry, two squadrons of cavalry and a hundred troopers of Captain Anderson's Irregular Horse, with a hundred Sappers; but "with a fatuity only to be accounted for by the belief that the curse of God was upon those unhappy people", the force took only one gun, a single Horse Artillery gun under a Sergeant Mulhall.

Of the British officers who accompanied Shelton on this occasion the senior was Colonel Oliver, the commanding officer of the 5th Native Infantry, a good soldier but very fat and very pessimistic, "one of the *great* croakers", as Lady Sale described him. Only the day before, when some of his men gleefully told him that a substantial quantity of grain had been procured for the battalion's rations, he had gloomily replied that "it was needless, for they would never live to eat it". Mackenzie had asked after his health

[1] Mackenzie.

one morning, to which the corpulent colonel answered, "Pretty well in body." "Well," said Mackenzie cheerfully, "that's always something in these hard times, Colonel." Oliver turned on him "with a most lugubrious countenance" and in a solemn voice intoned, "Dust to dust!" Mackenzie burst out laughing as Lieutenant Willie Bird disgustedly commented, "What can you expect of a man who is all *run to body*?" Oliver, who had been "from the commencement of our troubles most desponding and despairing of success", was not to survive the forthcoming battle on the Beymaroo heights.

As dawn broke, Shelton was in position on the high ground and Sergeant Mulhall, with his single gun, opened up with great effect upon the enemy with grape shot. The Afghans, taken aback by this unexpectedly resolute action on the part of the British, took shelter in the buildings of the village and began to return the fire with their jezails. They were ready to stand undaunted with only their rifles against cannon fire, and one recalls the generous tribute of Lady Sale: "I often hear the Afghans designated as cowards: they are a fine, manly-looking set, and I can only suppose it arises from the British idea among civilized people that assassination is a cowardly act. The Afghans never scruple to use their long knives for that purpose, *ergo* they are cowards; but they show no cowardice in standing as they do against guns without using any themselves, and in escalading and taking forts which we cannot retake." They were indeed proving themselves doughty foemen, and during the subsequent truce the British found that they had not even the satisfaction of having been opposed by the warrior tribes. "To our deep humiliation we found that instead of being stalwart and devoted clansmen, the troops who had chased the British banner from the field chiefly consisted of tradesmen and artizans from Caubul."[1]

Mulhall continued to spray these gallant citizen-soldiers with grape until they gave ground and began to evacuate the village of Beymaroo, leaving it wide open to a British assault. Belatedly, Shelton sent down a small storming party under Major Swayne, but Swayne, who had won no laurels in the abortive action on the previous day, again muffed his task. He lost his way, missed the main entrance, which was open and unguarded, and arrived in front of a side gate, which was barricaded. Here he was pinned down in helpless inactivity for half an hour or so by enemy sniping, until recalled by Shelton. The British had missed their opportunity, for by now it was light enough for the inhabitants of Kabul

[1] Lawrence.

to see what was happening, and soon thousands of horsemen and infantry were streaming out across the plain from the city to repel the Feringhees. It is hardly necessary to say that Elphinstone made no attempt to take these reinforcements in flank by a sortie from the cantonments. They quickly reoccupied the village and moved up on to a hill separated only by a narrow gorge from that on which Shelton's troops were posted. Here they opened up with their jezails with telling effect, and Shelton was compelled to take action in reply.

With extraordinary stupidity he formed his infantry into two squares on top of the hill, one a few hundred yards behind the other, with the cavalry posted in rear. As Eyre commented, the British square was a formation admirably suited to repel a cavalry charge, but at Beymaroo "we formed squares to resist the *distant fire of infantry*, thus presenting a solid mass against the aim of perhaps the best marksmen in the world, the said squares being securely perched on the summit of a steep and narrow ridge, up which no cavalry *could* charge with effect". Recalling that Shelton had seen active service in the Peninsula War in his younger days, Eyre added drily that any Peninsula general would consider this to be a novel fashion.

The British squares soon began to suffer heavy casualties from the fire of the jezails, which as usual far out-ranged their muskets. For a while Shelton could make an effective reply with his single gun, nobly worked by Sergeant Mulhall's crew. But taking the field with only one gun was another, in Eyre's opinion perhaps the most fatal, mistake of the many that were made that day. For years there had been a standing order in force throughout India which expressly forbade less than two guns to take the field under any circumstances whatever, and the practical reason for this prohibition was now to be painfully demonstrated. Mulhall's gunners were keeping up an incessant fire, pouring in round after round as quickly as they could load, and presently the vent became so hot that the gun could no longer be fired. And so the one effective British weapon fell silent and Shelton's men had only their muskets, at whose harmless fire the Afghans were openly laughing as from a safe distance they continued to mow down the British squares. Presently, in their contempt, they advanced so close to the leading square that five or six of the British officers began to pelt them with stones, these crude missiles proving rather more effective than the useless firearms.

Shelton refused to order a retreat, and was apparently prepared to stand all day watching his men shot down, unable to retaliate.

This was too much for the pessimistic Oliver. He remarked that the battle must inevitably end in a headlong flight to the cantonments and that as he was too stout to run, the sooner he got shot the better. With this, he got ponderously to his feet and advanced towards the enemy, who soon obliged him by shooting him dead. His body was found next day, headless and lacking a hand, which had been cut off for the sake of a ring on his finger. Another personal tragedy reached its climax about the same time. Two or three days earlier a British officer was standing behind a low rampart when a bullet whizzed past his head. Someone asked why he did not take cover. He turned round, pale as death, and with clenched teeth muttered, "I only wish it had been through my brain." He got his wish at Beymaroo, where he fell dead, "and all the blood rushing to his forehead, it became quite black".[1]

Shelton, who had immense physical courage, had stood all this time like a rock, endeavouring to cheer and rally his men. Five times he was struck by spent bullets, none of which did him much harm; "one spent ball hit me on the head and nearly knocked me down; another made my arm a little stiff". There came a moment, however, at which he started to go back to the second square to bring some more men to the front. The troops of the leading square, at the end of their tether, jumped to the conclusion that the Brigadier was retreating. Instantly deciding that all was lost, they turned and ran for it, and the next minute the whole British force was streaming in disorderly rout across the hill and back to the cantonments, pursued by the Afghan horse, who dashed in among them and cut them down as they ran. The slaughter would have been greater if the Afghan cavalry had not been commanded by Osman Khan, a nephew of Dost Mahomed, who was considered by Macnaghten to be "the most moderate and sensible man" of the insurgent party. Osman had no wish to annihilate the enemy and now, in the pursuit, was heard by the Sepoys to order his men not to fire on those who ran, but to spare them. And it was probably Osman himself who "rode round Kershaw three times when he was compelled to run with his men; he waved his sword over his head, but never attempted to kill him; and Captain Trevor says his life was several times in the power of the enemy, but he was also spared".[2]

At the time, however, few of Shelton's routed force realised that the enemy were not pressing home their victory, and they were panting with terror and exhaustion when they reached the shelter of the cantonments. Elphinstone, who had been watching

[1] Mackenzie.   [2] Lady Sale.

175

the battle with painful anxiety from the ramparts, hobbled down to the gate to meet them with some vague idea in his mind of rallying the fugitives. His efforts in this direction were not appreciated and he was heard saying plaintively to Macnaghten, "Why, Lord, sir, when I said to them 'Eyes right' they all looked the other way."

9

The defeat on the Beymaroo hills was enough finally to destroy what little spirit for resistance Elphinstone had ever possessed. It was enough, too, for Brigadier Shelton, who seemed quite unaware that it had very largely been his fault. "This concluded all exterior operations," he recorded without comment in his subsequent narrative of operations. It did indeed, but only because lack of leadership had now thoroughly demoralised the troops. "The total incapacity of Brigadier Shelton, his reckless exposure of his men for hours on the top of a high ridge to a destructive fire, and his stubborn neglect to avail himself of the several opportunities offered to him throughout the day . . . go far to extenuate the soldiers, who had lost all confidence in a leader who had proved himself so incapable to command."[1] Lieutenant Eyre was of the same opinion: "a general gloom hung over the cantonment; the most sanguine now began to despond; the troops had not only lost all heart—they had lost all discipline."

The news that had now come in from the north was not likely to encourage them. A day or two before Shelton's final defeat a sorely wounded Eldred Pottinger had limped into cantonments to report that the whole Kohistan was ablaze. His warnings, so airily dismissed by Burnes and Macnaghten as "croakings", had proved true after all. On the day after Burnes' murder a number of Kohistanee chiefs had appeared with about four thousand followers at Pottinger's post at Lughmanee and, after making some friendly noises, suddenly attacked. Pottinger's assistant, Lieutenant Rattray, was shot down during a parley and an Afghan, seeing that he was still breathing, put a musket to his head and blew out his brains. Somehow Pottinger managed to withdraw to the fort of Charikar, three miles away, where Captain Codrington commanded a garrison of the Shah's Gurkhas and some Punjabi artillerymen. The Kohistanee tribesmen, following up closely, at once launched an attack upon Charikar, in the course of which Pottinger received a ball in the leg and Codrington

[1] Lawrence.

was mortally wounded. The Punjabi gunners soon began to desert and in attempting to arrest two of them Lieutenant Haughton, the Gurkhas' Adjutant, had his hand lopped off by a sabre-blow from a mutinous jemadar, while a second blow "severed all the muscles on one side of the back of his neck, so that his head hung forward".[1]

The Charikar garrison, hopelessly outnumbered, held out for a few days, employing among other tactics "one curious device known to the Japanese; they put up curtains so as to prevent the Afghans taking aim at the men behind them, and as the Afghans will not throw away their shots at random, it stopped firing on that side".[1] But soon water was running short and after the daily ration had been reduced to a small wineglass-full per man, it was decided that the only hope lay in a fighting retreat to Kabul. The garrison broke out under cover of night and their retreat was not discovered by the enemy till long after daylight, thanks to the heroism of the bugle-major; too badly wounded himself to escape, he crawled to a bastion and sounded the usual morning call as if the garrison were still present. With the rest of the wounded he was put to death by the Afghans later in the day. Meanwhile the fugitives had soon become separated from each other in the darkness, and eventually only Pottinger, the wounded Haughton, with his head supported by a cushion under his chin, one little Gurkha sepoy, Pottinger's clerk and the regimental bunyah made their perilous way to Kabul, "where they were received by their brethren in arms as men risen from the dead".[2]

Pottinger found Macnaghten debating the possible courses and, as usual, putting them down in writing for Elphinstone. A retreat to Jalalabad was dismissed as "most disastrous", and to be avoided except in the last extremity. It would mean the sacrifice of much government property and it would mean the sacrifice of Soojah. Moreover, added the Envoy, 'I fear that in such a retreat very few of our camp followers would survive." He had thought of negotiation with the enemy, "or, rather, capitulation, for such it would be," but there seemed to be no Afghan with sufficient authority to protect the British if they were to surrender. A third possibility was to withdraw to the Balla Hissar, but this, too, he thought, would be "a disastrous retreat", involving the sacrifice of a great deal of property and probably of the heavy artillery; moreover,

[1] Mackenzie.
[2] Eyre. Haughton survived his terrible wounds and, though he got neither reward nor thanks for his heroic defence of Charikar, lived to distinguish himself as Governor of the Andaman Islands and as Commissioner of Assam and, later, of Cooch-Behar. (Mackenzie.)

in the citadel there would be neither food nor firewood. Perhaps, on the whole, the best course would be to hold on in the cantonments "in the hope that something may turn up in our favour. . . . If we could only bring in sufficient provisions for the winter, I would on no account leave the cantonment."

He was, however, being reduced to near despair by the helplessness of his military commanders and by the refusal of Elphinstone and Shelton to co-operate with each other in the slightest degree. The Envoy kept up an industrious and almost daily interchange of letters with his near neighbour, the General, in which each was now plainly writing with one eye on the record. At the same time he was writing daily to Sale's Political Officer, Macgregor, begging him in almost obsequious terms to get Fighting Bob and his men back to Kabul. "I have written to you four times," he wrote on 12th November, "requesting that you would come up with Sale's brigade as soon as possible." Two days later he was almost shrieking at him that "dozens of letters have been written from this, urging your immediate return with Sale's brigade to Caubul; and if you have not started by the time you receive this, I earnestly beg that you will do so immediately. Our situation is a very precarious one; but with your assistance we should all do well, and you must render it to us if you have any regard for our lives or for the honour of our country." But on the 17th he learnt with bitter disappointment that Sale, instead of returning from Gandamuck, where he had last been heard of, was still marching away from Kabul and on towards Jaalabad. "I have written to you daily," wrote the Envoy to Macgregor, "pointing out our precarious state and urging you to return here, with Sale's brigade, with all possible expedition. General Elphinstone has done the same and we now learn to our dismay that you have proceeded to Jalalabad. Our situation is a desperate one if you do not immediately return to our relief, and I beg that you will do so without a moment's delay."

It may seem curious that the British, dispersed at wide distances over a now thoroughly hostile country, were able to write with such apparent freedom to each other. These communications were completely dependent upon "cossids", native letter carriers who posted to and fro on foot or horseback. Captain Mackenzie of the 41st, not to be confused with Colin Mackenzie, tells us that "these men sometimes perform incredibly long journeys in the shortest space of time imaginable. They are very trustworthy and faithful, and capable of any amount of exertion and endurance of fatigue." They would conceal secret messages in a hollow stick, in their hair, their garments, their shoes or under their arm-pits.

If the risk was very great the despatch would be written on slips of tissue paper and wrapped in a little ball of wax so that, in emergency, it could be swallowed by the bearer. It was a hazardous profession and Mackenzie adds that "very little mercy is usually shown to a cossid; I have seen many a poor wretch lying by the road-side with his throat cut from ear to ear and his body otherwise mutilated, while the ground immediately about him was strewn in all directions with the contents of his dawk or letter-bag, torn in a thousand fragments".

The cossids safely carried Macnaghten's messages through to Macgregor, which was just as well, for they were written in terms by which the insurgents would have been greatly heartened if they had read them. They took several days in transit, and Macnaghten's last despairing appeal crossed with a letter from Macgregor which finally convinced the Envoy that all hope of receiving help from Sale must be abandoned. Sir Robert had decided, not without heartburning—for his own wife and daughter were still in the beleaguered cantonments—that he could not respond to Macnaghten's urgent appeals. It was rumoured among the British troops in Kabul, falsely, that the simple and shameful reason was that his troops had flatly refused to march back, and Shelton, spitefully or tactlessly, told Lady Sale that he believed that her husband was acting on the principle of "being out of a scrape, keep so".

Macnaghten was being forced to revise his ideas as to the feasibility of holding out in cantonments in the hope that something would turn up. On the day after Shelton's rout the enemy arrived outside the cantonments and began calmly to demolish a bridge across the river which the British had erected shortly before with the object of connecting the cantonments with the outpost on Seeah Sung. To Macnaghten's anger and astonishment the garrison, now in a state of paralysed inactivity, made no attempt to interfere, but looked on passively from behind the cantonment ramparts. At the same moment his nephew, John Conolly, who had remained in the Balla Hissar, sent a pressing message from Soojah, in which the Shah urged that the only course that could now secure the safety and honour of the British was an immediate withdrawal to the citadel. This course, which had had its supporters from the outset, was now once more brought forward.

The decision was essentially a military one, but old Elphinstone had no intention, if he could help it, of taking the sole responsibility. He therefore wrote to his "Dear Sir William", asking *his* views on the practicability of moving into the Balla Hissar. But he gave the Envoy a strong hint of the answer he wanted. To get the ammunition, the sick and the wounded into the citadel, he argued, would be an operation of the greatest difficulty, a difficulty increased by "the harassed and dispirited state of our troops". Moreover, he added gloomily, the move might fail, and "failure would tend to our certain destruction". In any case, what would be gained even if the move succeeded? "I am told that water is already selling in the Balla Hissar at a high price"—a rumour without foundation, said Eyre; then again, there were barely twenty days' supplies left; and if, in the end, a retreat to India became necessary, this would be even more difficult from the Balla Hissar than from the cantonments, for all the horses and transport would have had to be abandoned in the earlier move. In this pessimistic catalogue of objections, he added, Brigadier Shelton agreed. Impressed, perhaps, by the fact that for once Major-General and Brigadier were in agreement, Macnaghten could hardly do other than reply, rather curtly, that he "begged to state his opinion that the move into the Balla Hissar would be attended with the greatest difficulty and he did not see what advantage could accrue therefrom".

The Envoy was thus being driven by his Army commanders towards the last resort, the opening of negotiations with the enemy, a course from which all his instincts recoiled. Before finally taking the step that he knew in his heart must lead to disgrace and disaster, he determined to put the responsibility where it rightly belonged, upon the gouty shoulders of the unhappy Elphinstone. He therefore wrote formally to the General, requesting him to state specifically and in writing whether from the military point of view it was any longer feasible to maintain the British position in Afghanistan. Without hesitation, almost eagerly, Elphinstone replied that "after having held our position here for upwards of three weeks in a state of siege, from the want of provisions and forage, the reduced state of our troops, the large number of wounded and sick, the difficulty of defending the extensive and ill-situated cantonment we occupy, the near approach of winter, our communications cut off, no prospect of relief, and the whole country in arms against us, I am of opinion that it is not feasible any longer to maintain our position in this country, and that you ought to avail yourself of the offer to negotiate which has been made to you."

This catalogue of gloom decided Macnaghten and, with a heavy heart, he set himself to see what could be saved from the wreck by negotiation.

10

There were not a few Afghan leaders who, perhaps foreseeing that the utter destruction of the British would almost certainly lead to the arrival in due course of another and more powerful force from India, were ready enough to secure the safety of the Army of Occupation on what to Afghan eyes seemed reasonable terms. The Kuzzilbashes, descendants of Ahmed Shah's Persian mercenaries, would have gone further; they had no relish for the thought of a Barukzye restoration and would have come out in favour of Soojah if the spineless British leadership had not convinced them that his cause was lost. But even among the Barukzyes there were men of moderate views. One of them, Zemaun Shah Khan (no relation of the blind Zemaun, Soojah's brother), had been declared "King" by the insurgents, though it was understood that this was to be only a temporary appointment, pending the restoration of Dost Mahomed; Zemaun, who behaved honourably and with humanity in all that followed, was quick to write to Macnaghten to explain that he had accepted the throne "not from his own wish, but to prevent greater ills arising".

The Afghans had offered terms the very day after they had defeated Shelton on the Beymaroo. "They propose that we should leave the country," wrote Lady Sale in her diary; "giving hostages that we will send the Dost back to them. They say they do not wish to harm us, if we will only go away; but that go we must, and give them back the Dost." It was in response to his overture that Macnaghten, under the urgent promptings of his military commanders, agreed to treat.

The first small deputation sent to the cantonments by the Afghans was led by a Barukzye with crude ideas of negotiation. "Arrogant and offensive, he trode down, as with the heel of the conqueror, all the pretensions of his opponents; and declared that as the Afghans had beaten us in battle, they had a right to dictate terms of caputulation." He demanded that the British surrender at discretion as prisoners of war, and hand over all their arms, ammunition, stores and treasure. Macnaghten, with close on five thousand troops behind him in cantonments, resolutely rejected the proferred terms. "We shall meet, then," said the Barukzye, "on the field of battle." "At all events," replied Macnaghten, rather strangely, "we shall meet at the day of judgment."

The deputation departed, insisting that the British must surrender their arms and abandon Shah Soojah to his fate. Lady Sale later discovered that the Afghans did not intend to go to the extreme of putting Soojah to death, "but only to deprive him of sight". But it was little wonder, she thought, that the Shah "seemed quite *gobrowed* (an expressive Eastern term, to be rendered something between being dumbfounded and at one's wits ends)", and as being "in an awful state of alarm; for he has been told that we have been making terms for our free exit out of the country, and leaving him to his fate. He is certainly to be pitied (if not at the bottom of it all)". As Lawrence justly commented, "the proposal to abandon the Shah was in marked contrast to his Majesty's conduct towards ourselves, for we were aware that, although proposals had been made by the insurgents to him, inviting him to break with us and join them, his Majesty had summarily rejected them and remained staunch and faithful to us". For the moment, however, Macnaghten had no intention of abandoning the unhappy Soojah, and to the insolent demands of the Afghans he replied "that death was preferable to dishonour —that we put our trust in the God of battles, and in His name bade them come on". On this heroic note the first round of negotiations came to an end.

During the truce there had been strange scenes at the cantonments. Hundreds of Afghans, all armed to the teeth, had come crowding round to pass the time of day in the most amicable manner with their enemies of yesterday. Everything was settled, they declared, and now they could all be friends, as befitted good fighting men. The British soldiers of the Queen's 44th responded heartily and were soon mingling unarmed with the Afghans and shaking hands with them, "unchecked by Lieutenant Cadett, the officer on duty, who seemed to think this friendly meeting a very fine affair".[1] The Afghans were pressing gifts of vegetables, chiefly cabbages, upon their new-found British friends with a generosity which presently aroused ponderous suspicions among the British officers. Might it not be that bladders of spirits had been hidden among the outer leaves of the cabbages, nefariously intended to intoxicate the garrison in preparation for a sudden attack on the cantonments? The cabbages were sternly confiscated by the Adjutant, "but they proved on examination to be very harmless cabbages after all".[2]

These first negotiations came to an end on 26th November, and a day or two earlier a new and sinister actor had appeared upon the Kabul scene. Akbar Khan, Dost Mahomed's favourite son, had spent the two years of the British occupation of his country as an outlaw in Turkestan. But early in October, evidently knowing

[1] Lady Sale.   [2] Eyre.

182

that the rising was at hand, he had reappeared in Afghanistan, hovering about Bameean and watching the progress of events in Kabul from afar. Now, on the night of the 24th, he arrived in the capital. His appearance was greeted with loud delight and salutes were fired all through the night in honour of his arrival. He was rumoured in the cantonments to have brought six thousand fighting men with him to add to an insurgent force estimated as already 10,000 horse and 15,000 foot. Akbar's men, thought Lady Sale, were "probably Uzbeks, and not far removed from rabble; but even a mob may from numbers succeed against us". In himself, however, he supplied something more valuable to the insurgent cause than a reinforcement of Uzbek savages. At last the rebellion had a leader, one whose personal record in battle and whose membership of the royal house of Barukzye made him acceptable to the chiefs. From now on, Akbar guided events with a strong hand.

The young Sirdar was fiery and impetuous, with considerable personal charm. "In seasons of repose he was one of the most joyous and light-hearted of men; no man loved a joke better; no man laughed more heartily, or seemed to look more cheerfully on the sunny side of life." But he was a creature of impulse, and his impulses were as often bad as good. "He was, indeed, peculiarly demonstrative, and sudden in his demonstrations, passing rapidly from one mood to another—blown about by violent gusts of feeling, bitterly repenting to-day the excesses of yesterday, and rushing into new excesses to-morrow."

The British at first hoped that because his father and brothers were in detention in India, Akbar would use his influence to arrange an honourable evacuation of Afghanistan. But he quickly showed that he had no intention of easing the pressure upon the beleaguered army. Starvation was the weapon to beat the British to their knees and Captain Johnson soon found that, whatever price he offered, there was no more grain to be purchased in the Beymaroo district. Akbar had been there before him, had destroyed every house in the village and had threatened death to the headman and all his family if any more supplies were sold to the British commissariat.

The garrison's situation at once became precarious in the extreme. There were only eight days' supplies in store, of which the force must take five-eighths with it if it were decided to attempt the five days' march to Jalalabad. Johnson pointed out to Macnaghten that this meant a decision, one way or the other, within three days. The Envoy agreed that the present situation could not continue; "but let us wait two days longer," he pleaded, "as something may turn up".

The troops were on short rations, the followers on rations shorter still, and the animals, with nothing to eat but twigs and the bark from trees, were suffering dreadfully. Horses had been seen gnawing desperately at tent pegs and Lady Sale saw her own mare champing away at a cart-wheel. She found it hard to believe a story that the artillery horses had eaten a gun trunnion and was sceptical about the rumour that one artillery horse had eaten another's tail; "but," she added, "that he bit it off, there is no doubt".

The wretched animals at least provided a temporary supply of meat; a committee was set up to decide which of them should be sacrificed, and for the time being there was plenty of cheap meat. "Tattoos (ponies) and camels have for some time past been eaten," wrote Lady Sale at the beginning of December. "Even some of the gentlemen ate camel's flesh, particularly the heart, which was esteemed equal to that of the bullock. I was never tempted by these choice viands, so cannot offer an opinion regarding them."

To the misery of hunger was added the misery of cold, for the bitter Afghan winter had descended upon the wretched inhabitants of the cantonments. Before the end of November sleet and snow became a daily occurrence, with the thermometer at freezing point, and from mid-December onwards the ground was inches deep in snow. The Indian troops suffered particularly from the cold, but although there was a complete winter stock of firing laid in, fires were not allowed. Sturt pressed Elphinstone and Shelton that at least fires might be permitted at night, so that men coming off duty from the ramparts might warm themselves and dry their frost-encrusted clothes, but nothing was done and the miserable troops sank deeper into apathy and numbed despair. There was some misguided self-help in the effort to keep warm and Sturt, sent out hastily by Shelton on a story that the bastion of an outlying fort had been fired by the enemy, came back furious, having found the troops burning some defences that he had just put up. The garrison was jumpy, too: "last night," says Lady Sale scornfully, "they popped away 350 rounds at shadows, probably of themselves." Fortunately, she added, there was plenty in store, despite Elphinstone's fears. To be sure, Shelton had swallowed whole a rumour that the Afghans were coming with 80,000 foot and 10,000 horse to set fire to the magazine with red-hot balls. "How these balls were to be conveyed here red-hot is a mystery," commented Lady Sale sarcastically, "as the enemy have no battery to erect furnaces in: but nothing is too ridiculous to be believed; and, really, any horrible story would be sure to be credited by our panic-struck garrison."

On the subject of supplies Elphinstone, said Lady Sale, "appears to be kept in a deplorable state of ignorance. Although reports are sent in daily, he scarcely knows what supplies are in store, or what is our real daily consumption." By now, however, the situation was in reality almost as bad as he had always imagined, and he was writing to Macnaghten to express the hope that "your negotiations may prosper, as circumstances are becoming extremely critical; I don't wish to croak, but think it right that you should be constantly informed of the real state of things". A retreat to the Balla Hissar, he reiterated, was out of the question; retreat to India without terms was almost impossible, and few would reach Jalalabad; Sir William really *must* come to an agreement with the enemy. "Are we justified in risking the safety of so many people when we can no longer do anything? When reduced to the last extremity (where we now are almost), I think honourable terms better for our government than our being destroyed here, which, without food, is inevitable. All this I write in confidence for your own consideration, that you may think what is best to be done."

Macnaghten had understandably lost patience with a Commander-in-Chief who did nothing but point out difficulties, had no constructive suggestion to offer and left all the decisions to him. He replied curtly that he was perfectly aware of the state of supplies; when the cantonments had first been attacked, there were only one or two days' supplies in store, now there were nine. "I conceive that we are better off now than we were a month ago." If the force were to retreat it could not carry more than two or three days' supplies; with nine days' rations in store, there seemed no necessity to come to an immediate decision.

Wearily, he went once more through the various courses which he and Elphinstone had raked over so many times before. Once more retreat to Jalalabad without terms was dismissed not only as impracticable but as something that would cover the British with "everlasting infamy", since it would mean the abandonment of Soojah. Once more he dismissed the possibility of retreating to India on negotiated terms; there were so many factions among the insurgents that none was in a position to promise effectual protection; in any case, "the consequences would be terrific as regards the safety of our Indian Empire and our interests in Europe". So back he now came to the oft-debated, oft-dismissed proposal to fling the garrison into the Balla Hissar and there stick it out. It would be strange, he thought, if with four or five regiments under command they could not obtain fuel and provisions; they would be in a position to overawe the city, and to encourage the Kuzzilbashes and other well-wishers to rally to their support. And therefore, he concluded—and he was almost certainly right—this course, "though certainly attended by risk, would be by far the most safe and honourable which we could adopt". But it was bound to involve fighting and therefore could not be undertaken unless the troops retained at least a modicum of warlike spirit. They were now to give conclusive proof that this no longer existed.

The British, thanks to the energy of Sturt, had finally dislodged the Afghans from the small building known as Mahomed Sheriff's fort and had installed a garrison of a hundred men, forty of the Queen's 44th and the rest from the 37th Native Infantry. The Afghans decided to retake the fort and, on 6th December, came creeping unseen through the gardens and orchards, planted crooked sticks against the wall to serve as scaling ladders, pulled out the mud with which a window had been blocked up and climbed in. As Lady Sale said, "a child with a stick might have repulsed them". But the garrison, who had been lounging about with their equipment off, fled in panic when they saw Afghan faces at the window, leaving arms, ammunition and bedding behind them. "It was," says the same authority, "the most shameful of all the runaways that occurred."

There followed some unedifying recriminations between the 44th and the 37th as to who had run first, but the garrison commander, Lieutenant Hawtrey, who had at least stayed long enough to hurl six grenades at the enemy before following his rabble to the cantonments, angrily reported that "there was not a pin to choose —all cowards alike". It was, however, remarked that two of the 37th's Sepoys were left dead in the fort and two others wounded, "while not a man of the 44th was touched, excepting one whose hand suffered from the accidental explosion of a grenade".[1] The sad fact was, that as Eyre gloomily noted, "it was notorious that the 44th Foot had been for a long time previous to these occurrences in a state of woeful deterioration. . . . The regiment fell a prey to a vital disease, which the Horse Guards alone could have remedied, which is now beyond the reach of proper investigation. May a redeeming glory and renown rise from its ashes!"

For the moment, however, there was to be no redeeming glory for Her Majesty's 44th Foot. Some of the men were stung by

[1] Eyre.

shame into volunteering to recapture Mahomed Sheriff's fort, and Elphinstone, as usual seeking the opinions of his juniors, asked Sturt whether it was practicable and tenable—in other words, whether the men could capture and hold it. Laconically the subaltern replied—"Practicable if the men will fight, tenable if they don't run away." Elphinstone lugubriously reported to Macnaghten that "if the 44th have any sense of shame left, they must do better, and their officers *must exert* themselves. Shelton is disposed to attribute the blame to the Sepoys—from all I hear, I fear unjustly; but this must be inquired into when we have time."

Just now, however, there was no time. There were only four days' provisions left. The wretched camp followers were living on the carcases of camels that had died of starvation. The trees, stripped of all bark and twigs to supply fodder of a sort for the animals, were now bare and useless, and the horses were eating their own dung, which was served up to them over and over again. And the Envoy was angrily writing to Macgregor that "our troops are behaving like a pack of despicable cowards and there is no spirit or enterprise left among us".

11

Macnaghten now again set himself to attempt to save by diplomacy an army that had proved incapable of saving itself by military exertion. Determined that posterity should recognise that his generals had left him no alternative, he wrote formally to Elphinstone on 8th December, peremptorily requesting "that you will be so good as to state, for my information, whether or no I am right in considering it as your opinion that any further attempt to hold out against the enemy would merely have the effect of sacrificing both His Majesty and ourselves, and that the only alternative left is to negotiate for our safe retreat out of the country on the most favourable terms possible".

"Sir," replied Elphinstone without hesitation, "In reply, I beg to state my opinion is that the present situation of the troops here is such, from the want of provisions and the impracticability of procuring more, that no time ought to be lost in entering into negotiations for a safe retreat from the country." He cautiously disowned any responsibility for the possible consequences to Soojah, whom he did not regard as his concern. "As regards the King, I must be excused entering upon that point of your letter . . . but I may be allowed to say that it little becomes me, as commanding the British troops in Afghanistan, to regard the necessity of negotiating in any other light than as concerns their honour and welfare, both of which I should be answerable for by a further stay here." What Macnaghten made of this reference to honour can only be guessed. The General ended on his usual note: "In conclusion, I can only repeat my opinion that you should lose no time in entering into negotiations." To lend weight, he had enrolled the support of his senior officers. "I concur in the above opinions," wrote Brigadier Shelton beneath Elphinstone's signature. "I also concur," wrote Colonel Chambers, who commanded the cavalry. But Brigadier Anquetil, who signed as commander of Shah Soojah's forces and perhaps felt some qualms at the possible consequences to Soojah, qualified his verdict. "*In a military point of view*," he wrote, "I concur in the above." There was apparently no attempt to conceal this exchange of views between Envoy and General; Lady Sale had it all down in her diary the same evening, including Anquetil's qualification.

On December 11th Macnaghten rode out of the cantonments and met a dozen or so of the Afghan chiefs, headed by Akbar and Osman Khan, on the banks of the Kabul river, about a mile away. After some courteous preliminaries, in which both Akbar and Osman, with apparent sincerity, expressed their personal regard for the Envoy, the meeting got down to business. Macnaghten had brought a draft treaty, written in Persian, which he now read aloud. It began truly enough, "Whereas it has become apparent from recent events that the continuance of the British army in Afghanistan for the support of Shah Soojah-ool-Moolk is displeasing to the great majority of the Afghan nation"; there followed a rather more dubious limb to the preamble: "and whereas the British Government had no other object in sending troops to this country than the integrity, happiness and welfare of the Afghans, and therefore it can have no wish to remain when that object is defeated by its presence." The chiefs nodded approvingly and waited for the meat of the treaty. "1st," read Macnaghten, "the British troops now at Caubul will repair to Peshawar with all practicable expedition, and thence return to India." Again there were approving nods. "2nd," continued Macnaghten, "the Sirdars engage that the British troops shall be unmolested in their journey, shall be treated with all honour, and receive all possible assistance in carriage and provisions." Akbar impatiently burst in that there was no need to supply the British with provisions, since they could start for home the very next day. The other chiefs gravely rebuked him for his unmannerly interruption, and Macnaghten was allowed to proceed with the reading of the draft.

It amounted to complete capitulation. The garrisons at Ghuznee, Jalalabad and Kandahar were to follow the Kabul troops back to India, and as soon as they had arrived safely at Peshawar Dost Mahomed would return to Afghanistan. Soojah would have the choice either of accompanying the British or of remaining in Afghanistan, and in either event was to receive a pension. There was to be a general amnesty. (This stipulation brought another angry interruption from Akbar, but again he was silenced by his elders.) There was always to be friendship between the Afghans and the English; and, finally, and of more immediate importance, as soon as the treaty had been signed, the British in the cantonments were to be supplied with provisions, for which they would pay.

After two hours' discussion, conducted "with as much calmness and moderation as could have been expected", the terms were accepted in principle by the chiefs and it was agreed that the British should quit the cantonments within three days; meanwhile, the chiefs would at once send in provisions. Macnaghten, playing the weakest of hands, might fairly claim to have done as well as could be expected, and in an unfinished report, found among his papers after his death, he made a strong case for the course which he had been reluctantly compelled to follow:

"The whole country," he wrote, "as far as we could learn, had risen in rebellion; our communications on all sides were cut off; almost every public officer, whether paid by ourselves or his Majesty, had declared for the new governor, and by far the greater number even of his Majesty's domestic servants had deserted him. We had been fighting forty days against very superior numbers, under most disadvantageous circumstances, with a deplorable loss of valuable lives, and in a day or two we must have perished from hunger, to say nothing of the advanced season of the year and the extreme cold, from the effects of which our native troops were suffering severely. I had been repeatedly apprised by the military authorities that nothing could be done with our troops; and I regret to add that desertions to the enemy were becoming of frequent occurrence among our troops. The terms I secured were the best obtainable, and the destruction of fifteen thousand human beings would little have benefited our country, whilst our government would have been almost compelled to avenge our fate at whatever cost. . . . We shall part with the Afghans as friends, and I feel satisfied that any government which may be established hereafter will always be disposed to cultivate a good understanding with us."

But the outcome was indeed to be the destruction of fifteen thousand human beings and in due course another army would be reluctantly sent from India to avenge their fate. The negotiations were doomed to failure from the start by a deep mutual distrust. Suspecting that the British would never evacuate the cantonments until they were actually starving, the Afghan leaders withheld the bulk of the promised supplies, and such small quantities of provisions as were sent were intercepted under the muzzles of the cantonment guns by a crowd of thieves and Ghazis swarming outside the ramparts. The Ghazis, said Captain Johnson, "are without exception the most barefaced, impertinent rascals under the sun. Armed with swords, daggers and matchlocks, they acknowledge no chief, but act independently—they taunt and insult the whole of us. People from the town, bringing in grain or bran, are often plundered and beaten. Although our cattle and men are starving, no measures are taken by our military authorities to check all this." The chiefs, professing that they were quite unable to control the Ghazis, refused to interfere.

It seems that it was the Afghan leaders' breach of their promise to supply the starving garrison that made Macnaghten decide to embark upon a dangerous game of intrigue. From the outset he had hoped to sow dissension among the rebels, and had complained to Macgregor that "it is perfectly wonderful how they hang together". Now he saw a ray of hope, for some of the Douranee leaders, remembering the strong hand with which Dost Mahomed had ruled them, began again to turn towards Soojah. They proposed that he should remain on the throne on condition that he would allow his daughters to marry the leading chiefs and would make the Barukzye family his hereditary viziers. They also insisted, since "the Afghans hate ceremony, which Shah Soojah carried at all times to an absurd length", that he must give up "the offensive practice of keeping the chief nobles of his kingdom waiting for hours at his gate, in expectation of audience".[1] Soojah gave a reluctant consent to these conditions but a few days later his pride got the better of him and he withdrew it. His lack of co-operation caused what Lady Sale described as "a very evident change of politics. The 'good King', as Sir William used to call him, is now thrown over by us, as he refused to deviate from his accustomed hauteur towards his nobles, or to admit of his daughters marrying the chiefs, as they proposed."

Macnaghten continued to try to play off one set of Afghans against another. Ostensibly in treaty with Akbar's Barukzyes, he

[1] Eyre.

was simultaneously attempting, by bribes and large promises, to get the Ghilzyes and Kuzzilbashes to declare in favour of Soojah and the British. His chief instrument in this tortuous business was Mohun Lal, the late Alexander Burnes' secretary, a born intriguer who had remained in Kabul after his master's murder, keeping in with all parties. Macnaghten, who at this time "never knew, from one day to another, with whom he would eventually conclude a treaty for the extrication of the unhappy force," was writing constantly to Mohun Lal, urging him on to see what arrangement could be reached with this or that faction. "If any portion of the Afghans wish our troops to remain in the country, I shall think myself at liberty to break the engagement which I have made to go away, which engagement was made believing it to be in accordance with the wishes of the Afghan nation." It was darkly whispered that the Envoy had gone even further and had offered blood money for the heads of the more dangerous Afghan leaders. This was not true, but that it was believed to be true was enough to seal Macnaghten's doom.

Late on the evening of the 22nd December Captain Skinner, with two Afghan companions, rode down from Kabul to dine with Macnaghten in the cantonments. Skinner ("commonly called 'Gentleman Jim' from his more than usually pleasing manners and cultivated mind"[1]) had been trapped in the city at the start of the rebellion and had for some time remained hidden by Afghan friends. He had now emerged, in some strange fashion, to become the guest of Akbar Khan, and it was on Akbar's behalf that he had come to see the Envoy, "charged with a message of a most portentous nature". Of his two companions one was Akbar's cousin and the other a close friend of Burnes, a man who throughout the occupation had been a firm supporter of the British. Macnaghten looked eagerly across the dinner table when Skinner remarked, with a nervous laugh, that he felt "as if laden with combustibles", but it was made plain that the portentous message could only be communicated in the presence of the two Afghans, who had refused to attend the infidel's table.

After dinner they joined the Envoy and Gentleman Jim in a private room, and there Akbar's proposal was revealed. It was to be a gigantic double-cross upon the great majority of the Afghan leaders. Soojah was to remain on the throne, with Akbar as his Vizir; the British might save their faces by remaining in Afghanistan for another eight months or so, and then withdraw from the country as if of their own free will; and as his reward Akbar was

[1] Mackenzie.

to receive from the British Government thirty lakhs of rupees, with an annual pension of four lakhs for life. The chiefs of the Eastern Ghilzyes were ready to co-operate, said Skinner, and the bargain must be sealed next day by Macnaghten's meeting them, with Akbar, at a spot outside the cantonments. Let the Envoy have a body of troops laid on, and at a given signal they might seize not only a key point known as Mahmood Khan's fort but their old inveterate enemy, Amenoolah Khan, one of the two ringleaders in the murder of Burnes.[1] Akbar's cousin hinted pretty broadly that for an extra payment the Envoy might be presented with Amenoolah's head as an earnest of Akbar's good intentions, but from this suggestion Macnaghten recoiled in horror.

The rest of the plan he swallowed hook, line and sinker and rashly signed a paper written in Persian to record the fact. This document finally convinced Akbar that there could be no trusting Macnaghten.

Later, British heads were to be shaken censoriously over Macnaghten's readiness to break faith with the Afghan chiefs and make a private compact with Akbar. But it should be remembered in his defence that he had good reason to believe that the chiefs were equally ready to break faith with him. He had been under a tremendous strain for seven weeks and the military were useless. By now he was like a drowning man, clutching at any straw that might save him from the shipwreck of all his splendid hopes for Afghanistan. His fatal mistake was to suppose that he could match the Afghans at intrigue. "Poor Macnaghten should never have left the secretary's office," commented George Broadfoot, when he heard of the Envoy's death, "he was ignorant of men, even to simplicity, and utterly incapable of forming or guiding administrative measures."

There were others, with cooler heads, who saw his danger. Mohun Lal, himself an expert in intrigue, recognised a kindred spirit in Akbar and had already warned the Envoy that the young Sirdar was deceiving him. Now, after the dinner party with Skinner, he wrote again to Macnaghten and "begged him to take very great care of himself, and do not go so often to meet Mahomed Akbar out of the cantonments, as he is the man that nobody can trust his word upon oath". Hasan Khan, the jemadar of Mackenzie's jezailchis, was another who "repeatedly warned Sir William of the likelihood of a fatal termination to his hazardous interviews with the Afghan chiefs. He argued that surely he was a better

[1] The other, the ferocious Abdoolah Khan, had been mortally wounded at the battle of the Beymaroo Heights.

judge of the intentions of his own countrymen than Sir William could be, and that among them no dishonour was attached to what we call treachery."[1] Mackenzie too had his doubts, and when Macnaghten told him of Skinner's proposal, at once exclaimed that it was a plot. "A plot!" replied the Envoy hastily, "let me alone for that—trust me for that!"

But there was indeed a plot. Akbar never had any intention of letting Soojah remain upon the throne, nor yet of sacrificing Amenoolah, who had readily agreed to the proposal that he should be used as bait for the trap. The whole story had been concocted to test Macnaghten's good faith. If he fell for it, he was damned; and he had fallen.

On the morning of 23rd December Macnaghten told Elphinstone of these new developments, and of the part that the troops would be required to play. The General, slow in the uptake, asked naïvely about the attitude of the other Barukzyes, who had hitherto been playing a leading part in the negotiations. They were "not in the plot" explained Macnaghten impatiently. This talk of a plot worried Elphinstone, who asked anxiously whether the Envoy did not fear some treachery. "None at all," snapped Macnaghten, "I wish you to have two regiments and two guns got ready, as speedily and as quietly as possible, for the capture of Mahmood Khan's fort; the rest you may leave to me." Elphinstone still had doubts. "Very well," said Macnaghten, "if you will at once march out the troops and meet the enemy, I will accompany you, and I am sure we shall beat them." "Macnaghten, I can't," said the General despairingly; "the troops are not to be depended on." He returned to harping upon the dangers of treachery, but to Macnaghten his warnings sounded so like the old imbecile croakings that he had been hearing from Elphinstone from the start that he turned away with the snubbing remark that, "I understand these things better than you." An hour later, accompanied by Lawrence, Mackenzie and Trevor, he rode from the cantonments to his rendezvous with Akbar Khan.

Shelton was to have led out the two regiments who were to seize Mahmood Khan's fort and arrest Amenoolah, but the troops were not ready. Even the small cavalry escort commanded by Lieutenant Le Geyt of the Bombay Cavalry had failed to parade in time, and the Envoy rode almost alone, except for his three staff officers and a handful of chuprassis of the Mission guard. He commented bitterly that this slackness on the part of the military was all of a piece with every arrangement that had been left to

[1] Mackenzie.

them since the start of the outbreak. Lawrence again asked whether there was not a risk of Afghan treachery. "Treachery!" exclaimed Macnaghten; "of course there is, but what can I do? The General has declared his inability to fight, we have no prospect of aid from any quarter, the enemy are only playing with us, not one article of the treaty have they fulfilled, and I have no confidence whatever in them. The life I have led for the last six weeks you, Lawrence, know well; and rather than be disgraced and live it over again, I would risk a hundred deaths; success will save our honour, and more than make up for all risks."

The Envoy was not going empty-handed to the meeting. A day or two earlier Akbar had admired a handsome pair of double-barrelled pistols belonging to Lawrence, which Macnaghten had at once purchased from his aide and presented to the Sirdar. Akbar promptly went on to express admiration of a beautiful Arab horse, the property of Captain Grant, the Adjutant-General. Gloomily aware of what would come next, and reluctant to see his beloved mare go to this barbarous young Afghan, Grant at once put its price at the exorbitant figure of 5,000 rupees, but Mackenzie, urged by the Envoy, had persuaded the unwilling vendor to accept 3,000, and the Arab mare now accompanied the little cavalcade. "Sir William appeared much pleased with the prospect of gratifying Mahomed Akbar by the present."

A mere three hundred and fifty yards from the cantonment, on a slope where the snow lay less thickly and where a carpet had been spread, Akbar and the chiefs were waiting on horseback. After the usual courteous salutations Grant's mare was handed over. "Many thanks," replied Akbar, "and also for Lawrence Sahib's pistols, which you see I am wearing. Shall we now dismount?" Even now, it seems, he was ready to give Macnaghten one last chance to disprove the suspicions of his good faith, for as the Envoy took his place beside him on the carpet, he asked whether Macnaghten was "perfectly ready to carry into effect the proposition of the preceding night". "Why not?" was the reply, and Akbar hesitated no longer.

Macnaghten's three British captains now found themselves engaged in the friendliest conversation by various Afghans. The former chief of the Kabul police was an old friend of Mackenzie's whom he took on one side with anxious inquiries as to the whereabouts of his pistols. The smell of treachery was strong in the air, and the British officers, noticing that a crowd of armed Afghans were gradually closing in upon the conference and encircling it, suggested that they should be ordered back. Akbar jovially called out that it was unnecessary, "we are all in the same boat, and Lawrence Sahib need not be in the least alarmed". But Lawrence, who was still uneasy and was, as Lady Sale says, "a very spunky active man", refused a solicitous invitation to sit down and relax. He remained crouching on one knee, close behind Macnaghten, ready to spring into action. He got no chance to do so. There was a sudden shout from Akbar—"Begeer! Begeer!" (Seize! Seize!) and Lawrence's arms were gripped from behind, his pistol and sword firmly held. Mackenzie found himself staring at a pistol levelled at his head by his old friend the chief of police. Trevor too had been seized and all three officers were hurried to horses and mounted pillion behind their captors. They caught a last glimpse of Macnaghten, his face blanched with horror and astonishment. His little escort had fled, except for Ram Sing, a Rajput jemadar of the Chuprassis, who heroically rushed to the rescue and was instantly cut to pieces by the Afghans. Meanwhile Akbar—"with an expression in his face of the most diabolical ferocity"—had gripped the Envoy by one arm while his cousin, Sultan Jan, had seized the other. They seemed to be trying to drag Macnaghten head first down the slope. Before they were forced from the scene the three British officers heard a hoarse cry of despair from the Envoy—"Az barae Khooda!" (For God's sake!). The survivors would remember that cry, and the look upon Macnaghten's face, until the day they died.

The horses were galloping for Mahmood Khan's fort, their Afghan riders now anxious to save their prisoners from the Ghazis, who were closing in with yells of "Why spare the accursed? Drop the infidel! Let us shed the kaffir's blood!" The unlucky Trevor fell, or was dragged, from his horse and died instantly beneath the Ghazi knives. Lawrence and Mackenzie, more fortunate, clung on desperately while their escorts, at considerable personal risk, parried the blows of would-be assassins. At one point Mackenzie found himself again face to face with Akbar, who was now being congratulated by the crowd upon his successful stratagem. The Ghazis continued their furious attempts upon Mackenzie's life but Akbar drew his sword and "laid about him right manfully" in the British officer's defence. Then, having saved him, he could not resist gloating over him. "*You'll* seize my country, will you?" he jeered. "*You'll* seize my country?"

Mackenzie found himself thrust into a cell of the little fort, with Lawrence alongside him, while a crowd of blood-lusting Ghazis milled around outside, trying to break down the door. Two Ghilzye chiefs joined the prisoners and tried to cheer them up with false though well-meant assurances that Macnaghten and Trevor were safe. At this point the ancient Amenoolah, the supposed victim of the kidnapping plot, burst furiously in upon them and told the two officers that they would shortly be blown from the guns, a display of bad manners that greatly shocked the two Ghilzyes, who persuaded the old monster to withdraw. Outside, the hatred of the Ghazis was unabated and the muzzle of a blunderbuss appeared through the bars of the window, but was struck up by the Ghilzyes just as it was about to be fired. There came another yell of hate and derision from the window, where a human hand, impaled upon a pole, was being bobbed up and down in mockery. "Look well!" screamed the Ghazis; "your own will soon be in a similar plight." Later the two officers learnt that this was the hand of Sir William Macnaghten. The head and limbs of Her Majesty's Envoy and Plenipotentiary at the Court of Shah Soojah were already being paraded in triumph through the streets of Kabul, while the trunk, alongside the corpse of Captain Trevor, was hanging from a meat hook in the bazaar.

Author's note

Nearly all contemporary accounts put the responsibility for the choice of Elphinstone to command the Kabul force on Lord Auckland (cf page 166). But the choice of Elphinstone seems to have originated in London. "Great blame attaches to the Horse Guards here," wrote Lady Palmerston to her brother in May, 1842; "Hobhouse objected to Elphinstone's Appointmt, thinking him not up to it, either in mind or body, but Fitzroy Somerset insisted because he was a friend of his, and the Duke of Wn would not support Hobhouse in his objections. It is shocking to think of such loss of life, all owing to a job, for there is no doubt they might still be safe in Cabul, had the troops behaved as they ought."

It seems that the future Lord Raglan bore some responsibility for the Kabul disaster as well as for the charge of the Light Brigade.

PART IV

THE CATASTROPHE

I

AKBAR was later to protest with tears in his eyes—on one occasion weeping for two hours to prove his point—that he was innocent of Macnaghten's death, which he blamed upon the uncontrollable Ghazis. It is probably true that, in the first place, he had never intended to do more than kidnap the Envoy and hold him as a hostage. But the evidence is strong, and the British always believed, that Akbar's own hand had precipitated the murder. A letter from his cousin to an uncle at Kandahar seems to put the matter beyond doubt. "The Sirdar," said this account, "at last said to the Envoy: 'Come, I must take you to the Nawab's.' The Envoy was alarmed, and rose up. Akbar seized him by the hands, saying: 'I cannot allow you to return to cantonments.' The Sirdar wished to carry him off alive, but was unable; he then drew a double-barrelled pistol from his belt and discharged both barrels at the Envoy, after which he struck him two or three blows with his sword, and the Envoy was thus killed on the spot." The Ghazi knives swiftly completed the work of dismemberment.

It had all happened in broad daylight, less than a quarter of a mile from the British lines and practically in full view of the garrison. Indeed, the taciturn Lieutenant Warren, who had kept his eye fixed on Macnaghten from the moment he left the cantonments, was now stoutly maintaining that he had distinctly seen the Envoy fall to the ground and the Afghans hacking at his body. Eyre might well ask, "What were our troops about all this time? Where was the bodyguard that followed the Envoy and his friends from the cantonments?"

The troops were, as usual, doing nothing, because no one had ordered them to do anything; the bodyguard was safely back in the cantonments. Le Geyt's lancers had seen the Envoy attacked as they cantered up to join him, and had instantly wheeled to ride full stretch for the safety of the lines. Le Geyt, after vainly yelling at them to follow him to the rescue, came galloping in behind them, shouting as he came that Macnaghten had been kidnapped.

Elphinstone, to whom a trooper of the escort had come panting with the news that "they have seized the Lord Sahib and taken him to the city", chose to ignore these disturbing reports and the still more alarming version that Warren was loudly proclaiming. The General later recorded that, for reasons unstated, "by myself and others it was thought at the time that Sir William had proceeded to the city for the purpose of negotiating". The Adjutant-General, Captain Grant, now put this version into official circulation by riding to each regiment in turn with the news that, because the Ghazis had interrupted the conference, Macnaghten and his companions had been removed to the city, but would be returning to cantonments immediately. Despite this comforting assurance, many remained gloomily certain "that they would never hear the Envoy's voice or look upon his living face again".

The British remained inactive in their cantonments as the day wore on, until after dusk they were startled by a hideous din. The Ghazis, apprehensive of British retaliation, had been mustering to defend Kabul against the attack which they believed must now surely be launched to avenge the Envoy's murder. The result, about nine o'clock that evening, was "a great disturbance . . . horrible shouts and cries, with rattling of musketry".[1] The British, however, nervously interpreted the horrible shouts as meaning that *they* were the ones who were about to be attacked; they therefore stood to, manned the ramparts, and waited helplessly. "The only certain thing," wrote Lady Sale that evening, "is that our chiefs are at a nonplus."

Next day, Christmas Eve, there came authentic reports from Lawrence and John Conolly of the fate of Macnaghten and Trevor, and Lady Sale "had the sad office imposed on me of informing Lady Macnaghten and Mrs. Trevor of their husbands' assassination; over such scenes I draw a veil. . . . All reports agree that both the Envoy's and Trevor's bodies are hanging in the public chouk (bazaar); the Envoy's decapitated and a mere trunk, the limbs having been carried in triumph about the city."

These reports seemed to excite no spark of indignation from Elphinstone, who showed more interest in the news that the Afghans wished to continue negotiations on the basis of Macnaghten's draft treaty; moreover, as a first step, they were now demanding that the British prisoners already in their hands should at once be replaced by married officers, complete with their wives and families. Far from rejecting this preposterous demand out of hand, Elphinstone sent Major Thain round the camp to call for volunteers, with the promise of a salary of 2,000 rupees a month to any who would agree to his wife being handed over.

[1] Lieutenant Melville's account (quoted by Kaye).

With the bodies of Macnaghten and Trevor still hanging in the chouk, the married officers' response was chilly. Sturt protested that his wife and mother-in-law should only be taken at the bayonet's point, while Captain Anderson sternly declared that sooner than see his wife in Afghan hands he would put a pistol to her head and shoot her. Only Eyre said that if it would really help towards a solution, he and his wife would stay.

Elphinstone, in need of someone to take over the business of negotiating, now remembered that there was a Political Officer available in the person of Major Pottinger, who all this time had been nursing the unpleasant wound he had received at Charikar. Pottinger was astonished to find that the British apparently intended to overlook Macnaghten's murder as an unfortunate accident. He knew the troops to be in a mood of furious anger and had vainly urged the General to lead them at once to an attack upon Kabul, "which in their then temper they would no doubt have stormed and carried".[1] Now, after recording a formal protest against the renewal of negotiations, he reluctantly accepted the task assigned to him by Elphinstone, "plainly perceiving our affairs to be so irretrievably ruined as to render the distinction anything but enviable, or likely to improve his hardly-earned fame".[2]

Negotiations went on throughout 25th December. "A more cheerless Christmas Day perhaps never dawned upon British soldiers in a strange land; and the few whom force of habit urged to exchange the customary greetings of the season did so with countenances and in tones indicative of anything but merriment."[2] The draft treaty had now crystallised into a curt document prepared by the Afghans, and entitled "Agreement of peace that has been determined on with the Frank English gentlemen." It began with a peremptory demand "that the going of the gentlemen shall be speedy", and went on to stipulate that the British forces at Kabul, Ghuznee, Kandahar and Jalalabad should promptly return to India; Dost Mahomed and his family were to be restored to Afghanistan and hostages must be left behind to guarantee his release. In the same dictatorial vein it was stipulated that all the cash in the British treasury was to be handed over and—greatest of humiliations to military honour —the guns must be surrendered. The British might take six only for the retreat. "They are enough. More will not be given." The final paragraph, presumably aimed by Akbar at his cousin, Mrs. Warburton, declared menacingly that "if any of the Frank gentlemen have taken a Mussulman wife, she shall be given up."

[1] Mackenzie.   [2] Eyre.

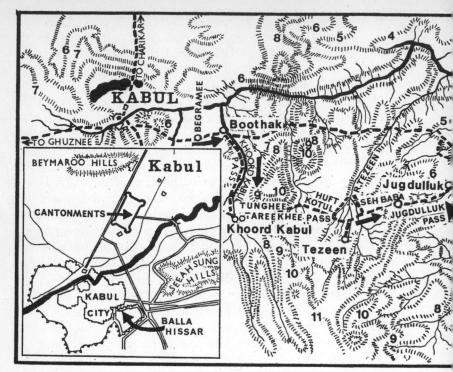

The retreat from

All that the British were offered in return was a promise of doubtful value that their safety on the retreat would be secured by an escort of chiefs.

Convinced that acceptance of these humiliating terms would be as disastrous as it would be disgraceful, Pottinger urged an emphatic refusal. The Afghans, he argued, were almost certainly deceiving the British and had no intention of letting them retreat unmolested; it was Elphinstone's duty, he urged, to refrain from making promises that would tie his government's hands; it was disgraceful for the Kabul force to think of purchasing its own safety at the cost of many lakhs of public money; and, finally, Elphinstone had no right to order the commanders of the garrisons at Jalalabad, Ghuznee and Kandahar to surrender their posts, since he had no power to compel them to obey the order.

Pottinger argued, as others had done before, that there were better courses open. Already messages had come in from Macgregor, in Jalalabad, and from Mackeson, in Peshawar, promising that reinforcements were on their way from India and urging the Kabul garrison to hold out to the last. In these circumstances,

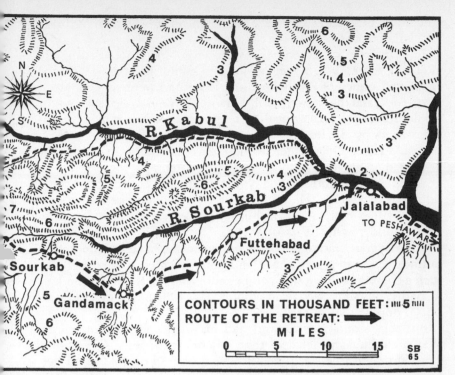

Kabul to Jalalabad

thought Pottinger, "we had but two courses open to us which, in my opinion, promised a chance of saving our honour and part of the army. One was to occupy the Balla Hissar, and hold it till spring. By this we should have had the best chance of success. The other was to have abandoned our camp and baggage and encumbrances, and forced our way down. This was perilous but practicable. However, I could not persuade them to sacrifice baggage; and that was eventually one of the chief causes of our disaster."

It was argued against him that it would be impossible to get the cantonments guns through to the citadel, and that although there were guns already in the citadel, they were short of ammunition. Pottinger thereupon proposed a desperate improvisation, believed to have been successfully tried in the Peninsular War. This "excellent suggestion", recorded Lady Sale, training her sarcasm on one who ill deserved it, was to "erect a battery on the Seeah Sung hills (of course, to be the work of fairies during the night), fire our shots from cantonments into this battery where, of course, guardian sylphs would protect the lives of our men, who were quickly to pick them up and send them on in like manner into the Balla Hissar!"

This interesting experiment was never tried, for Pottinger, after all, was only a Brevet Major and could make no headway against a Council of War whose hearts were set upon a negotiated retreat to Jalalabad. Anquetil, Chambers, Grant, Bellew—none would respond to his appeal to take a braver line, for all were dominated by Shelton. "We were prevented from going into the Balla Hissar," Pottinger would later report, "by the obstinacy of Brigadier Shelton, who declared the attempt impracticable." For Elphinstone himself the young Political Officer had considerable sympathy. He admired the "noble courage and resignation with which he bears himself under such a load of misfortune and physical suffering" (Elphinstone, in addition to his rheumatic gout, had somehow managed to get "a shot through the buttock") and deplored that "he should have been fated to hold such a command when so incompetent from disease; and seconded so badly, that the second-in-command would never give advice but to oppose that of the other".

But the second-in-command had his way, and the Council of War unanimously decided that Major Pottinger's suggestions were impracticable. This decision was reached in the face of the many warnings that were coming in to support his belief that treachery was in the air. Even before Macnaghten's murder Taj Mahomed, a distinguished Afghan who had always shown himself pro-British, had cautioned that Akbar was plotting deceit and that the force was to be annihilated. A Ghilzye chief in his cups had blurted out the truth to Mackenzie and Skinner, while they were Akbar's prisoners after the Envoy's murder. "You think that your troops will get safe to Jalalabad?" he jeered; "If there was no one else to intercept them, I and my friends would do it." Eyre was noting in his journal that "numerous cautions were received from various well-wishers to place no confidence in the professions of the chiefs, who had sworn together to accomplish our entire destruction". And on Boxing Day Lady Sale confided to her diary that "the chiefs do not mean to keep faith; and it is their intention to get all our women into their possession; and to kill every man except one, who is to have his hands and legs cut off and is to be placed with a letter *in terrorem* at the entrance of the Khyber passes, to deter all Feringhees from entering the country again."

On New Year's Day the treaty in its final form was duly sealed by eighteen of the Afghan chiefs, its language a mixture of the friendly and the dictatorial. The various contingents of the Army of Occupation, both at Kabul and elsewhere, were to be escorted to the borders of Afghanistan by "trustworthy persons . . . so that none shall offer molestation on the road". The sick and wounded might be left at Kabul and would be free to return to India on recovery. In the same vein, "should any English gentleman be unavoidably detained in Caubul, we will treat him with all respect and consideration, and on his departure dismiss him with honour". But running all through the treaty was the reiterated theme that the British must *go*, go quickly, and go without further argument. And they might take with them only six horse-artillery guns and three mule guns; all the rest, with all the muskets and ordnance stores in the magazine, were to be surrendered to the Afghans. This, it was said, was to be done "as a token of friendship", but Elphinstone's army knew, and all the world would know, that the surrender of its guns was the hallmark of a beaten and humiliated force, and an indelible stigma of disgrace.

Since the ordnance stores were to be surrendered, it was fortunate that a fortnight earlier Elphinstone had ordered that all old muskets were to be exchanged for new ones, of which there were plenty in the magazine. No attempt had been made to organise the exchange, the troops being casually told to go to the magazine and help themselves. The result was a scene described by Lady Sale as "curious", and by Eyre as one of "disgraceful confusion and plunder", a free-for-all scramble in which the camp followers had joined. Eyre sombrely noted the incident as symptomatic of "the unsteadiness of the troops, and of the recklessness that now began to extend itself amongst all ranks of the force". At least, however, the troops had new muskets.

With departure imminent, Captain Johnson was busily engaged in buying up camels and ponies to carry the baggage. His efforts were, as usual, impeded by Ghazi fanatics, who "still infest our gates and insult us in every possible way". He noted angrily that Elphinstone took no notice, although both officers and men were "burning for revenge". It was small consolation to the Paymaster to be told by his Afghan friends that "we have brought the whole of our misfortunes upon ourselves, through the apathy and imbecility displayed at the commencement of the outbreak". The chiefs had said as much during the negotiations. They explained that on the morning of Burnes' murder, every one of them had kept his horse saddled, ready for instant flight if the rising failed; now, having experienced Shelton's ineptitude in command at the Beymaroo battle, they were satisfied that they had nothing to fear from British generals. This opinion was shared even by civilians in the British camp. Mr. Baness, a merchant variously described as a Greek or an Indian, came to Mackenzie and said that if Elphinstone would give him just twelve or fifteen men he would personally go out and drive off the Afghans. When this spirited offer was not accepted, Baness "heaped imprecations on Elphinstone, Shelton and all concerned" and departed angrily.

Johnson's friends warned him that the safety of the British on the retreat would depend on themselves alone, and urged that no trust be placed in the promises of the chiefs, least of all in those of Akbar Khan. More practically, these lugubrious well-wishers sent the Paymaster some food for the journey, "some very excellent cakes", for which he was duly grateful, gloomily observing that there would not be a particle of firewood for cooking for the whole of the march to Jalalabad. "How dreary a prospect we have before us," he added; "ninety miles! And the greater part of this distance through snow upwards of a foot deep, and the thermometer at night below zero." The snow had been falling heavily since mid-December and was likely to prove at least as great a danger as the threatened Afghan treachery. Pottinger, who had noticed that as soon as the first snows fell, every Afghan appeared with his legs "swathed in rags", now urged that old horse-blankets should be cut into strips which the troops could roll puttee-fashion round their feet and legs. This sensible suggestion presumably seemed to the high command both slovenly and unsoldierly, for nothing was done, and the troops were left to the misery of their hard leather boots. Within a few hours of the start of the march the frost had done its work and hundreds were suffering the agonies of frost-bitten feet.

As 1841 drew to its end, the British were kept in almost hourly expectation of departure. Each day they would be warned that the retreat would begin next morning; and next morning, at the last moment, a postponement of twenty-four hours would be announced. Always the excuse was that the chiefs had been unable either to organise the escort that was to see the British safely out of Afghanistan, or to collect the stocks of food and firewood that would be needed for the journey. Elphinstone was in a dilemma. On the one hand was the strong suspicion that these pretexts for delay were mere cover to give the Afghans time to perfect their preparations for the destruction of the force. "Every day's delay," wrote Johnson on New Year's Eve, "increases our difficulties on the road." On the other hand, to embark without fuel or rations on a ninety miles' march through deep snow and freezing cold, encumbered with a mass of women, children and other non-combatants, was to invite disaster. Not surprisingly the letters and diary entries written at Kabul at this time are full of foreboding. "The troops march to-morrow," wrote Lawrence; "treachery is feared. We have no money and no friends." "We are to depart without a guard," wrote Lady Sale, "without money, without provisions, without wood." Tempers were beginning to wear thin under the strain. The supercilious Captain Bellew came with an order to Lieutenant Sturt to "scarp" the banks of the canal so that the baggage camels could get down them. "To scarp?" asked Sturt; "to slope, I suppose you mean?" "You may suppose what you please," snarled Bellew, "but the General's orders, sent by me, are to scarp the banks; and now, do as you like!"

Meanwhile, the dreary business of packing for departure was going on. What could not be carried was destroyed, and this at least provided some welcome fuel. It had been getting steadily colder and at sunrise on 3rd January the thermometer showed over thirty-two degrees of frost, while even in an officer's quarters, with a blazing fire, the temperature at noon rose only eight degrees above freezing-point. Boxes and chests of drawers were now broken up for firewood, and Lady Sale's last dinner and breakfast in the Kabul cantonments were cooked on the wood of a mahogany dining table. A curious little incident had cast a chill over her which the leaping flames of mahogany could not dispel. Sturt, her son-in-law, had been jettisoning his books and she picked up one at random. It was Campbell's poems and it opened by chance at "Hohenlinden." Lady Sale found herself reading a verse that would haunt her in the days to come:

> Few, few shall part where many meet,
> The snow shall be their winding sheet;
> And every turf beneath their feet
> Shall be a soldier's sepulchre.

"I am far from being a believer in presentiment," she confided to her diary; "but this verse is never absent from my thoughts." Some months earlier another eerie vision of the forthcoming tragedy had been experienced. Back in July, 1841, Major Hamlet Wade had attended a ceremonial parade in Kabul at which the 44th had trooped their colour before General Sale. "Sir Robert Sale inspected the 44th this morning," he wrote in his diary that evening, "the colours of the regiment are very ragged, and when they passed in review I was suddenly startled by what I took to be a large funeral procession. What put such a thought into my head I know not, as I was thinking of very different subjects. I cannot help recording this, it has made such an impression."

Now, on 6th January, 1842, the funeral procession of the 44th Regiment, and of many thousands of others, was about to begin.

3

6th January, 1842

"Dreary indeed was the scene," wrote Eyre, "over which, with drooping spirits and dismal forebodings, we had to bend our unwilling steps. Deep snow covered every inch of mountain and plain with one unspotted sheet of dazzling white, and so intensely bitter was the cold as to penetrate and defy the defences of the warmest clothing." The troops were already half starved with cold, their only rations for days past having been a handful of flour with melted ghee or dhal, and the non-combatants had fared even worse. Ahead lay many days' march through the grimmest of mountain country. They must pass through a succession of formidable defiles, Khoord-Kabul, Tezeen and Jugdulluk. Unopposed, the journey would have been one of the utmost difficulty. If the force was attacked, it would be doomed.

The one faint hope would have been a quick start before dawn and the use of every available road so that the Khoord-Kabul pass could have been cleared on the first day. But in their two years of occupation the British had made no attempt to reconnoitre a number of lateral routes that might have been used, and now the whole force, in one great unwieldy mass, had to march by the one main road, ten miles due east through Begramee to Boothak, and then south through the Khoord-Kabul pass for the same distance to the village of that name. Nor was there any sense of urgency on the morning of departure. Shelton, who from now on would play a valiant part that went some way to atone for his earlier stupidities, knew nothing of the arrangements for the retreat until they were published the evening before. He at once urged that the baggage be loaded and ready to move by moonrise, but nothing was done and it was not in a position to start until eight o'clock on the morning of the 6th, when Shelton again called on Elphinstone to emphasise the need for haste. He found the General at a leisurely breakfast and was snubbed for his interference or, as he put it, "got offended for my trouble".

With their usual folly, Elphinstone's staff had introduced another prime element of delay into the move from cantonments by ordering Sturt to build a temporary bridge of gun-waggons across the Kabul river, half a mile away. Sturt sensibly pointed out that the river was fordable in many places and that with the snow over a foot deep, there was little point in trying to keep the men's feet dry. He was overruled, and it was midday before the bridge was ready. A monster traffic jam immediately built up. The camp-followers, some twelve thousand in number, were determined not to put foot in the water and jostled in a disorderly queue at the bridge. The delay at the bridge, thought Lady Sale, was "the origin of the day's misfortunes, which involved the loss of nearly all the baggage and the greater part of the commissariat stores".

Even now, Elphinstone was dithering in an agony of indecision whether finally to commit his force to the march, and when half the column had moved out of cantonments he tried to call off the operation, ordering Mackenzie to ride to Shelton with a command to stand fast. Mackenzie, convinced that this would be fatal and that, with the garrison half in and half out of the cantonments, they would be "ignominiously butchered by the enemy", took it on himself to overrule the General and galloped off to Shelton, who had halted in bewilderment, to order him to resume the march. As he rode he could hear old Elphinstone bleating piteously behind him; "Mackenzie, don't! Don't do it!"

The force that marched from Kabul on that ill-fated 6th of January amounted to some 4,500 fighting men. Of these nearly seven hundred were European troops, six hundred men of the Queen's 44th and a troop of horse artillery. The Indian troops consisted of nearly a thousand cavalry, more than half of them from Soojah's levies, three sepoy battalions of the Company's infantry and the Shah's 6th. A mixed handful of sappers and miners, Mackenzie's gallant little band of Afghan jezailchis, who had decided to stand by their British masters, some mountain gunners and the mission escort made up the total. The camp followers and their families were, however, nearly three times as numerous.

To the inhabitants of Kabul, looking down from the city, it

must have been an extraordinary sight, a long black snake of human beings and animals winding its slow way across the dazzling snow. From the Balla Hissar, to which he had repeatedly and in vain urged the British to withdraw, Soojah too now gloomily watched the exodus. His own troops were going with the rest. He had addressed a poignant appeal to Anquetil, the commander of his army, asking him "if it were well to forsake him in the hour of need, and to deprive him of the aid of that force which he had hitherto been taught to consider as his own?" There was no reply. As Eyre said, "The General and his council of war had determined that we must go, and go we accordingly did."

There had been some attempt to organise the retreat in military fashion. There was an advance guard, commanded by Anquetil and consisting of the 44th, the sappers and miners, one squadron of Soojah's cavalry and the three mountain guns. Shelton commanded the main body, while Colonel Chambers was left in charge of a rearguard of two infantry battalions—the Company's 54th and the Shah's 6th—the 5th Light Cavalry, and four Horse Artillery guns.

This order of march looked business-like enough on paper, but milling about in the main body were two thousand camels and ponies, laden with stores and baggage, and at least twelve thousand camp followers, with their terrified wives and children. These were the people who were now expected, half-starved as they already were, to march for miles through deep snow and freezing temperatures, without tents or firewood to help them through the bleak nights that lay ahead. The British wives, headed by Lady Macnaghten and Lady Sale, were slightly more fortunate. There were about a dozen of them, with rather more than twenty children between them, and they moved at the head of the main body, which was considered the position of greatest safety. Some rode ponies, others jogged along in *kajavas*, panniers slung one each side of a camel. But some nursed at their breasts babies a few days old and could not stand without assistance, others were so advanced in pregnancy that "under ordinary circumstances a walk across a drawing-room would have been an exertion".[1] Before long, thousands of the wretched camp followers, bewildered, numb with cold, terrified and undisciplined, had come surging forward and thrown the whole line of march into confusion.

When only half the column had cleared cantonments Pottinger received an urgent message from Zemaun Khan, the acting

[1] Eyre.

"King", protesting that the army had moved before their Afghan escort was ready or the fuel and supplies for the march had been collected. Zemaun's concern was genuine and Pottinger, to whom the project of a ninety miles' trek through the snow without food or firewood seemed insane, would willingly have taken the "King's" advice to halt. But it was too late. Already there were Afghan looters in the Mission Compound at the eastern end of the cantonments, and before the rearguard had moved out of the camp the jezails had begun to crack. Fifty of the 5th Light Cavalry, with Ensign Hardyman, were left dead or dying in the snow.

The Afghans realised with glee that the British force was too demoralised to prevent them from engaging with impunity in their favourite pastimes of plunder and murder. They grew bolder and began to harass the straggling column like wolves, a trail of bodies along the line of march and bloodstains in the snow marking the success of their efforts. Many of the camp followers had already given up in despair and sat apathetically by the road-side, waiting for death. Mackenzie would remember all his life the sight of a little Indian child sitting in the snow, stark naked, alone and deserted. "It was a beautiful little girl about two years old, just strong enough to sit upright with its little legs doubled under it, its great black eyes dilated to twice their usual size, fixed on the armed men, the passing cavalry and all the strange sights that met its gaze." Mackenzie reflected that if an Afghan boy of twelve came across it, he would amuse himself by drawing back the baby's head and cutting its throat. "The Afghan children were seen stabbing with their knives at wounded grenadiers, one of whom, the day before, could have put a dozen of those children's fathers to flight with his bayonet." Mackenzie longed "to take up this poor little native of a foreign climate and cuddle it in his arms", but what would have been the good? There were many other children as young and innocent lying slaughtered on the road, and women with their long dark hair wet with their own blood.

The frightful confusion at Sturt's bridge had at last sorted itself out. It had been "an enormous mass of struggling life, from which arose shouts and yells and oaths—an indescribable uproar of discordant sounds; the bellowings of the camels, the curses of the camel-drivers, the lamentations of the Hindostanees, the shrieks of women and the cries of children; and the savage yells of the Ghazis rising in barbarous triumph above them all". But at last the tortured force had struggled free and now, to reach the Jalalabad road, found itself marching *towards* Kabul for the best part of a mile, with the great grey mass of the Balla Hissar looming up ever closer in front. Pottinger, Lawrence and others still hoped against hope that at the eleventh hour Elphinstone would come to his senses and order the army to march straight in and occupy that formidable stronghold before the Afghans could rally to prevent them. But Elphinstone was not the man to be capable of such an audacious change of plan. The crossroads were reached, the advance guard turned left towards Jalalabad and the Balla Hissar died away in the winter dusk behind them. Soon the murky scene was lit up by the flames of the cantonments, which had been set alight by the exultant Afghans and were now blazing furiously. As the force halted for the first night of its Purgatory, men looked back through the frosty darkness and saw the night sky lit up like a stormy sunset by the great fire, which shed a red glare over the waste of snow for miles around. In their exuberance the looters also set fire to the guns which Elphinstone had left behind, in strict observance of the treaty. At least these could not now be turned against their former owners.

Friendly Afghans—and there were still many of them—had been insistent that for the British the only hope of safety lay in pushing on at all costs and covering the fifteen miles necessary to clear the terrible pass of Khoord-Kabul on the first day. The late start, the muddle and delay at the bridge, the milling crowd of non-combatants and Elphinstone's lack of any sense of urgency made this out of the question. The column was still a bare six miles from Kabul when, at four o'clock in the afternoon, the General called a halt for the night at Begramee. It was freezingly cold and in a few short hours the force had already lost the bulk of its supplies, such as they were, for when the Afghans swooped on the cantonments "the servants threw away their loads and ran off. Private baggage, commissariat and ammunition were nearly annihilated at one fell swoop."[1] Now, as the wretched force bivouacked for the night, there were, as Lady Sale laconically noted, "no tents, save two or three small palls. All scraped away the snow as best they could, to make a place to lie down on. The evening and night were intensely cold. No food for man or beast procurable."

Mackenzie, with twenty or so of his jezailchis still loyally following him, passed a better night than most, thanks to his men's local knowledge. They cleared a circle in the snow, laid

[1] Lady Sale.

half of their poshteens on it and lay down in a ring, feet inwards. The remaining poshteens were then spread over the circle and Mackenzie, "who himself shared their homely bed, declared that he had felt scarcely any inconvenience from the cold".[1] But Mackenzie and his jezailchis were about the only ones to pass a tolerable night. The rest shivered on the icy ground. "The night was pitch dark and excessively cold," said Lawrence, "the silence of the men betrayed their despair and torpor, not a voice being heard." When the bleak dawn broke over the dreary scene it was found that many had perished in the night, and Lawrence found, lying close to his tent, "stiff, cold and quite dead, an old grey-haired conductor named Macgregor who, utterly exhausted, had lain down there silently to die". The only signs of life in the night had been at two o'clock in the morning when the rearguard came straggling in, shouting loudly for their regiments and getting the general reply that "no one knew anything about it". They had fought the whole of the way to Begramee, and had passed through what Lawrence described as "literally a continuous lane of poor wretches, men, women and children, dead or dying from the cold and wounds, who, unable to move, entreated their comrades to kill them and put an end to their misery".

So passed the first twenty-four hours of the retreat. The force had covered a mere six miles. There were more than eighty miles still to go.

7th January, 1842

The advance guard (the previous day's rear-guard) moved off without orders at seven-thirty, but found the camp followers and many of the sepoys already surging on ahead of them. Discipline was almost at an end, and when the sepoys were asked why they were not with their units, "One had a lame foot, another could not find his regiment, another had lost his musket, any excuse to run off."[2] More than half the sepoys, said Lawrence, were unable to handle their muskets from cold and hunger and were throwing them away and mixing with the crowd of non-combatants. Most of Soojah's 6th Infantry and his Sappers had already deserted and returned to Kabul, "preferring becoming prisoners there to the certain death which they saw clearly must result from continuing any longer with the main body".[3]

The order of march of the previous day had been reversed, "if that could be called *order* which consisted of a mingled mob of soldiers, camp followers and baggage cattle, preserving not even

[1] Eyre.   [2] Lady Sale.   [3] Lawrence.

the faintest semblance of that regularity and discipline on which depended our only chance of escape from the dangers which threatened us".[1] Up to now, indeed, apart from the attack on the rearguard and the cantonments, which had been as much an orgy of looting as anything, the Afghans had not shown much active hostility. But the Afghan winter was enemy enough. "The very air we breathed froze in its passage out of the mouth and nostrils, forming a coating of small icicles on our moustaches and beards."[1] The horses had great lumps of snow frozen to their hooves so solidly that they had to be dislodged with hammer and chisel. The infantry sank a foot deep in the snow with each step, even on the regular track, and several feet if they wandered off it. "It was bitterly cold, freezing hard," said Lawrence, "and I pitied from my soul the poor native soldiers and camp followers, walking up to their knees in snow and slush."

It was now noticed that small parties of Afghan horse and foot were hovering on the flanks of the column and moving parallel with it. It was at first optimistically supposed that the protective escort had arrived at last but disillusionment came swiftly as they suddenly charged down on Anquetil and the rearguard. The British broke before the onrush and the three 3-pounder mountain guns were captured. Valiantly, Anquetil rallied his men and with a gunner subaltern, Lieutenant Green, recaptured the guns. But the 44th, the main constituent of the rearguard, "precipitately *made themselves scarce*", as Lady Sale recorded with scornful under-linings, and the three little guns had again to be abandoned, though not before Brigadier and subaltern had spiked them with their own hands, "amid the gleaming sabres of the enemy". Elated with their success, the Afghan cavalry now charged head-long upon the main baggage column and carried off large quantities of stores, "creating the greatest confusion and dismay".[1]

These attacks threw the British command into an agony of doubt and indecision. The attack on the cantonments might have been overlooked as an outburst of the usual Afghan turbulence. Now, however, it began to seem as if all Akbar's promises of a safe conduct had been a mere trap, and many remembered the warnings they had received from Afghan friends before leaving Kabul. Shelton was all for pressing on, and if the Afghans were plotting treachery, he was certainly right. But meanwhile the "King", Zemaun Khan, one of the few whose efforts to save the British from destruction can be accepted as genuine, had written to Pottinger, again urging that the column be halted so that the

[1] Eyre.

chiefs might have time to send in food and firewood and disperse the marauders who had been attacking them. Pottinger saw Akbar Khan hovering in the distance with a body of some six hundred horsemen and sent Captain Skinner to remonstrate with him for his failure to ensure a safe conduct. Gentleman Jim returned to report that Akbar had maintained that the British had only their own premature start to thank for their misfortunes, but had reassuringly said that he had now come to escort the column on its way; also, added Akbar, six hostages must be surrendered as a guarantee that the force would not march beyond Tezeen until it had been confirmed that Sale had evacuated Jalalabad.

Pottinger urged a halt, as advised by both Zemaun and Akbar, even though it was now only noon and the force had covered barely five miles since its start that morning. While Shelton raged at the suggestion of further delay, arguing that "a halt on the snow, without tents or food, would destroy the troops", Elphinstone, shaken by "the utter confusion which prevailed, the exhausted state of the sepoys, who had been under arms in deep snow from daylight of the 6th, with scarcely any rest, and neither food nor water at the bivouac", decided to stay where he was until night-fall. "Here was another day entirely lost," commented Shelton sourly, "and the enemy collecting in numbers."

Elphinstone had intended to resume the march after dark, but after Grant had persuaded him that to attempt a night march with such a disorganised rabble as he now commanded would bring utter disaster, it was decided to spend the second night of the retreat at Boothak. The force had covered only ten miles in two days and there were still eighty miles to go, with two-fifths of the rations already consumed.

The second night was even worse than the first, the snow more than a foot deep and the men, without cover of any kind, "perfectly paralysed with cold".[1] "Our camp," said Lawrence, "if camp that can be called which consisted of thousands of human beings and animals all promiscuously huddled together in such a dense mass that it was hardly possible to move through them. . . . The night was intensely cold, the thermometer ten degrees below zero. Most of the officers and all the men were forced to lie down upon the snow, without food or fuel." The wretched sepoys, now past caring for the morrow, were burning their caps, accoutrements and even their clothes in the effort to get a little immediate warmth, and Lieutenant Melville of the 54th would

[1] Lady Sale.

later tell how he and eleven others "crowded round the hot ashes of a pistol-case and, with some bottles of wine still remaining, tried to keep off the effects of the cold. They then all huddled together and lay down on the ground to sleep." It was, said Eyre, "a night of starvation, cold, exhaustion, death; and of all deaths I can imagine none more agonising than that where a nipping frost tortures every sensitive limb, until the tenacious spirit itself sinks under the exquisite extreme of human suffering".

And the morning and the evening were the second day.

8th January, 1842

The third day of the retreat dawned upon a force almost completely demoralised by two nights' exposure to the frost and snow, which "had so nipped the hands and feet of even the strongest men as to completely prostrate their powers and incapacitate them for service".[1] Nearly every man, said Lady Sale, was so paralysed with cold as scarcely to be able to hold his musket or move. The troopers of the cavalry, though they had suffered less than the rest, were so stiff with cold that they had to be lifted on to their horses. Now, with their physical strength at its lowest ebb and their morale fast disintegrating, Elphinstone's men rose from their frozen bivouac at Boothak to attempt the passage of the dreaded pass of Khoord-Kabul, five miles long and shut in on either hand by cliffs so high that the rays of the winter sun never reached the valley floor. The only sound in the grey stillness of the pass was that of a mountain torrent racing down the trough of the defile, a torrent that must be crossed and recrossed twenty-eight times before the column would be clear of the Khoord-Kabul.

The day opened in unexpectedly promising fashion as the 44th made a spirited bayonet charge that cleared out of the path several hundred Afghans, who had massed menacingly at the entrance to the pass. It seemed that there were still soldiers who, to the right leadership, would give the right response, and at about this time Lawrence, seeing a body of Afghan horsemen collected under the hillside, asked his men if they were willing to attack them. "Yes, we will follow you anywhere," was the confident reply, and he ordered the advance. The enemy promptly fled. This incident confirmed him in his belief that "even at this, the eleventh hour, we might, if properly led, have driven the enemy like sheep into Caubul and occupied the Balla Hissar."

Now Akbar again appeared upon the scene. He was still

[1] Eyre.

willing, he protested, to escort the force to safety, but he must have hostages to guarantee Sale's evacuation of Jalalabad, and he demanded Shelton and George Lawrence. Lawrence agreed; Shelton had always resolutely refused to be made a hostage and Pottinger, who felt that his leg wound made him something of a passenger, volunteered to take his place. Accordingly, Pottinger, Lawrence and Mackenzie (whose jezailchis had by now been almost annihilated "and his services with them, therefore, could be of little further use") now surrendered to the Afghan Sirdar, who received them with a friendly kindness. No sooner had the hostages been handed over than a note arrived for Lawrence from Conolly, "telling him to be cautious, to put ourselves as little as possible in Akbar's power, and above all things to push on as fast as we could".

To push on was just what the force was incapable of doing. There was the usual delay while an attempt was made to form an order of march, with the remnants of the 5th Native Infantry and Anderson's Irregular Horse acting as advance guard, "but the baggage was mixed in with the advance guard and the camp followers all pushed ahead in their precipitate flight towards Hindostan".[1] Forty-eight hours of frost and snow and Ghilzye sniping had reduced the effective strength to a few hundreds of men, who now "commenced their passage through the dreaded defile in no very sanguine temper of mind".[2] There had been the usual waiting about for orders, during which Lady Sale, who during the long delay had been sitting for hours on her horse in the snow, gratefully downed a tumbler-full of sherry, "which at any other time would have made me very unladylike but now merely warmed me, and appeared to have no more strength in it than water". Children of three and four years old, she added, were drinking sherry by the cupful without the least effect on their heads.

A sudden hubbub broke out as a handful of British horse-artillerymen, priming themselves on brandy from the 54th's mess stores, decided in a haze of Dutch courage that it was really all very simple. "They mounted their horses; and with the best feeling in the world declared that they were ashamed of our inactivity, and vowed that they would charge the enemy." Their battery commander, Captain Nicholl, failing to enter into the spirit of the occasion, called them a pack of drunkards and rode off, "having showered curses and abuse on them, which had irritated them dreadfully". More tactfully, Sturt assured the

[1] Lady Sale.   [2] Eyre.

pot-valiant gunners that they were fine fellows, but that their lives were too valuable to be risked at the moment; at the right time, he promised, he himself would charge with them, and "this in a certain degree restrained their ardour; yet still they kept on talking valiantly".[1]

And now the jaws of the grim pass began to echo a new sound that rose above that of the mountain stream, one that came on and on in a swelling crescendo, the sound of the thousands of footsteps of an army hastening to its doom. As the pass narrowed the waiting Ghilzyes on the hillsides, recklessly disobeying the shouts of Akbar and his lieutenants, opened fire with their jezails. "They had erected small stone breastworks behind which they lay, dealing out death with perfect impunity to themselves."[2] Elphinstone's men, now stumbling through the icy waters of the burn, now floundering through the snow, and all the time hemmed in by the steep walls of the defile, were an easy target, and the slaughter was fearful. The force disintegrated in panic as thousands surged forward in a blind attempt to get clear of this terrible pass, abandoning their arms, ammunition, baggage, their women and children. Three or four of the British wives, including Lady Sale and her daughter, were riding with the vanguard and now, as the Ghilzye fire grew hotter, they fairly dug their spurs in and galloped hell-for-leather the gauntlet of the Afghan bullets. "Fortunately," recorded Lady Sale stoically, "I had only *one* ball in my arm." Her poshteen had stopped three others, and the wound was slight. None of the other women was hit, and Emily Sturt was the first of Elphinstone's force to gain the southern end of the Khoord-Kabul.

Her husband was less fortunate, and fate was now to reward him cruelly for the gallantry with which he had behaved from the start of the rising. Somewhere along the pass he had come across a wounded horse which he recognised as Major Thain's and despite the protests of his wife and mother-in-law had insisted on riding back to look for his friend, only to have his own horse shot under him. As he stumbled to his feet a Ghilzye bullet struck him in the stomach. Lieutenant Mein, still convalescent from the head wound he had received in the October fighting, stood bravely by the wounded man until he was joined by a passing sapper, Sergeant Deane, and together they brought Sturt down through the pass on the back of a pony. Lady Sale watched anxiously while Dr. Bryce of the Horse Artillery dressed her son-in-law's wound (and afterwards "kindly cut the ball out of

[1] Lady Sale.   [2] Mackenzie.

my wrist") but the doctor's expression showed only too plainly that the case was hopeless. Sturt lingered through the night in agony, suffering intolerable thirst, which Mein relieved by constantly fetching water from a near-by stream. The dying man's last night was far from peaceful. "Half a sepoy's pall had been pitched, in which the ladies and their husbands took refuge . . . there were nearly thirty of us packed together, without room to turn. The sepoys and camp followers, half frozen, tried to force their way not only into the tent but actually into our beds, if such resting place can be so called—a poshteen half spread on the ground and the other half spread over one."[1]

Further back in the column other British wives and children had jogged their way down the pass in camel *kajavas*. Each camel was led by a sepoy at a maximum speed of two miles an hour. "How can we sufficiently admire the behaviour of the Hindustan-is, who unflinchingly remained at their posts and led the camels through the murderous fire?" asks Mackenzie. The British women's servants had nearly all deserted or been killed, and as a result they had lost all their baggage and had nothing left but the clothes they wore; "those," says Eyre in horrified italics, "in the case of some of the invalids consisted of *night-dresses*, in which they had started from Caubul in their litters." A camel carrying Mrs. Boyd and her four-year-old son Hugh on one side and Mrs. Mainwaring and her three-months-old baby on the other was hit by a bullet and pitched to its knees. As the passengers scrambled out a cavalry trooper mounted Mrs. Boyd pillion behind him, while his companion did the same for Hugh. But Ghilzye bullets were still taking their toll, the second trooper was hit, and the frantic mother looked round to see that the little boy had vanished. Meanwhile Mrs. Mainwaring, "a young merry girl, whose husband was at Jalalabad,"[2] ploughed doggedly on on foot, stumbling through the snow, wet to the knees, picking her way over the bodies of the dead and dying, shoved and jostled by men and animals. She was carrying her baby while little Mary Anderson, the four-year-old daughter of "Irregular Horse" Anderson, clung to her arm. By now, however, the more daring of the enemy were riding in among the column, cutting down stragglers in wanton savagery and snatching muskets out of the hands of unresisting sepoys. In the confusion Mary Anderson was whirled away from Mrs. Mainwaring's side and she saw her no more.

There were others who on this day fell into Afghan hands. "Mrs. Bourke, little Seymour Stoker and his mother, and Mrs.

[1] Lady Sale.   [2] Mackenzie.

Cunningham, all soldiers' wives, and a child of a man of the 13th have been carried off," recorded Lady Sale. She does not, however, mention the far more numerous wives of the sepoys, and ·their children, whom the Afghans did not bother to take prisoner, and who were either mercilessly butchered or left to perish in the snow. All the British contemporary accounts exhibit an unconsciously callous disregard towards the fate of these "natives". No thought was given as to who it was who had persuaded the camp followers to leave the warmth and peace of their own Hindustan to come to this savage land of mountain and snow. When they are mentioned at all, it is only to comment with exasperation on the way in which their cowardice and panic impeded the operations of the fighting men.

By evening on the 8th January the force had struggled through to the southern end of the Khoord-Kabul, one of those who got through being the indomitable Mrs. Mainwaring, still carrying her baby. But three thousand souls had perished in that awful pass, and before long the survivors were to envy the dead. As they settled down to bivouack in the highest and coldest spot they had yet met, the snow began to fall and continued throughout the night. By this time there were only four small tents left. Elphinstone had one, the British wives and children had two of the others and the fourth was earmarked for the sick. But there were far more of these than one small tent could accommodate, and "an immense number of poor wounded wretches wandered about the camp destitute of shelter, and perished during the night. Groans of misery and distress assailed the ear from all quarters."[1]

9th January, 1842

At dawn there was the usual confusion, three-quarters of the fighting troops and all the camp followers shambling off without orders in the direction of India. Any who could had appropriated to their own use ponies and camels from the transport column, and there was complete chaos. The only order, said Lady Sale, appeared to be "Come along; we are all going, and half the men are off, with the camp followers in advance!" But before a mile had been covered in this disorganised fashion Elphinstone ordered a halt. Surprisingly, the order was obeyed, although it caused despair. "Mothers threw their children from them in utter desperation, and the general feeling was that there was no hope left."[2] The instinct of the whole force was to push on at all costs, and the instinct was right. Whatever their human enemies

[1] Eyre. [2] Mackenzie.

might have done, one more march would have carried them clear of the snow, and the snow was as great a threat to survival as the Afghan jezails. By now more than half the force were frost-bitten or wounded and most of the men, said Lady Sale, could scarcely put a foot to the ground. On top of this, many were suffering the agony of snow blindness. Captain Johnson found that his eyes had "become so inflamed from the reflection of the snow that I was nearly blind, and the pain intense", and he adds that several officers were completely blind.

The brief march, before Elphinstone called a halt, had finished off the unfortunate Sturt, his last agony intensified and his death accelerated by being jolted along on a camel. "We had the sorrowful satisfaction," said his mother-in-law, "of giving him Christian burial," and according to Eyre he was the only man in the force who received this rite.

Akbar had turned up once more, and it was he who had urged that a halt be ordered so that he could make proper arrangements for the protection of the force and the provision of supplies. This hoary excuse had been heard so often in the past few days that no one except Elphinstone was prepared to believe it. There was, says Eyre, "scarcely even a native soldier who did not plainly perceive that our only chance of escape consisted in moving on as fast as possible". Shelton too was hotly opposed to the order to halt. "I went to Elphinstone and told him such a measure would cause the total destruction of the whole force." The General, however, persisted in trusting not only to Akbar's good faith, which might conceivably have been genuine, but also in his ability to perform his promises, which had been repeatedly disproved.

The unhappy force was therefore compelled to spend a day of inactivity, waiting in the snow for the provisions promised by Akbar, "which, as I foretold," recorded Shelton with sour satisfaction, "never came". It was the fourth day that the animals had gone without food, noted Lady Sale, "and the men are starved with cold and hunger." The Indian troops were now beginning seriously to consider desertion, an idea which had more than once been temptingly dangled before them by the Afghans. The symptoms first developed among the troopers of Soojah's cavalry, who had hitherto behaved remarkably well in the face of the temptation to secure their own safety by abandoning their British masters. But they were mostly very young soldiers, and they "foresaw full well the fatal results of all these useless and pernicious delays. The love of life is strong in every breast."[1]

[1] Eyre.

Eighty of the Shah's 2nd Cavalry still remained true to their salt, but the rest now rode over to the enemy, Eyre generously commenting that not until they saw that the situation of the force had become incurably hopeless did they put self-preservation before loyalty. Elphinstone, however, sent a reproachful message to Akbar and Akbar, apparently prepared to play to what Elphinstone seemed to think were the rules, sent a chief to explain to the British force, through the mouth of Captain Grant, that anyone who succeeded in deserting to the Afghans would be shot. Grant added that any who made the attempt and failed would receive the same fate from his own side. A foolish, or unlucky, chuprassie of the Mission guard, choosing this very moment to try to desert, was instantly executed by a firing squad, but this belated attempt to re-assert discipline in a demoralised force was futile, for already death, desertion, wounds and sickness had whittled Elphinstone's fighting strength down to two hundred men of the 44th and about 120 men in each of the four battalions of Indian infantry; the Irregular Horse and the 5th Light Cavalry between them could muster about 170 troopers. And there were still seventy miles between the force and safety.

To the three hostages, Pottinger, Lawrence and Mackenzie, Akbar now made a new and startling suggestion. He proposed that the wives and children should be taken out of the column and handed over to his protection, in which event he promised to bring them down in safety, one day's march behind the army. No one supposed for a moment that he was referring to any but the *British* wives and children, nor was any plea put in for the far more numerous wives and children of the sepoys and camp followers. These were natives and expendable, and by now the attitude of all the British was simply one of exasperation at the way in which they cluttered and disorganised the fighting troops. Akbar's proposals were therefore considered in relation to the British families alone, and the three officers unhesitatingly recommended to Captain Skinner, who was acting as the link between Elphinstone and Akbar, that they should be accepted. Akbar's good faith was always suspect and it was fairly plain that even if he had been moved in part by genuine feelings of chivalry—the destitute situation of the widowed ladies and married families, according to Eyre, "rendered them objects of universal pity and sympathy"—his main motive was to acquire some valuable hostages. On the other hand, to accept his proposal was the only hope of saving the women and children from certain death and the fact that his own father and brothers were in the hands of the

British in India might restrain him from any excesses. Skinner therefore brought the proposal to Elphinstone with a strong recommendation for its acceptance, and Elphinstone, "desirous", as he said, "to remove the ladies and children, after the horrors they had already witnessed, from the further dangers of our camp", agreed.

At midday, therefore, the wives and children set off under the escort of some Afghan chiefs to a little fort where Akbar had set up his temporary headquarters. Lady Sale, the widowed Lady Macnaghten, the widowed Mrs. Trevor and her seven children, and Mrs. Sturt, widowed that very morning, with her only child, headed the party. There were about seven other wives, including Mrs. Mainwaring, whom we last met wading through the snow with her baby in her arms, and as many small children. At Akbar's fort there were some happy re-unions. Mrs. Boyd was overjoyed to find the four-year-old Hugh, safe and sound in the arms of George Lawrence, and little Seymour Stoker had also turned up unharmed. Mrs. Boyd's delight, said Lawrence, "was in striking contrast with the anguish of Captain and Mrs. Anderson at not finding their little daughter among our number, as they hoped and expected". And in the dark grim little fort these cold and famished refugees were presently regaled to a midnight feast of mutton bones and greasy rice.

They had not come alone. Whether Akbar had intended it or not, Elphinstone had read his suggestion of taking under his wing "all the widowed ladies and married families" as including the husbands, and Akbar did not disagree with an interpretation which would deprive Elphinstone of a few more officers and furnish the Afghans with additional hostages. More surprisingly, there is no record of any of the officers concerned showing any misgivings at the suggestion that they should abandon their men.[1] They evidently regarded their first duty as being to their wives, and accordingly Captain Anderson, the commander of the Irregular Horse, Captain Boyd of the Commissariat and several others joined the party that was escorted to the questionable safekeeping of Akbar Khan. Elphinstone had also intended that wounded officers (wounded other ranks being apparently of no account) should have the opportunity of seeking Akbar's protection, but the party was taken away by the Afghans so hurriedly that the only two who had time to join it were Troup, the Brigade-

[1] Mackenzie was indignant at Lady Sale's insinuation that the married officers abandoned their posts of their own accord. It was, he says, "by General Elphinstone's express command".

Major of Soojah's levies, and Mein, who had become the friend and protector of Lady Sale and her daughter. Eyre and Waller (Bengal Horse Artillery), who accompanied their wives, were also qualified as wounded, for in the Kabul fighting they had received injuries that totally disabled them from active service.

10th January, 1842

Dawn broke over the dreary snow-covered wastes to reveal the usual confusion, "a rush to the front by the mixed rabble of camp followers, sepoys and Europeans in one huge mass",[1] with everyone dreading above all things to be left in the rear. The European troops were now the only effectives left, for the sepoys were all suffering from frostbitten hands and feet and few could even hold a musket, let alone pull a trigger. The freezing cold had numbed them both mentally and physically and "hope seemed to have died in every breast. The wildness of terror was exhibited in every countenance."[2]

Two miles from the morning's starting point the force faced the gorge of Tunghee Tareekee, only fifty yards long but a bottleneck so narrow, less than four yards wide, that the column had practically to go forward in single file. The Afghans, having chosen this as the appointed place for the next shambles, had hurried on ahead to occupy the heights commanding the pass. The advance guard, comprising the 44th, some fifty troopers of the 5th Light Cavalry and the one remaining Horse Artillery gun, managed to fight their way through with heavy casualties, but when the main body reached the death-trap there was a massacre. The Afghans on the hillside poured in volley after volley upon their close-packed and helpless target, and "the unfortunate sepoys, seeing no means of escape and driven to utter desperation, cast away their arms and accoutrements, which only clogged their movements without contributing to their defence, and along with the camp followers fled for their lives". But there was to be no escape. The Afghans, realising that there was no need now to waste valuable ammunition, moved down among them sword in hand and, at their leisure, cut the throats of their defenceless and unresisting victims. By the time they had finished, "there was not a single Sepoy left of the whole Caubul force".[3]

The advance guard had struggled on through deepening snow for another few miles before halting to let the main body catch up, but now, as a few scattered stragglers came through, they were

[1] Lady Sale.   [2] Eyre.   [3] Lady Sale.

appalled to realise that the main body had ceased to exist and that they themselves were the only survivors of those who had marched from Khoord-Kabul that morning. Every particle of baggage was gone. Four days earlier Elphinstone had marched from Kabul with four and a half thousand fighting men. Nine tenths were gone, and he was now left with 250 men of the 44th, 150 cavalrymen and 50 horse gunners. The camp followers had perished in their thousands. But the Afghans had not yet had time to kill them all, and there were some three thousand left to clog the movements of the four hundred and fifty troops still intent on winning through to Jalalabad.

If the wounded could not keep walking they must resign themselves to being left by the side of the track to await death from cold or the Afghan knives, and after death would come mutilation. Retaliation, when it was possible, could be equally merciless, as one savage little incident revealed. A colour-sergeant had been killed and his body left lying where it fell. "A soldier of the same corps, happening to pass by the same spot some time after, saw a Khaibari boy, apparently about six years of age, with a large knife which his puny arm had scarcely sufficient strength to wield, engaged in an attempt to hack off the head of the dead sergeant. The young urchin was so completely absorbed in his savage task that he heeded not the near approach of the soldier, who coolly took him up on his bayonet and threw him over the cliff."[1]

There was the occasional near-miraculous escape. Lieutenant Melville, in endeavouring to save the colours of the 54th Native Infantry, was speared in the back, slashed over the head with a sword and stabbed in the back with a knife, yet still managed to crawl after the column on his hands and knees through the snow until he reached a spot where the 44th, with one gun, still preserved order of a kind. He was tied on to the gun, but presently it was needed for action and he was left by the roadside to wait for death. A little later a passing Afghan, recognising him as an acquaintance from the old days in Kabul, lifted him on to his own horse and led him to Akbar, "who received him most kindly and, binding up his wounds, gave him a *loonghee*, a cloth worn as a turban commonly by the Afghans and is generally of blue check with a red border, his regimental cap being cut to pieces".[2] Eyre

[1] *Frontier Expeditions.* This incident in fact occurred during General Pollock's advance into Afghanistan a few months later.

[2] Lady Sale. Lawrence explains that Akbar made Melville wear the turban and a poshteen so that he might escape detection by the Afghans.

seemed to think that Melville could have done more, and rather slightingly described him as having "a few slight cuts only".

The remnant of the force was struggling on towards Tezeen, still under the surveillance of Akbar and his cavalry. Continuing to protest his inability to stop the Ghilzye sniping from the hillside, the Sirdar now promised that if the few hundred surviving Europeans would lay down their arms and surrender, he would guarantee to bring them safely to Jalalabad. He could do nothing for the three or four thousand camp followers, and they must be left to their fate. Elphinstone, either feeling that he could not abandon the wretched civilians—though they were all doomed to die anyway—or perhaps shrinking from the crowning humiliation of unconditional surrender, refused; the march continued.

As the column came down the long steep descent from the Huft Kotul, they left the snow behind them at last, but at the foot of the hill, where the track entered a narrow defile, they came upon a ghastly sight. A crowd of camp followers had gone on ahead with the walking wounded and had run into an ambush. Once again it had been a slaughter of unresisting men, women and children, and the pass was almost choked with corpses. As the troops, sickened at the butchery, started to pick their way past the bodies, they were themselves relentlessly attacked, and only the unflinching courage of Shelton and his little rearguard saved the force from annihilation at this point. Shelton was now performing prodigies of valour, and his own regiment, the 44th—"nobly and heroically these fine fellows stood by me," he reported—was doing much to retrieve a reputation that had been so tarnished in the early days of the rising.

At about four o'clock in the afternoon the force reached the camping ground at Tezeen. In five days more than twelve thousand of those who had started from Kabul had perished and the survivors knew that death waited implacably for them too, but the instinct of self-preservation still flickered in their hearts. Twenty-two miles on from Tezeen there awaited them another grim and formidable defile, the dreaded pass of Jugdulluk, two miles long, very narrow, and commanded on both sides by precipitous hills. Shelton suggested, and for once Elphinstone agreed, that the only hope lay in a forced night march. They might thus have a chance of getting through Jugdulluk early the following morning, before the Ghilzyes had got ahead of them to block the pass.

After two or three hours' rest at Tezeen the force moved off at 7 o'clock in the evening, having told Akbar that they planned to march only as far as Seh Baba, seven miles on. The few hundred fighting troops started off as quietly as possible, hoping to shed their incubus of camp followers, but the followers were sleeping with one ear open and were at once on their feet, milling round the column and getting in the way. It was here that Doctor Cardew of the medical branch, wounded and unable to walk, had to be left behind. He was tied to the last remaining, and now useless, gun; the soldiers, who loved him, said their sad good-byes and there, next morning, Akbar's men found him cold and dead. He had come to Kabul from Ghuznee in order to travel to India to meet his fiancée, "whose anticipations of happiness were thus for ever blighted by the stern vicissitudes of war".[1]

The night was frosty and bright with moonlight and the force, unmolested, made good time until they reached Seh Baba, where a few shots fired at the tail of the column brought the camp followers crowding to the front. But now the tribes ahead were alert and they too opened fire. "The panic-stricken camp followers now resembled a herd of startled deer, and fluctuated backwards and forwards *en masse* at every shot, blocking up the entire road and fatally retarding the progress of the little body of soldiers who, under Brigadier Shelton, brought up the rear."[2]

And so, with the force still miles from its destination, the fifth day of the retreat came to its end.

11th January, 1842

At daybreak the advance guard, still more than ten miles from Jugdulluk, halted to let the remnants of the rearguard catch up before forcing their way onward. But it was now daylight, the enemy were on the heights above them, and the delay caused by the wretched camp followers had wrecked the last hope of escape. The ten miles to Jugdulluk were one long running fight, with Shelton and his gallant little rearguard facing overwhelming numbers of the pursuers with dauntless courage. In mid-afternoon the advance guard paused at the village of Jugdulluk, which lay at the entrance to the pass, to watch Shelton and his handful of the 44th fighting their way in. Elphinstone decided to assist them with an odd manoeuvre and ordered the British officers, about twenty in number, to form a line and "show an imposing front". What impression this parade made on the enemy is not recorded, but it proved disastrous to Captain Grant, the Adjutant General, who was hit in the face by a bullet which broke his jaw. Grant had been an abominable staff officer and, in many respects,

[1] Lawrence.   [2] Eyre.

Elphinstone's evil genius, but he did not lack courage; the wound "was so far from quelling his spirit that up to the final massacre at Gandamack he was among the foremost to encourage his companions in arms to fight manfully while they had life and limb".[1]

Meanwhile, the survivors of the "imposing front" were cheering Shelton as he fought his way on towards them with bulldog courage until at last the rearguard joined them behind some ruined stone walls under which the force had taken cover. The Afghans, being in no hurry, patiently took up their own positions and kept the British pinned down by accurate sniping. Elphinstone's men, who were almost frantic with hunger and thirst, greedily ate what little snow lay on the ground, but it only increased their thirst. A tantalising hundred and fifty yards from their position ran a stream of clear water, but any who tried to reach it were at once shot down. As for food, Johnson was lucky enough to find, among the camp followers, three bullocks, "which were instantly killed, served out to the Europeans and as instantly devoured, although raw and still reeking with blood".[2]

12th January, 1842

Throughout the night of the 11th and for the whole of the next day the force lay at Jugdulluk, continually harassed by the fire of the enemy jezails. At one moment the Afghans ventured too close, whereupon Captain Bygrave, the Paymaster of the British troops, led out a handful of the 44th in a bayonet charge and the enemy fled. "There is no weapon like the bayonet in the hands of a British soldier," complacently noted the anonymous contributor to *Frontier and Overseas Expeditions from India*, "the Afghans would stand like swarms against firing, but the sight of the bristling line of cold steel they could not endure." Others might have said that the Afghans were fighting with an intelligent economy of force, for when Bygrave's charge had wasted itself on the empty air and his men had again withdrawn behind the ruined walls, the Afghans at once returned to their former positions and resumed their deadly sniping.

Gentleman Jim Skinner, still going to and fro between the two armies, now brought an invitation from Akbar suggesting that Elphinstone, Shelton and Paymaster Johnson come to a conference. After Elphinstone had handed over command to Anquetil the three officers made their way to Akbar's encampment, where the

[1] Mackenzie.
[2] Johnson's journal, quoted by Kaye.

Sirdar received them with every appearance of kindness and regaled them with food and great draughts of tea to slake their thirst. They were then taken to a small tent to enjoy the first night's sleep since leaving Kabul. Akbar had been free with the usual empty promises that food would at once be supplied to the starving troops, but Johnson later noted that "we had the extreme mortification to learn that not one particle of food or water had been tasted by the troops from their arrival to their departure from Jugdulluk". The troops had watched their General go off to the conference with a feeling of despair, "having seen enough of Afghan treachery to convince them that these repeated negotiations were mere hollow artifices, designed to engender confidence in their victims, preparatory to a fresh sacrifice of blood".[1]

On the morning of the 12th a number of the local Ghilzye chieftains arrived at Akbar's camp to discuss the fate of the remnant of Elphinstone's force. The General and his two companions were present and Johnson, who understood the language, was not reassured. Akbar, to all appearances, "but possibly only as a blind to his real feelings", seemed to be doing his best to persuade the Ghilzyes with offers of large bribes to let the British pass through in safety to Jalalabad. The Ghilzyes, however, "were most bitter in their expressions of hatred against us; and declared that nothing would satisfy them and their men but our extermination, and money they would not receive". Akbar reminded them that his father and his family were in British hands and would be exposed to British vengeance. But the Ghilzyes "from their expressions of hatred towards the whole race of us . . . appeared to anticipate much more delight in cutting our throats than even in the expected booty". To Akbar's expostulations they answered, "When Burnes came to this country, was not your father entreated by us to kill him? or he would go back to Hindostan, and on some future day return with an army and take our country from us? He would not listen to our advice, and what is the consequence? Let us, now that we have the opportunity, take advantage of it and kill these infidel dogs."

The debate went on, until at last avarice seemed to be winning the day over the blood-lust and Akbar's father-in-law was sent to arrange matters with the chiefs of Jugdulluk pass. But the chiefs were dogs, said Akbar, "and no faith was to be placed in them". Akbar's own proposal was that at dusk he and his Barukzye horsemen would gallop into the British encampment, when each

[1] Eyre.

rider would whisk a European soldier up pillion behind him and ride off to safety. The Ghilzyes, he explained, would not dare open fire for fear of hitting the Barukzyes, "but he could not allow a single Hindostanee to follow, as it was impossible for him to protect two thousand people". Johnson passed the suggestion on to Elphinstone, but the General turned it down "as, from past experience, we had seen how impossible it was to separate the non-combatants from the fighting men".

Elphinstone was by now impatient to get back to his troops. A whole day had been spent in argument while his men had been left without food or drink and still, though he did not know it, under constant attack. At last it dawned upon him that Akbar had no intention of letting him go, but meant to keep him and his two companions as hostages. Elphinstone pleaded that he would be thought to have deserted his men and that his honour as a soldier would be indelibly tarnished; let him but go back to his troops and he would send Anquetil to take his place. Akbar was still procrastinating when his father-in-law returned from his talks with the Ghilzyes to report smilingly that all was satisfactorily settled; the remnant of the force would be allowed to proceed unmolested to Jalalabad.

This cheerful news was instantly contradicted by an outburst of firing from the direction of the British camp, where Anquetil had remained all day without news of Elphinstone, the men starving, and helpless under the leisurely Ghilzye sniping. At last, after the chief liaison officer, Jim Skinner, had been shot in the face by a treacherous tribesman and brought into the camp to die in agony, Anquetil had decided on his own initiative to resume the march.[1] His effective force was now down to 120 men of the 44th and 25 artillerymen, but there was still a teeming rabble of camp followers to come huddling against the fighting men. "A deep feeling of anguish and despair now pervaded the whole assemblage," and ahead there still lay the pass of Jugdulluk.

In this grim defile the Kabul force was finally annihilated. When the troops at last struggled to the narrow summit of the pass, it was to find that the Afghans had blocked it with two barriers of prickly holly-oak, "well twisted together, about six feet high",[2] stretching completely across the defile. Officers and men fought frantically to tear away the spiky branches with their bare hands

[1] Mackenzie, however, says that when Elphinstone realised that Akbar intended to detain him, he sent a note to Anquetil, telling him, "March at once; there is treachery!"

[2] Mackenzie.

while the waiting Afghans poured in a deadly fire from all sides. Then the enemy charged in with scimitar and knife to wreak wholesale slaughter among the pent-up mass of troops and followers. Here, sword in hand, fell Anquetil;[1] here was killed Colonel Chambers, the commander of the cavalry, and three fellow-officers of the 5th Light; here Major Thain, Elphinstone's *a.d.c.*, met his death and here Captain Nicholl of the Horse Artillery died gallantly. Here we meet for the first and last time Captain Dodgin of the 44th, who had only one leg but was "a most powerful and active man, who killed five Afghans with his own hand before he was slain".[2] At last it became a matter of *sauve qui peut*. The infantry had at last managed to tear a gap in the holly barricades; they were ridden over by mounted officers and men, rushing for the gap, and in their fury retaliated by firing on their own side. "Despair seized the survivors; many submitted unresistingly to be murdered, and some crawled into caves and holes in the rocks to die." [3] When that fearful pass was finally cleared there were left of Elphinstone's 4,500 men but twenty officers and forty-five European soldiers.

A dozen of those who got through Jugdulluk, still reasonably well mounted, rode on ahead, determined to make their way as best they could to Jalalabad. The rest, perhaps fifty strong, marched on in small straggling parties under different officers. The country was more open now, the going was easier, and for a while the Ghilzyes were too busy plundering the dead to pursue the living. But the pace was slowed by the men's determination to bring their wounded comrades with them, and presently they were again under fire from bands of the enemy, posted on the heights above the road. Several more fell at the crossing of the Sourkab river, where they found the bridge in enemy hands. The rest could do nothing but push on hopelessly through the night.

13th January, 1842

Gandamack was reached at dawn and the enemy was gathering round once more. "Every hut," said Captain Johnson, "had poured forth its inhabitants to murder and to plunder." Daylight revealed how pitifully small was the British remnant. They could muster a mere twenty muskets, with not more than two rounds of ammunition apiece. But the Afghans often preferred to achieve

[1] There is a tablet to his memory in St. John's Church, Calcutta.
[2] The Afghans eventually drew back and shot the redoubtable Dodgin down from a safe distance.
[3] Lawrence.

by trickery what might easily have been accomplished by force, and the senior surviving officer, Major Griffiths of the 37th Native Infantry, was called to a parley. Meanwhile Afghans came strolling up to the little band of survivors and engaged them in apparently friendly conversation. Soon, however, they were trying to take the men's muskets from their hands and the British, by driving them fiercely away, sealed their own doom. The Afghans began to shoot them down at leisure and then rushed in, sword in hand, to finish off the survivors. The only prisoners taken were Captain Souter of the 44th, who saved the regimental colours by tying them round his waist,[1] and three or four privates of his regiment. Griffiths, too, with Mr. Blewitt, a civilian clerk who had gone with him as interpreter, was spared. The rest, including eighteen officers, were slaughtered without pity. It was here that Captain Grant, who had been suffering agony from his bullet-shattered jaw, finally paid with his life for the wrong advice he had given from the outset. His courage at least was unquenched and, "being at length rendered powerless by wounds in both arms, he ordered an artillery sergeant who had lost his own weapon to draw his sword and rush yet once again upon the Ghazis, which the poor fellow did and, after maiming several, himself received a mortal wound".[2]

There were now only six left of all Elphinstone's force, for of the twelve mounted men who had ridden on ahead from Jugdulluk half had fallen by the way by the time they reached Futtehabad, a mere sixteen miles from their goal. Grant's supercilious fellow staff-officer Bellew, Captain Collier and Captain Hopkins, Lieutenant Bird and two doctors, Harpur and Brydon, were still travelling onwards. Brydon's own horse had been shot under him and he owed his survival to the self-sacrifice of a veteran subadar, who insisted on giving his own horse to the doctor, with the words, "Sahib, my hour has come; I am wounded to death, and can ride no longer. You, however, still have a chance; take my horse, which is now useless to me, and God send you may get into Jalalabad in safety."[3]

At Futtehabad the fugitives were met with the smiling friendship that, as only too often, masked a murderous treachery. The inhabitants urged them to rest while food was made ready for them and Bellew, in command of the little band, unwisely agreed. The Afghans used the delay to get their weapons and then rushed

---

[1] The Afghans therefore supposed him to be someone of great importance and worth a substantial ransom.

[2] Mackenzie.   [3] *Frontier and Overseas Expeditions.*

at the six officers. Bellew and Bird were hacked to bits while the other four scrambled to their horses and rode for their lives. But the horses were tiring fast, armed men rode in pursuit and Collier, Hopkins and Harpur were overtaken and killed within four miles of Jalalabad.

And now, of all the Kabul army, there was only Surgeon Brydon, riding desperately onwards on a sorely wounded pony. When twenty enemy horsemen barred his way, with large stones in their hands to greet him, he kicked his pony into a gallop and broke through the cordon. A second body of horsemen loomed up in his path and a second time he was able to burst clear, though a stone broke his sword-blade, leaving a mere six inches in the hilt. Yet a third time enemy troopers crossed his path, men in scarlet tunics whom for one joyous moment he mistook for a cavalry patrol of the Jalalabad garrison. He realised his error when one of them rode at him with a shout, his sabre swinging. Brydon parried with his broken sword and the last six inches of blade were knocked from the hilt. Unarmed and desperate, the surgeon flung the hilt in the other's face and stooped to gather the reins, which had dropped from his hand; the assailant, thinking that he was drawing a pistol, wheeled his horse and galloped off. The Afghans, unpredictable as usual, lost interest, and Brydon suddenly found himself alone, free to ride slowly on to where Sale and the garrison of Jalalabad were waiting for him.

4

Sale had been instructed to wait for further orders at Gandamack, which he had reached at the beginning of November. He had assumed that he was to wait there for Elphinstone and the Macnaghtens, whose departure from Kabul he knew to be imminent, so that they could all travel on together to India. But now, early in November, rumours began to come seeping down through the passes that some disaster had occurred at Kabul and on the 10th a cossid got through with a letter from Macnaghten, informing Sale that Burnes and his companions had been murdered and that all Kabul was up. "It alluded in the most desponding language to the progress of the revolt, described the embarrassment of their position and reiterated in pressing terms the request he had previously made[1] for the immediate return of Sale's brigade."[2] George Lawrence had added a short postscript, curtly

[1] In letters which had never reached Sale.
[2] Marshman.

stating that "they were in a fix". At the same time came a message from Elphinstone to Sale, ordering him back to Kabul, "provided the sick and wounded could be placed in security with the irregulars at Gandamack".

No one ever questioned Fighting Bob's personal courage, but as a commander he was timorous and unintelligent. At a loss whether or not to march his troops back to Kabul, he had recourse to what Havelock contemptuously described as "the Jackdaw Parliament", a Council of War that, on and off, would persist in bad-tempered argument at Jalalabad for many weeks to come. At its first meeting many officers were in favour of return, and Sale, whose wife and daughter were still up in Kabul, must have felt his personal preference pulling in that direction. According to Durand, some of the ablest officers in the brigade favoured this course, "foremost among whom was Broadfoot". As Sir Herbert Edwardes later wrote, "it will always remain a moot point whether Sale could have returned or not; and if he had returned, whether it would have saved the Caubul force. . . . But there were at least two men with Sale's brigade who would have made all the difference: one—Henry Havelock—who would have recalled the discipline and spirit of poor Elphinstone's subordinates, if mortal man could do it; the other—George Broadfoot—who, in the last resort, would have dared to supply the army with a leader."

As it happened, it was one of these two—Havelock—whose influence was cast decisively into the scales against the proposal to return. It was plain, he argued, that what had really shaken the British hold on Kabul was the loss of moral courage by those in command. How could one help a garrison that apparently could not, and would not, help itself? Yet again, how could it be in serious danger? It consisted of between five and six thousand men, with good artillery and an immense stock of munitions. Nor would return to Kabul be easy, for winter had set in and snow was falling in the passes. Sale's brigade was badly clothed, it had lost much of its equipment and nearly all its transport. It had only enough ammunition for three battles, yet might have to fight its way for every one of the eight marches that return would entail. Finally, he reminded Sale, they had more than three hundred sick and wounded on their hands and that to leave them at Gandamack, either with or without the dubious protection of the Afghan irregulars, would be to abandon them to certain destruction.

This formidable list of objections convinced the Jackdaw

Parliament, and it was decided not only to disregard the appeal to return to Kabul but to march even further away, to Jalalabad, "thus," as Sale later explained, "establishing a point on which the force at Caubul might retire if hardly pressed, and restoring a link in the chain of communications with our provinces".

The Ghilzye chiefs of the district had shown a prudent friendliness towards the British so long as the brigade remained encamped at Gandamack, but on the day Sale marched for Jalalabad the mask was thrown off; the Afghan irregulars whom he had left at Gandamack turned at once on their British officers, set fire to the cantonment and blew up the magazine, together with some of their fellow-traitors, who failed to get clear in time. The passes that lay between Sale's brigade and Kabul were now sealed.

The brigade took two days to march from Gandamack to Jalalabad, fighting a brisk action *en route*. Dennie, by a feigned retreat of his infantry, lured the tribesmen into the open plain and there destroyed them with his cavalry, whose "right arms were wearied with the blows which they struck; and the quantity of dead that might be seen scattered over the face of the valley proved that they had not struck at random". Or so wrote the Reverend G. R. Gleig, Chaplain to the Forces, with all a muscular Christian's satisfaction at this smiting of the Amalekites.

On 13th November Sale seized Jalalabad, much to the chagrin of the Afghans who had assumed that he would go on his way to India and had been looking forward to plundering his baggage in the passes between Jalalabad and Peshawar. There was not much to be said for the town as a fortress. "The walls of Jalalabad," wrote Havelock, "were in a state which might have justified despair as to the possibility of defending them"; the tracing of the perimeter was "vicious in the extreme". Except for a few hundred yards, there was no parapet more than two foot high, and so much rubbish had accumulated round the ramparts that roads into the surrounding country had been driven across them. "The population was disaffected," said Havelock, "and the whole *enceinte* was surrounded by ruined forts, walls, mosques, tombs and gardens from which a fire could be opened at twenty or thirty yards."

Broadfoot at once set himself to remedy this state of affairs and under his indefatigable leadership the work went energetically forward. His days were spent in superintending work on the fortifications, his nights in drawing plans and making calculations. The ramparts were rebuilt, fields of fire were cleared, and the result was that "an indefensible heap of ruins was, as if by a magic wand, transformed into a fortification proof against any but siege ordnance".[1] Macgregor meanwhile busied himself in obtaining supplies and soon a month's rations had been collected. Now, as the Afghans began to invest the town more closely, Sale's troops sallied forth and defeated them in a sharp little engagement, at the start of which an enemy piper stood on a hill and "ceased not to play upon his most unmusical instrument, regardless of the shower of balls that whizzed past him. As a matter of course the piper became the subject of many a rude joke among the men of the 13th. They laughed while they took deliberate aim at him, showing however this much of respect to his acknowledged bravery that in honour of him they forthwith denominated the heights 'Piper's Hill'."[2] (The piper escaped unhurt.)

The battle of Piper's Hill put Sale's men in high fettle. The ease with which they had routed the enemy, supplied themselves with provisions and created a fortress out of nothing made it hard for them to believe the rumours that were drifting down from Kabul. Elphinstone had three times their strength, was established in cantonments and had, they assumed, ample supplies. How came it then that he had written again to Sale (this time in French, an elementary effort at security) bewailing that "notre peril est extreme"? He had once more implored Sale to return to the rescue, but again there was the proviso—"provided the sick and wounded could be placed in safety with their allies, the Sikhs". Sale replied that the whole of his camp equipage had been destroyed; that he had more than three hundred sick and wounded on his hands; that there was no longer a single depot of provisions on the route; and that his transport was not sufficient to carry more than one day's rations with it. He was sure that he would have to fight his way back, "and even if the debris of my brigade did reach Caubul, I am given to understand that I should find the troops now garrisoning it without means of subsistence. Under these circumstances, a regard for the honour and interests of our government compels me to adhere to my plan already formed of putting this place into a state of defence, and holding it, if possible, until the Caubul forces fall back upon me or succours arrive from Peshawar or India."

So Sale stood fast at Jalalabad and when, at the beginning of December, the Afghans again crowded him too close, Dennie once more led out the garrison and without the loss of a single man routed them with great slaughter. Again the brigade's morale bounded.

[1] Marshman.   [2] Broadfoot.

But the news that was now trickling down through the passes, partly rumours, partly messages brought by those nameless heroic couriers the cossids, was increasingly disturbing. By December 17th the Jalalabad garrison had heard a report, which as it happened was premature, that the British leaders in Kabul had entered into a treaty with the enemy and agreed to a compulsory evacuation of the country. "There are certainly indications of something extraordinary having occurred," wrote Havelock; "if a compact has been entered into, no faith will be kept by the Afghans and our troops will be attacked in the passes; but whatever be the result of that contest, it is our duty to die behind the walls of Jalalabad, rather than abandon the country." Broadfoot commented that it would be insanity for the Kabul force to capitulate. "They would inveigle our troops into the passes, and on the horses dying of hunger and cold would attack them, seize the guns, and starve or massacre the men reduced by want of food, shelter or fuel."

On 2nd January, Sale received confirmation of his worst fears. It came in the shape of a letter from Pottinger to Macgregor, which had been written on Christmas Day.

"My dear Macgregor [wrote Pottinger],

"We have had a sad Comedy of Errors, or rather tragedy, here. Macnaghten was called out to a conference and murdered.[1] We have interchanged terms on the ground he was treating on for leaving the country; but things are not finally settled. However, we are to fall back to Jalalabad to-morrow or the next day. In the present disturbed state of the country we may expect opposition on the road, and we are likely to suffer much from cold and hunger, as we expect to have no carriage for tents and superfluities."

A few days later another letter from Pottinger arrived, written in French for greater security. (Rather oddly, he had also taken for the same reason to signing his name in Greek characters —ποττιγγερ). "Notre situation devient perilleuse de plus en plus," he wrote; the chiefs were finding all sorts of excuses to delay Elphinstone's departure, and their promises were worthless; accordingly, any orders that might purport to come from Macnaghten for the evacuation of Jalalabad should be ignored, and Sale must stand fast until he received further instructions.

The further instructions were brought in next day by three

[1] "I am truly sorry for him", wrote Broadfoot, when he heard of Macnaghten's death; "his late firmness redeemed many errors."

swaggering Afghan insurgents, who handed in a formal letter to Macgregor, signed by both Pottinger and Elphinstone, stating that it was their wish that Sale should at once evacuate Jalalabad, leaving behind all his artillery and such stores and baggage as the brigade could not carry with it. When Sale laid the letter before his Jackdaw Parliament, Broadfoot and Havelock hotly opposed the suggestion of evacuation. The latter had already written to his old commander in India, General Sir Harry Smith, to tell him that "there is a force at Jalalabad which would, I trust, sooner bury itself under its ruins than be saved by a convention, and which ardently desires, when reinforced, to be led against the treacherous and sanguinary foe, which has butchered our ambassador and must be defeated, if we would save our own in India".

Sale needed little urging to stay put, for he had heard through Macgregor that letters had arrived from Akbar Khan urging the tribes round Jalalabad to rise and attack the British. Clearly, treachery was intended, and in that case the retention of Jalalabad would be of great value to the force retreating from Kabul. Sale decided that it was his duty to hold Jalalabad and await a further communication from Elphinstone, "which," he wrote in his reply, "we desire may point out the security which may be given for our safe march to Peshawar". At the same time he reported to the Commander-in-Chief, Sir Jasper Nicholls, that in the absence of all instructions from India he considered himself free to refuse to be bound by the Kabul convention, "which was forced from our Envoy and military commander with the knives at their throats"; if he could be reinforced from Peshawar before his ammunition and provisions were exhausted, he would hold Jalalabad for the Government.

There was nothing that Sale's troops could do to assist the Kabul force except watch and wait, and it was as well that there was plenty of work to keep them from brooding too much on what might be happening in the western passes. A letter from Lawrence had come through, dated 4th January, stating that the force was to march next day. "Whether we are attacked on the road depends upon their good faith," he wrote. "I believe we do not run very much risk as far as Jugdulluk, except from the weather, which is very severe here." On 12th January another message came in from Elphinstone's force, reporting that it had left cantonments but had been held up for two days in the Boothak area; Akbar Khan was escorting them with cavalry but they believed that he had sent his emissaries ahead to rouse the tribes to attack them.

This, the last message to get through, filled Sale and his officers with despair, and on that day the whole garrison felt a strange uneasiness, a deep instinctive foreboding that some dreadful calamity had occurred. Sale and a few of his staff were, as usual, on the flat roof of the highest house in Jalalabad, levelling their telescopes westwards across the plain to where the Kabul road debouched from the hills, when Colonel Dennie was suddenly moved to prophesy. "You will see," he told the others; "you will see; not a soul will reach here from Kabul except one man, who will come to tell us the rest are destroyed."

Next afternoon, 13th January, there were again watchers on the roof top. Let Havelock, who was one of them, tell the story in his own words. "One of us espied a single horseman riding towards our walls. As he got nearer, it was distinctly seen that he wore European clothes and was mounted on a travel-hacked yaboo, which he was urging on with all the speed of which it yet remained master. A signal was made to him by someone on the walls, which he answered by waving a private soldier's forage cap over his head. The Caubul gate was then thrown open and several officers, rushing out, received and recognised in the traveller the first, and it is to be feared the last, fugitive of the ill-fated force at Caubul in Dr. Brydon."

At that moment the voice of Dennie was heard again, sounding it was later remembered, like an oracle of doom: "Did I not say so? Here comes the messenger."

The tragedy foretold by General Keane more than two years before had been consummated.

PART V

THE AFTERMATH

I

THE bad news from Afghanistan made its way to India by instalments, each more calamitous than its predecessor, and when the news reached Auckland at the end of November that Kabul had risen and that Burnes had been murdered, he was appalled. As his period of office drew to its close he had been looking forward to handing over a peaceful realm to his successor, Lord Ellenborough. Only a day or two earlier there had been letters from Macnaghten, confidently reassuring him that the disturbances were at an end. Now the Governor-General's eyes were opened. Afghanistan—serene and prosperous Afghanistan—was up in arms against its deliverers. The tranquillity of the country, boasted of in Kabul and believed in Calcutta, was suddenly seen to be a great delusion. "Across the length and breadth of the land," wrote Kaye, in a fine purple passage, "the history of that gigantic lie was written in characters of blood." The fact was that the Afghans were Afghans still, "still a nation of fierce Mahomedans, of hardy warriors, of independent mountaineers; still a people not to be dragooned into peace or awed into submission by a scattering of foreign bayonets and the pageantry of a puppet King."

Auckland reeled under the blow and it was rumoured that by day he was pacing for hours up and down the verandahs of Government House, by night throwing himself down on the lawn to press his face in anguish of spirit against the turf. Yet he kept his head and refused to send reinforcements blindly to the rescue, a step which he foresaw might well amount to throwing good money after bad. "It is not clear to me," he wrote at the end of November, "how the march of a brigade can by any possibility have any influence upon the events which it is supposed may be passing at Caubul. The difficulty will not be one of fighting and gaining victories, but of supplies, of movements and of carriage . . . the troops in Afghanistan are sufficiently numerous. They would but be encumbered by greater numbers, and reinforcements could not arrive before the crisis will have passed. If the end is to be disastrous, they would but increase the extent of the disaster. . . . I fear that safety to the force at Caubul can only come from itself."

This clear-sighted view found ready acceptance with Auckland's Commander-in-Chief, Sir Jasper Nicholls. "I really would not advise," wrote Nicholls, "our forcing either Soojah or ourselves upon a nation so distant and in all respects so dissimilar both to our Sepoys and ourselves, at an expense so decidedly ruinous . . . that we have no base of operations has always been clear; but now, were we to march a reinforcement on the best horses, we could not be sure of carrying the Khyber Pass, and if snow has fallen, the road to Caubul would still be closed."

There was, no doubt, good reason for believing that all thought of a reconquest of Afghanistan should be abandoned and that Elphinstone must be left to extricate himself from the net in which he had become enmeshed. But prestige, which really meant the security of British rule in North-West India, and perhaps even further afield, demanded an honourable withdrawal from the country. It was reluctantly borne in upon Auckland that, for this reason alone, a relief force would have to be sent; early in January, two days before Elphinstone marched from Kabul, two brigades were ordered to cross the Sutlej and concentrate at Peshawar.

When it came to appointing a commander for the relief force Auckland, incorrigible in this respect, did his best to saddle it with a second Elphinstone in the shape of the Adjutant-General, Major-General Lumley, who was yet another of the elderly invalids whom the Governor-General was so apt to favour. Lumley had recently been seriously ill and was described by Nicholls as "still very weak, though improved in health". Fortunately, he had the good sense to suggest that his appointment be made conditional upon a medical examination and the doctors were so emphatic that his state of health "would by no means admit of the required exertion and exposure" that even Auckland could no longer press his claims.

In the event the choice fell upon George Pollock, the Major-General commanding the Agra garrison. The appointment gave general satisfaction for he was a veteran of the Company's army and it was plain that neither snobbery nor nepotism had played any part in the choice. He was by now a somewhat venerable figure, for he had first arrived in India in 1803. He had seen plenty of fighting in his younger days though it was, perhaps, a disadvantage that he had not seen a shot fired in anger since the Burmese War of 1824; fortunately there had been little or no change in tactics or weapons since that date. He was, at least, calm and imperturbable, a rock of common sense. Broadfoot summed it up very well: "General Pollock, if not a Napoleon, is superior to any general officer I have yet chanced to meet in these regions."

As Pollock moved up from Agra to Peshawar to take over his command, he was confronted by three problems. What was to be done about the British garrisons still holding out at Kandahar, Jalalabad and Ghuznee? What was to be done about the British prisoners in Afghan hands? And what was to be done about Shah Soojah, who was still roosting uncomfortably in the Balla Hissar at Kabul, his constitutional position now increasingly obscure?

2

The news presently reached India that, surprisingly, Soojah still reigned in Kabul. After the initial success of the rising, feuds and jealousies had wrought such dissension among the Afghan chiefs that John Conolly, now their prisoner in Kabul, likened them to a set of Yorks and Lancasters. Among the older chieftains there was growing resentment at the rising power of Akbar Khan and there was, too, a strong feeling that Soojah was the person best able to mitigate the vengeance which the British were now expected to exact. He was therefore allowed to continue as King and Zemaun Shah, the acting monarch, although coins continued to be minted in his name, cheerfully resigned his claim. Zemaun became Prime Minister, with malevolent old Amenoolah Khan as his deputy. Amenoolah was eager to get his clutches on Conolly and the other British prisoners in Kabul, but Zemaun resolutely kept them under his own protection and even raised a private army of three thousand men to thwart his deputy's bloodthirsty designs.

Soojah regarded these goings on with gloomy suspicion. He was bombarding Macgregor, Mackeson and even the Governor-General with letters protesting that, despite appearances, he had always been a true friend to the British: "between us there were no differences, and there will not be." The Barukzyes, he explained, had managed to make him appear in the worst light to both sides: "to the British they said that I had instigated the rebellion and to the Mahomedans they said that I and the Feringhees were one, until they made me generally unpopular. Well, such was fated! It has caused me much grief and regret." However, if the British would only send him plenty of money, all would yet be well and "I shall have these people so much under my control that, if I order it, they will carry the shoes of the Sahibs on their own heads". Indeed, he promised, given the money, he would not only settle Afghanistan but undertake the conquest of Persia and Teheran.

These wild promises smack of desperation and in his heart Soojah must have known that he had little chance of surviving the vendettas that were now raging. At the end of March, 1842, since Sale was still holding out at Jalalabad, the chiefs demanded that Soojah now prove his sincerity for the true faith by placing himself at the head of the Afghan troops and marching against the British. The King was understandably reluctant to leave the shelter of the Balla Hissar. "I scarcely believe that he will ever march," wrote Mohun Lal, who was still engaged in his own form of diplomacy in Kabul, "and if he does, he will either be murdered or made blind by the Barukzyes." Zemaun Khan, appreciating Soojah's fears, sent his wife to swear to the King on the Koran that the Barukzyes would be true to him, and thus reassured Soojah arrayed himself in royal attire and was carried in a chair of state to the Afghan camp on the Seeah Sung hills. Zemaun had acted in good faith, but his son, Soojah-ool-Dowlah (whose first name indicated that the King had been present at his birth and was, as it were, his god-father) had other ideas. He had ridden ahead with a gang of Jezailchees, who waited in ambush. As the royal party made its way to the pavilion a volley of shots rang out and Soojah fell dead, a bullet through his brain.

Ool-Dowlah rode up and, after contemplating the corpse with satisfaction, had it stripped of its jewels and finery and flung into a ditch. A few weeks later he visited Eyre and his fellow prisoners, who thought him "a handsome quiet-looking man, whom few would have guessed to be the perpetrator of such a deed". But his father, Zemaun, swore with horror that never again should the murderer set foot in his house nor his name be mentioned in his presence.

Some sympathy might have been spared for Soojah as his long life of misfortune came to its predictably violent end, for he seems to have been by no means as bad as some people chose to paint him. Admittedly, he was not as attractive a character as the brave and freedom-loving Dost Mahomed and when the British, for their own ends, dredged him up from his comfortable exile in Ludhiana he was elderly, stout, pompous and unheroic. But he showed an imperturbable courage under fire, as at Ghuznee; he always behaved towards his British allies with a dignified courtesy and cut a not unreasonable figure for one compelled to run with the Afghan hare and hunt with the British hounds. He showed little skill in the art of government, not that the British gave him much scope to exercise it, but he was not brutal.[1]

Before long a number of British officers, perhaps unconsciously seeking for a scapegoat to explain the disaster, had persuaded themselves that Soojah had throughout been playing a double game of the blackest treachery and had been at the bottom of the whole insurrection. Mackeson, for example, wrote from Peshawar that to his mind "there had ever appeared but little doubt that his Majesty Shah Soojah was, in the commencement, the instigator of the Caubul insurrection". Macgregor was less certain: "I must agree with you," he wrote, "in thinking that the Shah was more or less implicated in the insurrection; but when he saw that it took such a serious turn, I really believe that he repented—even so soon as he heard of Burnes' assassination." The accusation seems outrageous; Soojah's behaviour from the very first day of the rising belied it and Lawrence, as we have seen, thought that Soojah was a good deal more faithful to his British allies than they were to him. Rawlinson, too, down at Kandahar, is a witness for the defence. "From everything I can learn," he wrote, "I should certainly say that the Shah was well inclined to us. . . . He has certainly done as little as he could, keeping up appearances with the Mussulman party, to complicate our position at this place." Most convincing of all is the evidence of John Conolly, who throughout was able to observe the Shah from close quarters in the Balla Hissar. "I believe that he is heart and soul in our interest," he wrote on 17th January, "it is contrary to all reason to suppose otherwise." There is a ring of truth, too, in a letter written by Soojah to the Governor-General about the middle of January. "I told the Envoy that sooner or later there would be a disturbance, but he listened not to me; I told him that they were deceiving him but he believed me not, and desired me to be at ease, for that he would settle the country with two Pultuns;[2] I sent word to the Envoy to come with all his baggage to the Balla Hissar, where the troops could hold out for a year or two, telling him that three or four thousand of the inhabitants might be turned out, and guns and stores brought. After much debate, no answer was given. I said, 'Very good! Please yourselves!'"

[1] J. K. Stanford (*Ladies in the Sun*) says that Soojah "had been originally deposed for cruelty, and if an Afghan is noted for that, it must be exceptional cruelty". The grounds for this statement are not stated. In fact Soojah seems to have been rather more humane than most Afghan rulers, and by the standards of his contemporaries even the massacre of the Ghazi prisoners (p. 99) was not unreasonable.

[2] Regiments.

The good faith of Akbar Khan was much more questionable. Right to the last he had protested that he and his horsemen were only accompanying the Kabul force in order to protect it, and loudly lamented his inability to control "those dogs of Ghilzyes". Johnson had heard him plead with apparent sincerity that the lives of the defeated enemy should be spared, and the sorrow which he expressed to Lady Macnaghten over her husband's death (he declared that he would give his right arm that the deed he so much regretted might be undone) seemed to be genuine.[1] On the other hand, there was no denying that matters had come to pass exactly as the British had been warned that Akbar intended. He can hardly have regretted that they should have been taught a terrible lesson that might deter them from ever again threatening the independence of his country. Eldred Pottinger, for one, had little doubt about Akbar's real intentions. He and Mackenzie, as hostages, had been riding with Akbar's party as it followed Elphinstone's force into the jaws of the Khoord-Kabul pass. "Mackenzie, *remember*!" said Pottinger with great emphasis, "if I am killed, I heard the Sirdar shout 'Slay them!' in Pushtu, though he ordered them to stop firing in Persian, imagining that we should understand the last, and not the first."

Perhaps the most that can be safely attributed to Akbar is a genuine desire to save the lives of as many of the British as he could, provided that the prospects of a resounding British defeat were not impaired. To the British prisoners in his hands he almost invariably showed a chivalrous courtesy. But to the Indians, whether soldiers, camp-followers, women or children, he was utterly without pity.

3

The British party handed over to Akbar for safe keeping on 9th January had consisted of seven officers, ten officers' wives or widows, and thirteen children, seven of whom were Mrs. Trevor's; Sergeant Wade "and family" brought up the rear. Presently they would join up with Elphinstone, Shelton and Johnson, and with the three original hostages, Pottinger, Lawrence and Mackenzie, together with children such as Hugh Boyd and little Seymour Stoker, who had been rescued from the maelstrom. Thereafter the party of captives was continually being swelled by the odd

[1] The widow, says Lady Sale, "sate in silent sorrow before him". Mackenzie thought that Akbar spoke "in grave mockery".

straggler, such as Lieutenant Melville, Captain Souter (still wearing the regimental colours round his waist) and others.

Harrowing sights had met their eyes as they were led back along the line of the retreat towards Tezeen. The road was strewn with the mangled corpses of their comrades and the stench of death was in the air. "The sight was dreadful," wrote Lady Sale, "the smell of the blood sickening; and the corpses lay so thick it was impossible to look from them, as it required care to guide my horse so as not to tread upon the bodies." Sometimes they recognised the dead faces of officers with whom they had been conversing a day or two before, Major Scott, Major Ewart, Dr. Bryce; further on they passed the last of the Horse Artillery guns, its carriage still smouldering and the bodies of Dr. Cardew and several gunners stretched beside it; they came upon the corpse of Dr. Duff, the chief medical officer, who a little earlier, to no purpose after all, had let Dr. Harcourt amputate his left hand with a pen-knife. At Jugdulluk they recognised the body of Captain Skinner and for him, at least, they were able to win from Akbar the tribute of a decent burial.

All along the route they had been passing little groups of camp-followers, starving, frost-bitten and many of them in a state of gibbering idiocy. The Afghans, not troubling to kill these stragglers, had simply stripped them and left the cold to do its work and now the poor wretches were huddling together naked in the snow, striving hopelessly to keep warm by the heat of their own bodies. There were women and little children among them, who piteously stretched out their hands for succour to Lady Sale and her companions as they passed. Later the Afghans were to report with relish that the unhappy fugitives, in their blind instinct to preserve life a little longer, had been reduced to eating the corpses of their fellows. But they all died in the end.

From time to time savagely triumphant Ghilzyes crowded round the hostages, brandishing their long bloodstained knives and yelling at the British to look well upon the heaps of corpses around them, for they would themselves soon be among them. "You came to Kabul for fruit, did you?" they jeered. "How do you like it now?" Lawrence was appealed to by a wounded sergeant of the 44th who called out, "For God's sake, Captain Lawrence, don't leave me here." At first his only wound seemed to be the loss of his left hand but when Lawrence, with two of the Afghan escort, started to lift him, it was seen with horror that "from the nape of his neck to his backbone he had been cut to pieces". The Afghans pointed out that he could not live many minutes and that the only thing to do was to leave him. "For God's sake, shoot me," pleaded the wounded man, but Lawrence could not bring himself to do so. "Then leave me here to die," replied the sergeant.

A little further on Lawrence recognised the body of a veteran subadar of the Envoy's bodyguard, Appumbul Singh. The Afghans reported with admiration that he had been offered his life if he would go over to them, but had sturdily replied, "No; for forty-one years I have eaten the Company's salt and I will now show myself ready to die for them."

The little band of English prisoners now made its way over stupendous passes, along the beds of mountain streams, passing springs "whose waters, arrested by the frost, hung suspended in long glittering icicles from the rocks",[1] until at length they came to what was intended to be their permanent abode in captivity, the fortress of Budeeabad. They had long realised that all the earlier talk of escorting them in safety to Jalalabad had gone for nothing; they were now Akbar's most valuable bargaining counter. All were agreed, however, that the behaviour of their Afghan captors had been beyond reproach. It was only their escort that saved them from having their throats cut by the bands of Ghazis that crossed their path. In one village they had to run the gauntlet of the sharp tongues of Afghan women, who pronounced the English ladies "not only immoral in character but downright scarecrows in appearance, and the gentlemen 'dogs', 'base-born', 'infidels', 'devils', with many other unpronounceable titles, equally complimentary, the whole being wound up with an assurance of certain death to our whole party ere many hours should elapse".[1] But the escort were throughout attentive to the safety of the women and children, and Eyre "found the Afghan gentry most agreeable travelling companions, possessing a ready fund of easy conversation and pleasantry, with a certain rough polish and artless independence of manner which, compared with the studied servility and smooth-tongued address of the Hindoostanee nobles, seldom fails to impress our countrymen in their favour".

The Afghans found it in no way inconsistent with their courtesy to relieve their prisoners of any material wealth upon which they could get their clutches. Thus Moossa Khan, who had been appointed quartermaster and major-domo to the captives, not only bullied Lady Macnaghten into giving him numerous presents of costly Cashmere shawls but twice himself stole her favourite cat in order to claim the reward of twenty rupees which she offered

[1] Eyre.

on each occasion. But then Moossa Khan, whom Lawrence described as "a man of indifferent character and low habits", was "so little restrained by scruples as to pass for a most consummate rogue, even among Afghans".[1]

The prisoners settled down to make themselves as comfortable as they could at Budeeabad. The food was one of the minor tribulations of their life, the daily diet consisting of rice, untempting lumps of tough mutton boiled to rags and thick half-baked cakes of unleavened dough. Matters improved when the crude Afghan cooks were persuaded to retire from the scene and the cooking was taken over by the prisoners' own Indian servants, who had faithfully followed their masters and mistresses into captivity. The absence of washing facilities and clean linen was another hardship to which the British soon became accustomed. "The first discovery of a real living l-o-u-s-e was a severe shock to our fine sense of delicacy," wrote Eyre, "but custom reconciles folk to anything, and even the ladies eventually mustered up resolution to look one of these intruders in the face without a scream".

The ladies' recovery of their morale was not an unmixed blessing, for snobbery, catty behaviour and selfishness soon made their appearance. Some of them, for example, "gave themselves great airs towards Mrs. Riley", which Mackenzie thought "not only most unfeeling but absurd; Conductor Riley and his wife were very superior people, he being a gentleman's son who had enlisted". Then again, Eyre's wife, who had only one gown, tried to borrow another from a lady who had trunks full, only to be rebuffed by the answer that she could not spare any. Mrs. Eyre was also short of needles and persuaded Mackenzie to try to wheedle one or two out of Lady Sale, who had plenty. He never exercised greater diplomacy in his life, he said later, but he failed. One result was that for the rest of his life, to the amusement of his friends, Mackenzie could not resist picking up every needle or pin that he saw.

Akbar, who frequently turned up to visit his prisoners and always talked to them with kindness and courtesy, did his best to improve their lot by supplying them with money, with which they could buy sugar and other little delicacies, with lengths of cloth and with needles and thread. Lawrence was given the task of distributing these gifts among the ladies, but found it so thankless that he quickly handed it over to a committee of three, on which he resolutely refused to serve. There was, however, one shining

[1] Eyre.

exception to the general selfishness, the young and merry Mrs. Mainwaring, who "on receiving a box of useful articles from her husband at Jalalabad, most liberally distributed the contents among the other ladies, who were much in need".[1]

Throughout January and February the boredom of their prison life was occasionally enlivened for the prisoners by the arrival of others who had escaped the final massacre. Major Griffiths and the other prisoners taken at Gandamack turned up in mid-February and a week later Captain Bygrave, the Paymaster, was brought in. He had got through the holly-oak barriers at Jugdulluk and with Mr. Baness, the enterprising merchant who had volunteered to drive the Afghans from the Kabul cantonments, had endeavoured to make his way to Jalalabad. They had travelled by night, lying up by day in the cover of the long rushes of a stream bed or under the thick foliage of evergreen shrubs. Their only food was a few dry grains of coffee, of which Baness had a pocketful, and some wild liquorice root which they found growing in the bed of the Sourkab river. After four days and nights of this harsh existence Bygrave, exhausted, and lame from frost-bite and worn-out shoes, declared that he could go no further and would throw himself on the mercy of the first Afghan he met. Baness replied that, for the sake of his large family, he must do his best to reach Jalalabad. Twice he started off and twice returned to try to persuade Bygrave to accompany him, but the Paymaster was finished. Left alone, he was lucky next day to find an Afghan friendly enough to take him to Akbar, and so he arrived at Budeeabad, "in a very weak state, having suffered much from frost in one foot, and having entirely lost the ends of his toes".[2] In his case the Afghan remedy for frost-bite, a cold poultice of cow-dung and water which, says Mackenzie, "proved most efficacious", was presumably applied too late. Meanwhile poor Mr. Baness with great determination managed to reach Jalalabad but was "in a dreadful state from lock-jaw, brought on by exposure and suffering, and died shortly after his arrival".[3]

On 19th February the prisoners had a terrifying experience, when Budeeabad was struck by an earthquake. It had been a morning of unusual warmth and stillness and at about 11 a.m. "a loud subterranean rumbling was heard, as of a boiling sea of liquid lava, and wave after wave seemed to lift up the ground on which we stood, causing every building to rock to and fro like a floating vessel".[4] Walls fell on all sides with a thundering crash

[1] Mackenzie. [2] Eyre.
[3] Lawrence. [4] Eyre.

and a building in the courtyard suddenly disappeared "as though through a trap door, disclosing a yawning chasm".[1] Everyone rushed into the open air and no one was injured. Lady Sale descended from a roof top with unladylike haste and old Elphinstone, bedridden with gout and dysentery, was carried to safety in the arms of his devoted batman, Private Moore of the 44th. "The poor General," said Eyre, "notwithstanding all that had occurred to cloud his fame, was greatly beloved by the soldiery, of whom there were few who would not have acted in a similar manner to save his life."

Brigadier Shelton had cut his escape fine. He had been sitting smoking a hookah on a roof with Mackenzie, the only officer with whom he was now on speaking terms, and had looked round angrily to see who was shaking the bench. "It's an earthquake, Brigadier," cried Mackenzie, and the two officers scrambled down the steps only just in time. Now, as the tremors subsided and willing hands set to work to dig Lady Macnaghten's precious cats from the ruins, Shelton re-established the military proprieties. "Mackenzie," he said, speaking "in a solemn tone to make him feel the enormity of his offence", "Mackenzie, you went downstairs *first* today." "So I did," replied the impenitent Mackenzie cheerfully, "I'm sorry; it's the fashion in earthquakes, Brigadier."

The prisoners were not wholly without amusements at Budeeabad. They had books, some of which were bought from Afghans who had picked them up along the line of the retreat and brought them in for sale. They had a few packs of old dog-eared playing cards and some home-made backgammon and draught boards; the occasional letter and out-of-date newspaper arrived from Jalalabad. The newspapers told more than was apparent to Afghan eyes, for individual letters had been unobtrusively marked with dots so as to form words and sentences and by this simple cipher the prisoners learnt of such events as the despatch of General Pollock to Peshawar and Brydon's arrival at Jalalabad.

For more strenuous recreation Lawrence used to race the Afghan guards round the courtyard every morning, generally managing to beat them, and "felt all the better for the excitement as well as the exercise". Then there was hopscotch and blind man's buff, which was a favourite game, "and when some ten or fifteen healthy and cheerful little boys joined in the sport, the mirth ran fast and furious".[1] The presence of the British children undoubtedly helped to warm the hearts of the Afghan gaolers

[1] Eyre.

towards their captives, for the Afghans were always fond of children. Sultan Jan, for example, Akbar's dashing and vain-glorious cousin, whenever he visited the prisoners, would always ask for his special favourite, little Edward Trevor. The fact that he had played a leading part in the murder of Edward's father did not seem to embarrass him in the slightest.

All things considered, the prisoners' spirits kept remarkably high, but there was at least one joker among them whose sense of humour was altogether excessive. Captain Johnson was woken one morning with the wonderful news that a letter had come in from Macgregor at Jalalabad; a ransom had been agreed and the prisoners were to start for home in five or six days' time. Johnson sprang up and rushed out, to find that the story was already all round the fort and was being eagerly discussed by the servants as well as the Europeans. Then, with a sense of sickening dismay, he remembered that it was April 1st and that the story was "all fudge". One can sympathise with him for feeling "half mad with rage at being made such an April fool of, on a subject which, of all others in our situation, should have been the last for any of our party to have expended his wit upon". At the time this heartless jest was perpetrated more than five months of captivity still lay ahead. Meanwhile the fate of the prisoners would largely hang on what happened at Jalalabad.

4

By mid-February, when it was known that Akbar and his army were on their way to attack Jalalabad, Broadfoot's labours on the fortifications had transformed the town into a very defensible stronghold, the parapets raised, the ramparts repaired, the bastions extended and a ten-foot deep ditch dug right round the walls. Now, in the twinkling of an eye, most of this devoted labour went for nothing. On 19th February the earthquake, of which we have already heard at Budeeabad, hit the town. There was a deep rumble like underground thunder, the earth shook, houses quivered and fell, the ramparts swayed and came down with a crash. "Now is the time for Akbar Khan," commented Broadfoot laconically as he saw his defences fall one after another. Sale, who was corresponding with Pollock in a quaint mixture of English and French which would scarcely have deceived a child, reported that "the dreadful earthquake of this day a fait tomber deux bastions. . . . Sans doute l'ennemi prend avantage de cet cala-mité". If the town had been bombarded for a month, he added, it could hardly have suffered more damage than the earthquake wreaked in a few seconds.

The Afghan army, camping in the open, had suffered no harm and Akbar's immediate conclusion was that the Almighty had obligingly intervened on his behalf to destroy the fortifications of the infidel. He had to wait a few days, while his men hastened to the neighbouring villages to assure themselves that their families were all right, and he then advanced upon Jalalabad, confidently expecting to find its defences laid flat by the hand of Allah. But Broadfoot had used those few days of grace to good purpose and the garrison had laboured manfully. Akbar was astonished and chagrined to find that the ditches had been cleared, the breaches filled and the ramparts doubled in strength. He concluded that Jalalabad alone had escaped the earthquake and that this phenomenon could only be ascribed to powerful English witchcraft.

Havelock, however, who never missed an opportunity to preach the virtues of total abstinence, had another explanation. There were no spirits, supernatural or otherwise, in Jalalabad. "If there had been a spirit ration, one-third of the labour would have been diminished in consequence of soldiers becoming the inmates of the hospital and guard houses, or coming to their work with fevered brain and trembling hand, or sulky and disaffected, after the protracted debauch. Now all is health, cheerfulness, industry and resolution."[1]

This was just as well, for Pollock was taking what the Jalalabad garrison thought was an unconscionably long time in coming to their relief. Though they could not know it, he had good reason for delay, having arrived at Peshawar to find that the leading brigade, Brigadier Wild commanding, had already been soundly trounced in the Khyber and had retreated in disorder to Peshawar with morale at a low ebb. The fugitives had done their best to spread pessimism, loudly asserting that the Khyber was impregnable. Nor was this defeatist spirit confined to the sepoys, for one British officer was openly proclaiming that it would be better to sacrifice Sale's brigade than to risk the loss of 12,000 men on the march to Jalalabad; another said that if an advance were ordered, he would do his best to dissuade every sepoy of his corps from again entering the pass.

In such a situation Elphinstone would have been racked with indecision, but fortunately Pollock was not an Elphinstone. Patiently but firmly he set about restoring the morale of his force,

[1] Marshman.

nursing them back to physical and mental health. Throughout February and March he remained at Peshawar, collecting his strength and determined not to move until success was assured, even though this meant resisting the increasingly urgent appeals now coming in from Sale. Hunger had become the main threat to the garrison. "Nous avons des provisionnements pour les soldats Brittanniques pour soixante-dix jours," Sale had written in mid-February: "pour les Sipahis et les autres natifs demi-provisionnements pour le même temps." The time was nearly up. But Pollock was ready at last, and on 5th April he ordered his troops to advance into the Khyber.

Avitabile, who still ruled at Peshawar for the Sikh government, was convinced that Pollock's force was going to certain destruction. He thought, apparently, that they would simply march straight ahead into the jaws of the pass, where they would surely meet the fate that had overtaken Elphinstone in Khoord-Kabul and Jugdulluk. But Pollock knew a trick worth two of that. Flanking parties swarmed up and over the hills, clambered up the precipitous sides of the pass and poured down a hot fire upon the disconcerted Afghans. The heights were crowned, the flanks of the enemy position turned; then, and not till then, the main body moved up and through the pass.[1] The Afghans melted away like snow in summer, and a few days later, with bands playing and colours flying, Pollock arrived at Jalalabad. But Sale's garrison too could raise a band and now, with a humour that had a bite in it, they played the relieving force in to the old Jacobite tune, "Oh, but ye've been lang o'coming."

Glad though they were to see Pollock's force, the Jalalabad garrison had, in fact, saved themselves already by their own exertions. On 1st April the threat of starvation had been averted when the garrison made a sudden sortie and in high glee drove in a flock of five hundred sheep and goats which the Afghan herdsmen had incautiously allowed to graze too near the walls. The Afghans were furious and Akbar swore to have the sheep back.

[1] Pollock had been insufficiently supplied with ammunition and was very short of transport. Broadfoot speaks of "the wretched way in which the force was equipped and provided; not a thought seems to have been bestowed on the nature of the country or the probable operations of the force". Pottinger commented that Pollock had been saddled with "some of the worst officers in the army". It is therefore the more remarkable that this was the first time in history that the Khyber had been carried by force of arms. Both Tamerlaine and Nadir Shah bought a safe passage from the Afridis. Akbar the Great, in 1587, was said to have lost 40,000 men in attempting to force the pass and Aurangzeb, in the seventeenth century, failed to get through.

He had better look sharp, then, commented Captain Backhouse, "as the flock is going the way of all flesh pretty fast". It was quickly rationed out to the troops and the 35th Native Infantry came forward with the request that, as meat was more necessary for Europeans than Indians, their share should be given to the 13th Light Infantry, "between whom and themselves there existed a romantic friendship which ought not to be forgotten".[1]

A week later Sale's Brigade had done even better. Again they sallied forth, advanced upon Akbar, who was waiting with six thousand men to receive them, attacked and routed him, captured his camp, retook four guns lost by Elphinstone and burnt Akbar's tents to the ground. "In short," said the official despatch, "the defeat of Akbar Khan in open field, by the troops whom he had boasted of blockading, has been complete and signal." Akbar took his defeat in sporting spirit and a few days later, visiting the British prisoners at Budeeabad, called George Lawrence over to him and "spoke in a free and soldierly manner of Sale's victory and his own defeat, praising the gallant bearing of our men, which nothing could exceed, with Sale conspicuous on his white charger at their head".

This unlooked-for British victory, marred only by the death in action of the veteran Dennie, was much to the liking of the new Governor-General, Lord Ellenborough, who had succeeded the unhappy Auckland in the second half of February. A flamboyant character, who wrote that although it was his misfortune not to be a soldier he knew how to appreciate soldierly qualities and soldierly acts, Ellenborough now celebrated Sale's victory with a resounding Order of the Day, which was to "be carefully made known to all troops, and a salute of twenty-one guns fired at every principal station of the army". In this proclamation Ellenborough referred to the defenders of Jalalabad as "that illustrious garrison" and the name stuck; the "Illustrious Garrison" they were from that day on, and Sale was a hero.

In this there was something of irony, for Sale had been forced into the heroic role only by the determination of his junior officers. After Brydon's arrival Fighting Bob had seen nothing for it but the immediate abandonment of Jalalabad and a negotiated retreat to Jalalabad. What was more, initially, all his Council of War save one agreed with him, after a session whose transactions are described by Fortescue as "the most astonishing, and perhaps the most disgraceful, recorded in the annals of the Army". It was left

[1] Mackenzie. In the National Army Museum can be seen the silver dish presented to the 35th by the British regiment as a memento of this friendship.

to the fiery, red-bearded, bespectacled Broadfoot alone to attack this pusillanimous proposal with a vehemence so incoherent that the rest of the Jackdaw Parliament burst into cackles of derisive laughter. Havelock, who was present but, not being a member of the Council, unable to speak, then quietly showed Broadfoot how to marshal his arguments in more orderly fashion and between them they won the members of the Council, one by one, to a policy, of "No Surrender". With the deepest misgivings Sale had bowed to the wishes of his subordinates.

Similarly, Sale—"stupid, unteachable old Sale" as Fortescue calls him—had been most reluctant to sanction the attack which had culminated in the capture of Akbar's camp. Havelock had been urging this course for days, but it was only when the senior officers came in a deputation to the General and pressed him to attack that he consented. "I love the old soldier," wrote Havelock, "and rejoice that, though he did not listen to my single voice, he was swayed by the united opinion of some older and some younger men, since it redounded to his own reputation and to the good of his country." It did indeed, and although the real credit belonged to Broadfoot and Havelock it was Sale, when he returned to India, who was everywhere greeted by bands playing "See, the Conquering Hero Comes!"

Meanwhile, however, it was still April and Pollock and Sale remained immobile at Jalalabad. From the end of the month onwards the heat became savage, with temperatures of 110° in the shade, and all who could lived in underground chambers called ty-khanas. Broadfoot headed one of his letters at this time "from my den six feet underground". He had been wounded in one of the sorties and Surgeon Brown peered anxiously into the dhooli in which he was carried back to the town, expecting to be told of his wound. He found Broadfoot contemplating his sword, which was covered with the blood and brains of an adversary, and thoughtfully remarking "Well, Brown, I had no idea a man's head was so soft."

Everyone was wondering what the next move was to be. The new Governor-General had been making a number of warlike noises which were greatly to the taste of those who believed that for the sake of British dominance in India the Afghans must receive signal chastisement. Ellenborough was fond of repeating that "India was won by the sword and must be maintained by the sword", and in a despatch of 15th March he had impressively declared that "in war, reputation is strength". All the greater, therefore, was the shock when on the very day that he had proclaimed the renown of the Illustrious Garrison he instructed his Commander-in-Chief, Jasper Nicholls, to issue orders to Pollock and Nott to withdraw from Afghanistan as speedily as possible. The recipients of the order were aghast. "The peremptory order to retire has come upon us like a thunderclap," wrote Rawlinson from Kandahar, for the order implied, incredibly, that the captives in Akbar's hands were to be abandoned to their fate. It was now remembered in Auckland's favour that "after the outbreak, he did all that was done. The whole of the force with which Pollock made his victorious march was sent up by Auckland; not a man was added to it by Ellenborough."[1] Moreover, Auckland's anxiety for the prisoners stood out in shining contrast to his successor's apparently callous disregard. "You will consider it *one of the first objects of your solicitude*," he had emphasised in his last directive to Pollock, in February, "to procure the release of British officers and soldiers, and their families, private soldiers and followers."

Nott and Rawlinson kept quiet about Ellenborough's order to retire, while Pollock adopted delaying tactics, producing a multitude of reasons to explain why retirement at the moment was out of the question. The argument continued through May, June and into July, when Ellenborough solved the problem by throwing the whole burden of decision upon his generals in the field. He wrote to Nott informing him that, although the decision to withdraw from Afghanistan must stand, the general might, if he chose, retreat by way of Kabul. At the same time he told Pollock that if Nott decided to take this course he "might advance to the capital and co-operate with that General". The Governor-General omitted to inform the Commander-in-Chief of what he had done and Sir Jasper Nicholls was left to explode in his diary that "Lord E.'s want of decent attention to my position is inexcusable".

If an immediate withdrawal from Afghanistan was intended, a retreat by way of Kabul was a very odd route indeed. Ellenborough had not attempted to minimise the burden of responsibility that he had put upon Nott. "It (retreat via Kabul)," he wrote to him, "is an object of just ambition, which no one more than myself would rejoice to see effected; but I see that failure in the attempt is certain and irretrievable ruin, and I would endeavour to inspire you with the necessary caution, and make you feel that, great as are the objects to be attained by success, the risk is great also."

Pollock's fear was that Nott might have already begun to re-

[1] Mackenzie.

treat to India before getting Ellenborough's letter giving him the choice. Provided that the letter had arrived in time, Pollock who knew his Nott, had little doubt what that choice would be. "As I have offered to meet him," he wrote, "he will find some difficulty in resisting the *glorious* temptation; but if he does resist, he is not the man I take him for." In mid-August all doubts were removed by the arrival of a brief note from Nott stating that, having been given the option to retire via Kabul and Jalalabad, "I have determined to take that route". To Ellenborough, within four days of the arrival of his letter at Kandahar, had gone a similar curt and unhesitating reply: "I have come to the determination to retire a portion of the army under my command via Ghuznee and Caubul. I shall take with me not a large but a compact and well-tried force on which I can rely."

If little has been heard of General Nott since the outbreak at the beginning of the previous November it is because, largely by his own choice, he played little part in the fortunes of the Kabul force. To some observers there seemed in his behaviour something of a suspicion of Achilles sulking his tent, something of the Black Sluggard in the Ivanhoe tournament, dealing out hearty buffets to any enemies who showed an inclination to molest him but not moving from his base to give active help to others of his own side. Within a fortnight of Burnes' murder he was reporting sturdily to India that "whatever may be the result of the outbreak at Cabool and its neighbourhood, I have no doubt of being able to hold the country, i.e. in the neighbourhood of Candahar". But he made no attempt to hide his feelings when, in December, he had been ordered by Elphinstone to send Maclaren's brigade to assist at Kabul. "Remember," he told Maclaren, "the despatch of this brigade to Caubul is none of my doing. I am compelled to defer to superior authority, but in my own private opinion I am sending you all to destruction." With this discouraging envoi, it is not surprising that within a few days Maclaren had brought his brigade back to Kandahar reporting that with snow falling in the passes it would be impracticable to get his Brigade to Kabul in a state of efficiency. Nott readily agreed, and one brigade at least had been saved from the holocaust.

As danger and the prospect of action drew nearer, the General's spirits improved. "Many happy returns of the day to you, fair ladies," he wrote to his daughters on New Year's Day, 1842; "I suspect it will prove a very troublesome year for me, I hope nothing worse than troublesome. The Afghans ... have not yet assembled in what I would call a tangible shape; when they do we shall give them a good licking. I fancy they do not like our state of preparation. Ah well, they are funny fellows—and so I go to tiffin." Twelve days later, when an insurgent army nearly twenty thousand strong appeared outside Kandahar, Nott was as good as his word. Marching out with five and a half battalions of infantry, the Shah's 1st Cavalry and a handful of Skinner's Horse, with sixteen guns, he routed the enemy with ease.

By the end of the month more bad news had come through from Kabul. "We have just heard of Macnaghten's death," wrote Nott to his daughter on the 31st. "Poor fellow! his end was like the rest of his proceedings from the day we entered the country. He ought *not* to have trusted those wretched half-savage people; but his system was always wrong. I fear his three years' doings cannot be retrieved, and that our blood must flow for it. Have I not for two years told you that we were drawing down the deadly hatred of these people upon us?" Nott, however, had no doubt where his duty lay. "I never will retire," he wrote stoutly in mid-February, "unless I receive orders from Government; at any rate, come what may, I never will enter into a treaty for retiring, and hope no Englishman will." He had now been instructed from India that he was no longer to obey any orders coming, or purporting to come, from Elphinstone. A despatch signed by Auckland himself, and three other members of the Council, confirmed that it was "of the highest importance that you should maintain your position at Candahar in concentrated strength, until you shall receive the further orders of Government". The same directive added that "on our present information we are disposed to view the conduct of Major-General Elphinstone with the most severe displeasure and indignation".

Nott considered that he was given shamefully little help by Government in the task which they had laid upon him. "The people in power are all mad," he wrote angrily to his daughters towards the end of April, "or Providence hath blinded them for some wise purpose. I am very tired, tired of working, tired of this country, and quite tired of the folly of my countrymen. . . . My soldiers are four months in arrears, there is not one rupee in the Candahar Treasury, and no money can be borrowed. I have no medicine for the sick and wounded, I have no carriage cattle for the troops, nor money to buy or hire, and therefore cannot move. I have no good cavalry and but little ammunition, I have been calling for all these for six months, *but not the least aid* has been given me." Given even one regiment of decent cavalry he felt confident of being able to subdue the country. But he was given nothing, not even an indication of Government's ultimate intentions. "All I have now to do," he wrote to the Brigadier commanding the troops in Scinde, "is to uphold the honour of my country in the best manner I can, without the assistance above stated, and in ignorance of the intentions of the Government I serve."

The alacrity with which this testy veteran now seized upon the opportunity that Ellenborough had given him to advance upon Kabul was, at least in part, inspired by a determination to show the world what the Indian sepoy, properly led, could do. He regarded his men with a touching pride and affection. "I have now several times seen European troops under fire with sepoys alongside of them," he wrote to his daughters, "and, believe me, the more I see of sepoys, the more I like them; properly managed, they are the best troops in the world. Some John Bulls would hang me for saying this." It was a theme of which he never tired. "I tell you, I never saw troops in such high trim, full of zeal, in high spirits—cheerful laughing dogs. Looking at them the last time I was in the field with them, believe me, I felt the tear of pride and joy dim my eye."

The readiness of some English critics to make the sepoys the scapegoats for Elphinstone's disaster aroused Nott's violent resentment. "These are the men," he wrote, after extolling the sepoys' virtues, "whom it has become the fashion to reflect upon, that they cannot face the Afghans! Even the Press whine forth 'the sepoys cannot cope with Afghans. They cannot bear the cold, and we want more Europeans.' *We want better officers*! I have it in my power to *prove* that the *Bengal* sepoys *did* bear the cold better than Europeans, that there was a greater proportion of deaths from cold among the Europeans than among the sepoys, although the sepoys stood sentry day and night, in frost and snow, while the European was snug in his barrack!"

Nott himself had no doubt that the blame for the debacle lay higher up than the loyal and brave sepoy. "The keen wind blowing over the bleached bones of our comrades, now in heaps on the rugged Afghan mountains, will whistle the imbecility and infamy of some high functionaries over Asia.... And now, just like Englishmen, the cry is 'sepoys cannot stand Afghans'. Not stand Afghans, indeed! One thousand sepoys, properly managed, will always beat ten thousand Afghans." Now he proposed to make good the boast, and as he marched on Kabul from Kandahar early in August, he wrote proudly to the Governor-General that "I and my beautiful troops are in high spirits".

Pollock too was on the move. As soon as he heard of Nott's decision to "retire" by way of Kabul he had ordered an advance westwards from Jalalabad. "Hurrah!" wrote Sir Robert Sale, almost incoherent with delight when he received the order, "this is good news. *All* here are prepared to meet your wishes to march as light as possible. *I* take no carriage from the Commissariat, and our officers are doubling up *four* in a small hill tent. . . . *I am so excited that I can scarce write!*" And with the prospect of rescuing his wife and daughter from their long months of captivity in the hands of the Afghans, who could blame him?

Pollock's force was marching back along the line of Elphinstone's disastrous retreat, through Gandamack, Jugdulluk, Tezeen and, at the end of the road, Kabul. At every point they came upon ghastly evidence of the fate of the Kabul force. Rotting corpses and skeletons already picked clean by carrion met them at every turn. At Tezeen they found a pile of fifteen hundred corpses of Elphinstone's sepoys and camp followers, who had been stripped naked by the Afghans and left to die in the snow. In the Khoord-Kabul pass, wrote Captain Backhouse, "the sight of the remains of the unfortunate Caubul force was fearfully heartrending. They lay in heaps of fifties and hundreds, our gun-wheels passing over and crushing the skulls and other bones of our late comrades at almost every yard, for three, four or five miles."

Twice the Afghans massed to meet Pollock's advancing Army of Retribution, once at Jugdulluk and once, under the personal command of Akbar Khan, at Tezeen. But Pollock's men were not only fighting fit but had been filled with a cold rage at the sight of their slaughtered comrades along the road, and there was no stopping them. Undismayed by the fact that their muskets were hopelessly outranged by the enemy jezails, they swarmed up the heights, with Broadfoot and his little Gurkhas ever in the thick of the fight, and charged with the bayonet. The Afghans scattered like sheep before the men whose comrades, a few months before, they had slaughtered in the shambles of Jugdulluk. Akbar fled westwards and by 15th September Pollock's force was camping on the Kabul race-course and the British flag flew once more from the heights of the Balla Hissar. Two days later, with creditable synchronisation, Nott's Kandahar force came marching in.

5

It now only remained to secure the British prisoners' release, inflict some exemplary chastisement upon the Afghans, the exact form of which had not been settled, and withdraw from Afghanistan. Negotiations for the release of the prisoners had been begun in April when Akbar, impressed by the arrival of Pollock's force at Jalalabad following his own defeat by Sale, had begun to reconsider his position. To George Lawrence he admitted that he "now sorely repents of the part he has taken in late events" and explained that he had rejected with horror a bloodthirsty proposal that all the prisoners should now be put to death, each chief killing one with his own hand so that all should be equally guilty and beyond the pale of British mercy.

In April, therefore, in an effort to put himself in a better light, Akbar had sent Mackenzie on parole to Jalalabad with his proposals for the terms upon which the prisoners might be released, either in return for the withdrawal of the bulk of the British forces from Afghanistan or in exchange for Dost Mahomed and his family. Mackenzie's unexpected arrival at Jalalabad had caused great excitement among the garrison and he was moved almost to tears by the affection with which Broadfoot's tough jezailchis received him. They swarmed round him, kissing his hands, clinging to his clothes and even to his boots as he sat on horseback. Then, having agreed among themselves that Mackenzie Sahib must by now be very poor and very hungry, they clubbed together and came forward to present him with a bag of rupees and five sheep, "as if to make up at once for past starvation". They were themselves all in rags and had been seven months without pay.

Akbar, through Mackenzie, was asking more than Pollock was empowered to promise and Mackenzie ("the modern Regulus" Havelock called him) insisted on returning to captivity. Of all the Afghans only Akbar had expected Mackenzie to keep his word. A second mission (Mackenzie had been sent back by Akbar to Jalalabad after only seven hours' rest), fared no better than the first and the Afghans, expecting Pollock to advance at any moment, moved their captives from Budeeabad. Over barren hills and through stony vallcys they went, with little or no food. At one stage "two old goats were sent us for dinner which, not being fit to eat, we returned, and were afterwards supplied with an awfully tough old sheep in exchange".[1] It was a gruesome journey. Marching towards Tezeen, they found the road lined

[1] Eyre.

with the corpses of those who had fallen in the retreat and their nostrils were sickened by the smell of decomposing bodies. They passed a cave, round whose mouth lay the corpses of many of the camp followers; some of the prisoners were sure that they could see "spectral figures" moving about inside the cave and heard cries for help as they passed.

Lawrence was moved to protest at the way the women and children were being dragged round the countryside, but their chief gaoler, Mahomed Shah Khan, turning on him "with a diabolical look", snarled back that "as long as there is an Afghan prisoner in India or a Feringhee soldier in Afghanistan, so long will we retain you, men, women and children. When you can ride, you *shall* ride; when you cannot, you *shall* walk; when you cannot walk, you *shall* be dragged, and when you cannot be dragged, *your throats shall be cut.*" Angrily Lawrence replied: "You a warrior and proposing to treat prisoners in such a manner! Warriors don't talk thus to men whose hands are tied." Akbar quickly intervened; "Oh, Lawrence Sahib, do not mind him; he is only trying you and does not mean what he says." Lawrence indignantly walked away, Mahomed Shah following him and rather unconvincingly declaring "he did not mean to offend me".

On 10th May there had been a joyous reunion when Captain and Mrs. Anderson had restored to them the little daughter who had last been seen in the Khoord-Kabul pass on 8th January. She had been taken into the family of Zemaun Khan, "where she was treated with the greatest possible kindness".[1] Now, looking "fat and well",[2] she had learnt Afghan manners and could speak nothing but Persian, though still understanding English. She had been taught to say, smugly, "My father and mother are infidels, but I am a Mussulman."

After moving from Budeeabad the captives had undergone considerable hardship. The heat was at first intense, with the sun scorching the skin from their faces, and then it rained without stopping for twenty-four hours. All this was too much for Elphinstone. He had been a very sick man even before the withdrawal from Kabul and now he had no wish to live. He recognised his responsibility for the disaster and regretted bitterly that he had not fallen in the retreat. Often he would tell Lawrence that he longed for death, for "sleeping and waking, the horrors of that dreadful retreat were before his eyes".[3] No one, he declared passionately, could blame him more than he blamed himself.

[1] Eyre.　　　[2] Lawrence.　　　[3] Mackenzie.

Cursing his folly in having left England to seek a bubble reputation in India, he applied to himself the lines of Gray:

Ambition this shall tempt to rise,
Then whirl the wretch from high,
To bitter scorn a sacrifice
And grinning infamy.

One man alone remained unmoved by the old man's remorse. Shelton made it brutally plain that, should he survive to put in a report, he intended to place responsibility squarely on his General's shoulders. But Elphinstone was now nearly beyond his reach. He was suffering from violent dysentery and there was no medicine left. Mackenzie supplied a lump of opium from his waistcoat pocket and, when that was done, they boiled a pomegranate to make a strong bitter drink which gave him some relief. But he was sinking fast and Mackenzie offered to read the prayers for the dying. Elphinstone agreed, but he had not lost his self-respect and he meant to go to his God clean and spruce. "Moore," he whispered to his batman, "I wish to wash; bring me that blue shirt which Captain Troup gave me." He was washed and his clothes changed. "Lift up my head, Moore," he said, "it is the last time I shall trouble you." The batman, who was in tears, raised the weary old head and Elphinstone died.

"To the very last moment of his being," said Eyre, "he exhibited a measure of Christian benevolence, patience and high-souled fortitude, which gained him the affectionate regard and admiring esteem of all who witnessed his prolonged sufferings and his dying struggles, and who regarded him as the victim less of his own faults than of the errors of others, and the unfathomable designs of a mysterious Providence."

Akbar heard of Elphinstone's death with apparently genuine sorrow and explained that had he realised in time how ill the old man was he would have followed Pottinger's advice and sent him to Jalalabad where he would have had medical assistance. Now, however, the young Afghan's chivalry was equal to the occasion. Elphinstone's body was crated up in "a rude framework constructed by an Afghan carpenter", the corpse wrapped in felt blankets and the interstices filled with the highly scented leaves of wormwood. It was slung across a camel and despatched with a small guard of Ghilzyes to Jalalabad, the faithful batman Moore in attendance. Elphinstone, however, was as unlucky in death as in life, and his cortege was intercepted by a band of tribesmen. Moore was wounded, narrowly escaping with his life. The "bigoted savages", as Eyre angrily called them, broke open the coffin, stripped the body, pelted it with stones and would have burnt it, but for the outnumbered escort's threats of Akbar's vengeance. And great was the Sirdar's wrath when he heard of this dishonour done to his opponent's corpse. A larger escort was sent, the body was repacked and eventually conveyed to Jalalabad, where it was buried with full military honours.

Death, having taken the oldest of the prisoners, did not spare the youngest. Little Seymour Stoker's mother had died and he had been put in the care of Sergeant Wade's half-caste wife. She was found to be an "infamous" person and cruelly beat the little boy, who was not yet three years old. (She also betrayed her husband and his friends by telling the Afghans where they had any money hidden; she even pointed out her husband's shoes, where he had hidden a few gold pieces, and the infuriated Sergeant declared that when Pollock's forces reached Kabul he would petition to have his wife hanged). Seymour Stoker was rescued from the clutches of this unpleasant woman but it was too late. Just before the prisoners were rescued Mackenzie saw him "lying on the ground, covered by a soldier's ragged cloak, moaning his little life away". He tried to comfort himself with the thought "of the tender arms of the Good Shepherd waiting to receive the little lamb, who had found this world such a rough one".

As well as death there were new lives. At least four of the wives gave birth to babies during the period of captivity, Mrs. Waller, Mrs. Boyd, Mrs. Riley and the wife of a soldier named Byrne. Akbar had greeted the news of the birth of the Waller baby with boisterous good humour, commenting to Lawrence, "the more of us, the better for him". The mothers had managed remarkably well without the help of doctor or midwife. "A peculiar Providence seemed on all occasions to watch over the ladies," said Eyre, "and nothing surprised us more than the slight nature of their sufferings on *these* occasions."

Relations between the prisoners and their gaolers were usually good and some of the British became adept at hoodwinking the Afghans when necessary. Gunner Dalton, for example, of the Bombay Horse Artillery, used to pretend to be mad and, if the Afghans asked him to do anything uncongenial, would begin to bellow and stamp his feet, finally charging at them "butting with his head like a ram".[1] "Truly," came the awed comment, "he is an inspired man!"

[1] Mackenzie.

This Dalton on one occasion indulged his "strange degree of savage humour"[1] by sitting all night in a tent with an Afghan who had been mortally wounded in a skirmish with the Jalalabad garrison. The dying man had evidently had some hand in Macnaghten's death, for he seemed to see the ghost of the murdered Envoy with him in the tent and kept shrieking at it in terror. "Ah, you may well cry out," said Dalton each time he did so, "for you are going to hell, my jewel." But the bitter words were uttered in such a gentle soothing voice that the Afghan's companions assumed that the artilleryman was praying for or sympathising with their friend, and kept patting him on the back, calling him a good fellow.

Now, as Pollock advanced on Kabul, the prisoners were hurried westwards to Bameean and there was a disconcerting rumour that it was intended to sell them all into slavery, somewhere in the wilds of Turkestan. Fortunately the commander of their escort was the genial trimmer Saleh Mahomed who, with his regiment, had deserted from Soojah's service two years before. He was fairly easily persuaded by Pottinger, that "grim and grumpy hero", as Mackenzie called him, to turn his coat a second time. Soon it became difficult to tell who were gaolers and who were gaoled. At Bameean, at Pottinger's instigation, the prisoners proclaimed their independence and hoisted their flag on the fort in which they were supposed to be imprisoned. They deposed the local governor and appointed a more friendly chief in his stead. They levied taxation on a passing caravan of merchants and with spirited effrontery Pottinger began to issue proclamations, calling upon the neighbouring chieftains to come in and make their submission. What was more, the chieftains came, and Pottinger collected any decent clothes which his fellow-prisoners still possessed and bestowed them as dresses of honour on those who recognised, however belatedly, that the authority of the British Raj, even when exercised by a handful of prisoners, was not to be defied.

The bluff did not have to be kept up too long for Pollock's first act on reaching Kabul had been to despatch six or seven hundred Kuzzilbash cavalry to rescue the Bameean prisoners. In command of the party went Pollock's military secretary, Sir Richmond Shakespeare, "a handsome and chivalrous officer," said Mackenzie, "who seemed to have a peculiar vocation for rescuing captives, having previously delivered many unfortunate Russians from Khiva". Shakespeare and his Kuzzilbash horsemen reached Bameean on 17th September, only two days after Pollock himself

[1] Mackenzie.

had entered Kabul, and there was a joyful reunion in which the only discordant note was the umbrage taken by the incorrigible Shelton "because Shakespeare had not reported his arrival *first* to him, before noticing his grateful countrywomen and countrymen whom he first met".[1]

No one had known how strenuously the Afghans might contest the rescue and Pollock thought it likely that a few hundred Kuzzilbash cavalry might not suffice. On the 17th, therefore, the day that Shakespeare reached Bameean and Nott's Kandahar force joined Pollock at Kabul, Pollock asked Nott to send one of his brigades to Bameean: "the object is merely to make a demonstration in favour of the party already gone; I therefore wish that the party you send should get into no difficulty and risk nothing." Nott was far from enthusiastic. He made it clear that he would obey a direct order but that it would be against his own better judgement. "I sincerely think that sending a small detachment will and must be followed by deep disaster. . . . I hourly expect to hear that Sir R. Shakespeare is added to the number of British prisoners." Nott had a well-founded dislike of splitting his force into penny packets, and his appreciation of the present situation was based on the fact that there was no positive information on the strength of the enemy between Kabul and Bameean; if they were dispersed, Shakespeare's handful of cavalry would be enough; if they were in force it would not be just a brigade that would be needed but the whole of Nott's army. His reluctance to rise to the occasion attracted much criticism. Mackenzie called him "that irritable and morose commander" and reported that his churlish response had been to say that "Government had thrown the prisoners overboard, why then should *he* rescue them"?

Pollock did not press his unwilling colleague and sent Sale instead, with the 3rd Dragoons and the 1st Light Cavalry. Sale, with the prospect of being reunited with his wife and daughter after nearly ten months of captivity, responded with alacrity and three days after Richmond Shakespeare he arrived at Bameean. The meeting was charged with emotion. "All hearts were full," said Mackenzie, "hardly anyone could speak." He himself rode beside Sale for a quarter of an hour before he could bring himself to blurt out, "General, I congratulate you." Sale was incapable of reply. "The gallant old man turned towards me and tried to answer, but his feelings were too strong; he made a hideous series of grimaces, dug his spurs into his horse and galloped off as hard as he could."

[1] Mackenzie.

By 21st September, Sale had brought the prisoners safe and sound to Pollock's camp at Kabul, twenty officers—half of them wounded—ten ladies and two soldiers' wives (the distinction is Mackenzie's), twenty-two children, six Bengal Horse artillerymen, thirty-eight men of the 44th and seven of the 13th Light Infantry. They found the inhabitants of Kabul in a state of apprehension; the day of British vengeance, dreaded since the murder of Alexander Burnes ten months earlier, had at last arrived. There were some, such as the Kuzzilbashes, who had taken little or no part in the rising and had been consistently friendly to the British, who now felt a natural sense of grievance at finding that they suffered as much at the hands of this new Army of Occupation as the clans who had been foremost in the rebellion. But a written submission of their complaints met short shrift from Nott. "If your friends suffer in this way," wrote the petitioners, "what may your enemies expect?" "We have not a friend in Afghanistan," wrote Nott in the margin, "and I know what our enemies ought to expect for their cruelty, treachery and bloody murders." His final comment was that the author of the document "should be instantly seized and punished for sending such a grossly false and insolent statement".

Pollock, under orders from India to leave on Kabul "some lasting mark of the just retribution of an outraged nation", but to do it in such a way as not to impair the army's reputation for humanity, had decided that an appropriate gesture would be the destruction of the magnificent Great Bazaar, where Macnaghten's quartered trunk and limbs had been displayed to the mob's gloating gaze. For two days Kabul echoed to the sound of explosions as Abbott, the Chief Engineer, methodically blew up the massive buildings with gunpowder. "War, even under so mild and just a commander as Pollock, is a terrible thing," commented Mackenzie, "and many a guiltless and friendly Hindu and Kuzzilbash was involved in the punishment which befel the bloodstained Caubuli." "This has always appeared to me rather a wanton mode of exciting the hostility of the harmless Bunnists," wrote Captain McKinnon, "to punish the unfortunate house owners of the bazaars was not dignified retaliation for our losses."

But Pollock had made his gesture and now, with his whole force, turned his back on Kabul and Afghanistan and set his face towards India. As the long columns wound through the passes the incorrigible Ghilzyes kept up an incessant sniping and at the Khyber the local tribesmen rushed down in the dark to beat up the rearguard. Lieutenant Christie of the Artillery and Ensign

Nicolson, 30th Native Infantry, lost their lives in this skirmish and so had the melancholy distinction of being the last officers killed in action in the First Afghan War.

6

The force halted for a month at Peshawar, where Avitabile entertained the officers with lordly hospitality. He seemed particularly pleased to see Mackenzie again and presented him with a Persian dress, a Bible and a prayer book. When the time came to resume the march to Ferozepore the Neapolitan soldier of fortune, "in spite of the savage cruelty of his nature", now took leave of Mackenzie with tears flowing down his cheeks, "pressing me in his arms as if I had been his son". At Ferozepore Lord Ellenborough, with India's Army of Reserve, was waiting to give the returning warriors a heroes' welcome. The Governor-General had been described by the wife of the legal member of his Council[1] as "flighty and unmanageable in all matters of business; shrewd enough, but wholly without ballast; violently enthusiastic on all military subjects, and they alone seem to occupy his interests or his attention. A soldier, as a soldier, is a thing he worships."

Pollock's return gave Ellenborough the opportunity not only to indulge his fondness for military display but to emphasise what he conceived to be the great superiority of his own policy over that of his predecessor. He had not forgotten that Auckland had opened the campaign with a grand military parade at Ferozepore; he would himself therefore ring down the curtain with an equally grand parade at the same place. In the same vein, to match Auckland's notorious Simla Manifesto of 1st October, 1838, he had carefully put the date of 1st October, 1842, upon a Proclamation of his own, rather anomalously headed "Secret Department, Simlah", in which he proposed to "lay bare to the very core the gigantic errors which had been baptised in the blood of thousands, and shrouded in contumely and disgrace". The long and short of it was that "the British arms in possession of Afghanistan will now be withdrawn to the Sutlej and the Governor-General will leave it to the Afghans themselves to create a government amidst the anarchy which is the consequence of their crimes. To force a sovereign upon a reluctant people would be as inconsistent with the policy as it is with the principles of the British Government." (Within the course of the next two years

[1] Mrs. Cameron.

266

the author of these noble sentiments was to annexe Scinde, attack Gwalior and get involved in the first Sikh war.)

Pollock's force arrived at Ferozepore to find that Ellenborough, perversely and in the face of his own Commander-in-Chief's protests, was determined for some reason to reserve all the honours for Sale and the Illustrious Garrison of Jalalabad. Pollock himself and Nott were to be ignored. This was less than fair and eventually both generals got their G.C.B., while Major Sir William Lloyd wrote to Nott that "the whole country rings in your praise; nothing is talked of but your gallant conduct and persevering endurance under the most untoward circumstances". Meanwhile, however, Ellenborough made himself ridiculous at Ferozepore by personally superintending the painting of the elephants' trunks for the victory parade and the erection of a triumphal arch of bamboos and coloured cotton under which the troops were to march. This contraption, which resembled nothing so much as a gigantic gallows, seemed to the Illustrious Garrison so ludicrous that they marched under it with shouts of laughter.

It was now the season of post-mortems and a search for scapegoats. Sir Jasper Nicholls, in a minute to the Governor-General, listed the causes of the disaster:

"1st: Making war with a peace establishment.

"2nd: Making war without a safe base of operations.

"3rd: Carrying our native army out of Egypt into a strange and cold climate, where they and we were foreigners, and both considered as infidels.

"4th: Invading a poor country, and one unequal to supply our wants, especially our large establishment of cattle.

"5th: Giving undue power to political agents.

"6th: Want of forethought and undue confidence in the Afghans on the part of Sir William Macnaghten.

"7th: Placing our magazines, even our treasure, in indefensible places.

"8th: Great military neglect and mismanagement after the outbreak."

Not one of Nicholls' reasons—a mixture of the strategical and the tactical—can be gainsaid. Yet given that the great basic error was to think that Soojah's rule could ever have been imposed upon the Afghans by British bayonets separated from their base by long, thin, vulnerable lines of communications, there need surely have been no signal catastrophe but for the maddening mischance that at the moment of crisis the man in command was

Elphinstone, Elphinstone who was about to be relieved by Nott, who had never wanted the appointment, who was crippled with gout, who was gentle, courteous and tender of his men's lives (he could hardly have written, as Nott did, "I am well aware that war cannot be made without loss"), who was racked with doubt and indecision, who was utterly incapable of gaining the co-operation of his second-in-command, and who finally died in misery in the hands of his enemy. Lance Naik Hoera, one of the few who got through from Kabul to Jalalabad,[1] summed it up pretty well when he said to Broadfoot that "truly, the want of bundobust ('arrangement, plan or method') was worse than the snow", and exclaimed, "Ah, sir, if we had had you to make the bundobust you made in the Punjab, we should all have arrived." Lawrence put it with brutal frankness: "Our Caubul army perished, sacrificed to the incompetency, feebleness, and want of skill and resolution of their military leaders."

Nicholls had listed among his reasons for the disaster the giving of undue power to the Political Officers. It was a sentiment very acceptable to such cantankerous fighting soldiers as Nott, who had written that "if a man is too stupid or too lazy to drill his company, he often turns sycophant, cringes to the heads of departments and is often made a Political, and of course puts the government to an enormous expense, and disgraces the character of his country." Ellenborough swam happily with the anti-political tide and it was noted that of all the Illustrious Garrison he ignored only Macgregor, the Political Officer, and could not bring himself to be civil to Eldred Pottinger. Yet throughout the captivity Pottinger's skill and courage had been such as to move his fellow-prisoners to a generous gesture. "Your exertions at Bameean for our release from captivity," wrote Lieutenant Webb,[2] "have elicited the warmest feelings of gratitude and admiration . . . and in token of our esteem and regard we beg your acceptance of a piece of plate, which will be forwarded to you on completion." Thirty-two signatures, headed by Lady Macnaghten's, followed Webb's; only Shelton churlishly refused either to sign the letter or contribute to the cost of the present.

Pottinger, as the officer whose signature was on the fatal treaty

---

[1] Brydon was the only *European* to arrive at Jalalabad, but in the days after his arrival a few Indian soldiers and a number of camp followers also completed the journey.

[2] The pewter tankard which Webb took with him into captivity can be seen in the National Army Museum. It is pitted with 266 notches cut into it by its owner, one for each day that he was a prisoner.

of capitulation made at Kabul, now found himself the central figure of a Court of Inquiry convened to inquire into his conduct. It soon became apparent to the Court that he had been resolutely opposed to the policy of surrender and had signed the wretched treaty only under protest and in obedience to the orders of his superiors. Even Shelton was compelled to admit as much. The opinion of the Council of War at Kabul, he told the Court, was that the Army should retire on Jalalabad. "State whether Major Pottinger coincided in that opinion," he was asked. "To the best of my recollection," replied Shelton, rather grudgingly, "he did *not* coincide." "Then what course did Major Pottinger propose?" came the next question. "The impression on my mind," answered Shelton, after deliberation, "is that Major Pottinger proposed that they should make the attempt to go from cantonments to the Balla Hissar." With this, and other evidence to the same effect, the Court was satisfied. "I consider," declared the President, "that Major Pottinger omitted nothing, so far as lay in his power, to maintain the honour of British arms and to secure the safety of the Army; and that he ultimately signed the treaty, contrary to his own judgment, through finding himself in his peculiar official position under the unavoidable necessity of acting as agent for the Council of War." In a final resounding tribute the President spoke for all the members of the Court: "The Court cannot conclude its proceedings without expressing a strong conviction that, throughout the whole period of the painful position in which Major Pottinger was unexpectedly placed, his conduct was marked by a degree of energy and manly firmness that stamps his character as one worthy of high admiration."

Although Shelton, true to his word, had put in a report placing all responsibility upon Elphinstone, he now found himself before a Court Martial. He was acquitted on three out of the four charges, rather surprisingly, since one of these was "using disrespectful language to the general within hearing of the troops". On the fourth charge, one of "entering into clandestine correspondence with Akbar to obtain forage for his own horses while Macnaghten's negotiations were in progress", he was found guilty, but the court decided that he had been duly censured by Elphinstone at the time of the offence and that no further action was required. They went further, for they added their opinion that he had "given proof of very considerable exertion in his arduous position, of personal gallantry of the highest kind and of noble devotion as a soldier".

Shelton returned to England and resumed command of the

44th, which had been practically raised afresh at its Colchester depot. In 1845, when the regiment was quartered at Dublin, he was thrown by his horse and died after three days of agony. The regiment, when it was known that their Colonel was dead, turned out on the parade ground and gave three hearty cheers. This bitter comment says all that need be said of the man's impossibly difficult nature. Yet he had served his country, in peace and war, for forty years; he had lost his right arm in the process; and for all this the only decoration he had received was Soojah's rather ridiculous Order of the Douranee Empire. Let us take leave of him with Fortescue's generous tribute: "the brightest figure in the retreat from Kabul is that of this little cantankerous man, with his right sleeve empty, ever at the point of greatest danger, watching every movement with untiring vigilance, securing every point of vantage, husbanding the strength of every man, inspiring every man of the rearguard with his own calm heroism, and foiling his fierce enemy with invincible energy and inexhaustible persistence. To so gallant a spirit surely much may be forgiven."

Eldred Pottinger, his reputation restored by the Court of Inquiry's verdict and their unqualified praise no doubt ringing in his ears, was looking forward to what would be his first home leave in sixteen years' service. But he was never again to see the beloved home in County Down that he had left as a sixteen-year-old cadet. His uncle, Sir Henry Pottinger, who had conducted the peace negotiations of the Opium War with China ("to all our requests," wailed the mandarins, "the barbarian Pottinger knit his brows and said 'No!'") was now the first Governor of the new British colony of Hong-Kong, and suggested that his nephew should travel home by the eastern route and stay with him on the way. At Hong-Kong Eldred Pottinger caught typhus and died at the age of thirty-two. Sir Henry Lawrence would later write of him that "India, fertile in heroes, has shown since the days of Clive no man of greater and earlier promise than Eldred Pottinger. Yet, hero as he was, you might have sat for weeks beside him at table and not have discovered that he had seen a shot fired."

Many of those who have made but a fleeting appearance in this story had lost their lives in the disastrous retreat. Lieutenant Warren, the taciturn bulldog-lover, had been killed on 10th January. Lieutenant Cadett of the 44th, whom we only hear of as being criticised by Lady Sale for enjoying the fraternisation between British and Afghans during the brief truce, had been killed at the Sourkab river on the 12th January.

At Neemla (where Eldred Pottinger's half-brother Tom, a jolly young subaltern of the 54th Native Infantry, had been killed) Lieutenant Le Geyt of the Bombay Cavalry, who had commanded the escort that had so signally failed in its duty when Macnaghten was murdered, met his end on 13th January. He had hidden in some reeds with a rissaldar of Anderson's Horse, who urged him to shoot his charger, "a fine old white Arab",[1] whose presence would otherwise betray them. Le Geyt could not bring himself to kill the horse that had so nobly carried him to that moment. But the rissaldar was right; the Afghans saw the animal wandering near the reeds, searched them and mercilessly put Le Geyt to death; his body was found there two months later. All in all, seventy-five British officers were killed in the retreat, while twenty-five had lost their lives in the earlier fighting.[2]

John Conolly, who had remained in the Balla Hissar throughout, died of a fever while still a prisoner in Afghan hands. Asia had indeed struck hard at the Conolly family for Edward had been killed by a sniper's bullet in the Kohistan in 1840; Arthur had been beheaded by the executioner in Bokhara; and now the last of Macnaghten's three young cousins was dead. British parents at home were learning that part of the bitter price to be paid for dominion in Asia was this sudden obliteration of a whole family of sons. In the same twelve months that saw the death of Eldred Pottinger his younger brother Tom had been killed in the retreat and another brother, Henry, serving in the Company's Civil Service, had died of disease. Death had been unsparing, too, of the Broadfoot family. One had been killed at Purwandurrah in 1840 while, a year later to the day, another was murdered with Burnes in Kabul; in 1845 the last of the three brothers, the gallant red-headed George, the real hero of Jalalabad, was killed at Ferozeshah in the first Sikh war. Two days earlier Sir Robert

[1] Lawrence.

[2] Mackenzie tells of the romantic tragedy of a young British officer who insisted on bringing with him on the retreat the lovely Afghan girl whom he intended to marry. His horse faltered under the double burden and the young lovers fell into the hands of Afghan villagers. The girl was forced to watch while her betrothed was stripped naked, cruelly whipped and, at last, slowly cut to pieces by the long Afghan knives. Her captors were minded to spare the girl for her beauty, but argued so fiercely as to which should have her that the dispute was settled by their chief's lopping off her head with his sword. *Si non e vero* . . . . But the story is suspect. The officer's name is not given, and no one but Mackenzie has the tale. Mackenzie's suggestion that the officer, but for his devotion to his sweetheart, would have escaped cannot stand; there were many others who rode unencumbered, but only Brydon, got through Jalalabad.

Sale, old Fighting Bob, fighting to the last, had fallen dead on the field of Mudki with a Sikh bullet through his heart.

Four of the young officers whose eye-witness accounts have been quoted in this book were more fortunate. George Lawrence, though he did not become as famous as his younger brothers, Henry and John, had a distinguished career and earned from Sir Charles Napier the enthusiastic tribute that "he is a right good soldier and a right good fellow and my opinion of him is high". He commanded in Rajputana in the Mutiny and died in London in 1884 aged eighty, Sir George Lawrence, K.C.S.I.

Lieutenant Eyre became in the fullness of time General Sir Vincent Eyre, after having been strongly, though unsuccessfully, recommended by Outram for the Victoria Cross in the Mutiny. When he was nearly sixty, and had retired, he took an ambulance service, organised under the English Red Cross, to help in France in the war of 1870. He died in 1881.

In the same year died Colin Mackenzie, now a Lieutenant-General and a Companion of the Bath. Durand, who had played a leading part in the early stages of the Afghan War, particularly in Keane's storming of Ghuznee, fought through both Sikh wars and the Mutiny. In 1870, now Major-General Sir Henry Marion Durand, he was appointed Lieutenant-Governor of the Punjab and a year later was killed when the howdah of the elephant on which he was riding was crushed against the roof of a low gateway.

Surgeon Brydon survived the siege of Jalalabad and fifteen years later, the siege of Lucknow. Here he was badly wounded and received the C.B. for his gallantry. He retired in 1859, forty-eight years old, and died in his bed in his native Scotland in 1873.

William Nott, that "umbrageous and cantankerous man, ever on the watch for slights, quick to take offence and slow to accept conciliation . . . an aggressive champion of the worth of the sepoy and furiously jealous of the Queen's service",[1] lived just long enough to get the plum appointment of Resident at the court of Oudh, to marry again in June and to return home in November to die. Of the renown achieved by Outram and Havelock in the Mutiny there is no need to speak.

Of the civilians, Auckland re-entered British politics on his return to England and in 1846, in Lord John Russell's ministry, became First Lord of the Admiralty, a post which he had held under Melbourne twelve years earlier. He died suddenly on New Year's Day in 1849. Ellenborough, who had announced that he

[1] Fortescue.

had come to bring peace to India, got involved in one war after another and in June, 1844, the Directors of the East India Company lost patience and recalled him. He was unabashed and in November of that year, when he visited the Duke of Wellington at Walmer Castle, "he seemed in the highest health and spirits and gave us many and most interesting details on Indian matters". When the Afghan debacle came up for discussion Wellington was moved to pronounce judgement. "The Duke observed that the opinion he had formed from reading all the reports of the Kabul expedition was that if, on the day after Sir A. Burnes' murder, the troops had marched in and occupied the Balla Hissar, removing thither the Commissaries' stores, they would have been perfectly secure; but that three weeks later, if even an angel had come down from heaven, he could not then have saved them."

In 1858, in Lord Derby's government, Ellenborough became President of the Board of Control for India for the fourth time in his life. He was an old man of over eighty when he died in 1871.

And what of the Afghans? The family of the murdered Soojah, including his old blind brother Zemaun Shah, had wisely asked to be allowed to return to India with Pollock's army and the General had appointed George Lawrence to take charge of them on the march. They lived out a more or less comfortable life of exile in India.[1] Immediately after Soojah's death some of the young princes of the Suddozye house had made sporadic attempts to win dominion, but Akbar Khan had descended upon Kabul and swept all before him, installing leading Barukzyes as governors of the main cities. "Everything," wrote Major Rawlinson, rather bitterly, "is reverting to the old state of things—as it was before we entered the country." And presently it was known that Dost Mahomed had been released by the British and was making his way back to his Kingdom. He always insisted that he had had neither part in nor knowledge of the plot that led to the

[1] Sir Robert Warburton, great-nephew of Dost Mahomed (see p. 122) remembered meeting them in his childhood at Ludhiana. Their kindness to him, he recalled, "was always of the same uniform character". Soojah's two youngest sons, Shahpur and Nadir, "particularly took my fancy. For resignation in the midst of their troubles, for gentleness to all who were brought in contact with them, and for a lofty regard for the feelings and wishes of others, I have seldom seen finer types of the true gentleman than those two brothers. The elder was in receipt of a pension of Rs. 500 and the younger of Rs. 100 a month from the Indian Government—small sums, indeed, with which to bring up their families and support the number of ancient servitors who had been driven out of house and home at Caubul and had followed the fortunes of this royal family into the heat and plains of India."

insurrection. In February, 1842, he had opened his heart to his escort and gaoler, Captain Peter Nicolson. "Recollect," said the Dost earnestly, "that I have from the day I came in been on your side, heart and soul. I swear by the most holy God that since my submission I have not communicated with Kabul and its people, except through you. . . . I am your guest or your prisoner, whichever you please. I came to you in the hope of being in time employed by you; and I should say what is not true if I denied still entertaining that hope; and I am ready to lay down my life in your cause." After his return to his throne, apart from an unfortunate intervention in the second Sikh war, he remained steadfastly true to the British and when the Mutiny broke out refused to listen to those who urged him to go to the aid of the rebels. He died in 1863, having long outlived his favourite son, Akbar, who had died at Jalalabad in 1847. Akbar was believed to have been poisoned by his Indian physician, and George Lawrence heard the news of his death "not without a feeling of regret".

Forty years after the retreat from Kabul it began to seem that history would repeat itself, when once again an Afghan ruler began to flirt ostentatiously with Russia and once again the British intervened. Again there were victories at the outset and again the Amir fled into exile. And again the Kabul mob rose in its fury and murdered the British resident[1] and his escort. But the parallel went no further for this time, instead of Elphinstone, Sir Frederick Roberts was in command. From time to time Roberts' men would come across strange little reminders of their predecessors of the earlier war. One avaricious old village headman appeared with a letter written by Captain Souter of the 44th (the saviour of the colours) while a prisoner at Gandamack. For nearly forty years the piece of paper had been carefully preserved and now the old Afghan decided that the market had come back to him and that he could claim his reward. In Kabul itself Roberts' officers were proudly shown a number of faded testimonials and chits that had been written long ago by Elphinstone's companions and one aged Kabul gatekeeper asked with anxious tenderness after the welfare of Janie Baba and Willee Baba. It was found that he was referring to Johnny and William Trevor, two of the baby sons of Captain Trevor, whose body had hung with Macnaghten's in the Great Bazaar all those years before; and the old man's joy was great when someone was able to tell him that both were now senior officers in the Army of the British Raj.

[1] Sir Louis Cavagnari.

But for the moment it is still 1843 as the curtain is rung down upon the follies and disasters and heroisms of the first Afghan war. With the victories of Pollock and Nott, and the release of the British prisoners, Ellenborough had made it appear as if it had all come right in the end. "It is a comfort to be able to look a native in the face again with confidence," wrote Colonel Sutherland, reckoned by his contemporaries as one of the ablest military statesmen in India. "Now all is right. How easily achieved! And we stand on surer ground now in all quarters than we ever did at any former period of our Indian history." The Mutiny still lay fourteen years in the future.

Back in England, indeed, the principal feeling by the end of 1842 was one of relief at the thought that the Afghan adventure was over and was not to be repeated. "The general and impartial opinion," wrote Greville in December, "is that Ellenborough is quite right to have withdrawn the army from Afghanistan, and to have announced a pacific policy for the future", though he added that the tone of Ellenborough's Proclamation was worthy of censure for the slur it cast on Auckland and for its unqualified condemnation of the errors of men who were no longer alive to defend themselves. Not that *The Times* hesitated to follow the same line: "we believe their policy to have been wholly false," it thundered, "we believe that the attempt to establish by *force* a British influence in Afghanistan was itself an error." And the *Standard* added that all now saw "the utter absurdity of any fears of an invasion of India through Afghanistan, whether from Russia, Persia or indeed at all".

The great men of state were of the same mind. With one exception, they had come to agree with Wellington, who had always believed Auckland's forward policy to be a mistake, and who now wrote to Ellenborough that: "Your Lordship, I am satisfied, would reject Afghanistan and Kabul, with their rocks, sands, deserts, ice and snow, even if Shah Soojah had bequeathed them as a peace offering to England." The exception was Palmerston, of whom Greville wrote years later that "his jealous and suspicious mind was inflamed by his absurd notion of Russia's intention to attack us in India, a crochet which led us into the folly and disaster of the Afghan War". He now continued to urge that the British must retain possession at least of eastern Afghanistan. Peel tartly replied that he had no intention of making war for the sake of promoting the study of Adam Smith among the Afghans.

Humbler folk, who neither knew nor cared where Afghanistan was, got most of their knowledge of the campaign next Christmas when it was made into a spectacular episode at Astley's circus. *Punch's Pocket Book* for 1844 carried an account of the performance under the title of "The Captives at Cabool", said to have been taken from a *Journal of the Astley's Afghanistan Campaign*.

"The Disasters of the Khyber

"Their situation was exceedingly distressing. No sooner had they traversed the pass than the dying English were obliged to throw a white tunic over their uniforms and climb up the ladders at the back of the set pieces, whence, as Afghan chiefs, they fired blank cartridges upon their fellows. The paper snow fell without intermission during the whole of this scene, and the cavalry were sadly harassed by the unceasing volleys of oaths from the prostrate supernumeraries who had laid down upon the sawdust to die.

"Akbar Khan

"The behaviour of Akbar Khan whilst in the green room, surrounded by our officers, was mild and courteous; but the instant he appeared upon the stage of his exploits, he became savage and ferocious, offering a fearful example of Afghan treachery.

"Supplies

"Amongst the auxiliaries supplies generally ran short, and a penny was frequently given in exchange for a meat-pie brought by a camp-follower, who proved to be the emissary of a Feringhee confectioner. Higher-priced luxuries were beyond the reach of the supers, who never got beyond the pies, for few could command the necessary sixpence to arrive at Jelly-le-Bad—from its indifferent composition very properly named.

"Return of the Captives

"The meeting between Lady Sale and her husband, for the first time after her imprisonment, took place in the prompter's box, through the exertions of the call-boy. . . . The heroic manner in which she fought the double sword combat with six Afghans, whom she put to flight, drew down the loudest praise; and her beautiful sentiment that 'the heart of the Briton, even amidst the snows of India's icy clime, still beats warmly for his native home upon the sea-bound isle,' threw an enthusiasm into the auxiliaries never before equalled."

Perhaps the cheering circus audiences were left feeling that the Afghan war must have been a very successful and splendid affair. But one clear-sighted observer found it hard to see what had been achieved at the end of it all by the blood, the tears and the expense. "Everything is reverting to the old state of things, as it was before we entered the country," Major Rawlinson had written. In London, Charles Greville summed it up in his journal with cynical realism. "In the midst of all our successes the simple truth is that Akbar Khan and the Afghans have gained their object completely. We had placed a puppet King on the throne, and we kept him there and held military possession of the country by a body of our troops. They resolved to get rid of our King and our troops and to resume their barbarous independence; they massacred all our people civil and military, and they afterwards put to death the King. We lost all hold over the country except the fortress we continued to occupy. Our recent expedition was in fact undertaken merely to get back the Prisoners, and having got them we have once for all abandoned the country, leaving to the Afghans the unmolested possession of the liberty they had acquired, and not attempting to place upon their necks the yoke they so roughly shook off.

"There is, after all, no great cause for rejoicing and triumph in all this."

No great cause for rejoicing or triumph, indeed. And if, in England and in India, there were still families who in their loneliness wept for those whose bones lay whitening in the passes from Khoord-Kabul to Jugdulluck, well, they must just become aware, like General Nott, "that war cannot be made without loss".

POSTSCRIPT—1963

MORE than a hundred and twenty years have passed since Elphinstone's ill-fated thousands perished in the grim passes that lie between Kabul and Jalalabad. In Britain today the disastrous retreat is all but forgotten, but in Afghanistan, along the line of the march, the tale is well remembered. Two years ago Dr. Louis Dupree, Associate Professor of Anthropology in the Pennsylvania State University, investigated Afghan memories of the great retreat as an example of how folklore is created and handed down from generation to generation. He has kindly allowed me to summarise what he found and to quote from the relevant chapter of his forthcoming book.

Dr. Dupree not only retraced the route of the Kabul force, almost entirely on foot, but—an imaginative touch—he did it at precisely the same time of year. The British had started from Kabul on 6th January, 1842; Dr. Dupree began his walk on 6th January, 1963. Each day he completed exactly the distance that the British had marched on the corresponding day a hundred and twenty-one years before. Begramee, where part of what was the British camping ground on the first night of the retreat is now a golf-course; Boothak; Khoord-Kabul, where it snowed heavily on the night of 8th January, 1963, just as it had in 1842: "the moon shone through the snow," says Dr. Dupree, "and the night landscape appeared as bright as day." Tezeen; Seh Baba; Jugdulluk, where Dupree found still growing on the hillsides the wild holly oak with which the Afghans had blocked the pass; Gandamack, scene of the last stand of the British, where "every hut poured forth its inhabitants to murder and to plunder"; and so to Jalalabad, where today the Afghan army occupies the old fort, as does the body of Elphinstone, lying in an unmarked grave.

As for the village story-tellers, Dr. Dupree found that his main problem was how to stop them once they had begun. They would constantly confuse wars and personalities. An aged raconteur, in the middle of tales of the war of 1839-42, would switch to the Third Afghan War of 1919 and then return to the first war, without pausing to clarify; the same confusion of thought could credit Elphinstone's army with the possession of tanks and aeroplanes. Similarly, others would begin with Roberts' campaign of 1879-80 before narrating, as if it were all of a piece, the British occupation of Kabul of 1839. Yet, when these confusions have been sorted out, Afghan memories today tally remarkably with the contemporary accounts left by British participants.

At Malik Khel, a Ghilzye village at the southern end of the Khoord-Kabul, one teller of tales gave Dr. Dupree a graphic account of the way in which the news of Macnaghten's murder was received in the cantonments. "Someone told the British that Macnaghten was dead. The British did not believe this and said, 'It is not possible that our lord is dead and the sky remains in the same position.' Then the British began to shoot their guns at the sky. And their guns were better than those of the Afghans. They were angry at God because it was true, their lord had been killed by Afghans and the sky still sat in the same position."

Macnaghten's name was the best remembered of all, and at Gandamack the story ran that it was he, and not Brydon, who had been the only survivor. "There is the place of the fight," said the story-teller, "there the British fought to the last man. Maybe one or two did not die right away and were made prisoner. But they did not all die on the hill, because many of the officers on horseback rode away from their men. And their men tried to shoot them down,[1] but some escaped. But only one, so I am told, lived to reach the fort at Jalalabad. The one to reach Jalalabad was Macnaghten, who said in Urdu when he rode into the fort '*Sah Makeh*' ('all is finished')." The narrator pointed to some large black boulders, reputed to be the ruins of the British fort at Gandamack: "See those black rocks? They have been made black by the blood of the English dead." He added that in his childhood, some fifty years ago, many British would pay a pilgrimage from India to the fatal hill at Gandamack: "they would stop their motors or horses close to the hill and would stand perfectly still, with a salute, and then they would leave."

In the Tezeen region Dupree found that by chance he had selected as his host for the night the grandson of Mahomed Shah Khan, who had at one time been in charge of the British prisoners and hostages. "My grandfather was a great man in the war against the British," said the grandson proudly, "it was he who was guardian of the British prisoners. They were not very brave, but my grandfather did all he could to make them comfortable. They were always offering bribes to the guards and

[1] This certainly happened at Jugdulluck. See page 229.

279

made insulting remarks about the Afghans, but my grandfather always was a gentleman."[1]

In two of the villages the legend persisted of two English ladies, wives of British officers, who to save their lives turned Moslem and married their Afghan captors, "the heroes who saved them". The villagers told Dr. Dupree that the descendants of these mixed, and forced, marriages are well known to this day. "One of those who remained here is the grandmother of Zarin; the other is the grandmother of Malang and Gulzar. The grandchildren of the British women everyone knows, because they have red hair and white skin."[2]

And so, as the snow falls and the winter wind howls through the mountain passes, the Afghan tellers of tales recite their legends and the names of Macnaghten and Burnes, long forgotten by their countrymen, are remembered by the descendants of their enemies. The countryside, discounting a modern road here and a golf-course there, remains as grim as ever. Its "desolate and rugged aspect," says Dr. Dupree, "emphasises the feelings of terror and hopelessness the British force must have felt, surrounded by hostile Afghans and a hostile environment." His Afghan companion was moved more than once to the spontaneous comment "the poor British!" Perhaps this may serve as a final epitaph upon the victims of that Signal Catastrophe.

The poor British!

[1] For a British view of Mahomed Shah's gentlemanly behaviour see p. 260. It seems more likely that he was the great-grandfather of Dr. Dupree's informant than the grandfather.

[2] But two years *before* the retreat Colin Mackenzie had noted that the red hair and white skin of many Afghans in the Kabul region were "very striking". (See p. 17).

NOTE ON SOURCES

The definitive account is Sir John Kaye's *History of the War in Afghanistan*. My own copy is the first (1851) edition, but in later editions Kaye added some useful footnotes and appendices. Other principal sources:

Henry Havelock. *Narrative of the War in Afghanistan.* 1840.

W. Hough. *The March and Operations of the Army of the Indus.* 1841.

Vincent Eyre. *The Military Operations at Caubul.* 1843.

Lady Sale. *Journal of the Disasters in Afghanistan.* 1843.

J. H. Stocqueler. *Memoirs and Correspondence of Major-General Sir William Nott.* 1854.

J. C. Marshman. *Memoirs of Major-General Sir Henry Havelock.* 1860.

Sir George Lawrence. *Forty-three Years in India.* 1874.

G. B. Malleson. *History of Afghanistan.* 1878.

Sir John Kaye. *Lives of the Indian Officers.* 1880.

Lieut.-General Colin Mackenzie. *Storms and Sunshine of a Soldier's Life.* 1886.

W. Broadfoot. *The Career of Major George Broadfoot.* 1888.

Sir Robert Warburton. *Eighteen Years in the Khyber.* 1900.

Sir T. H. Holdich. *The Indian Borderland.* 1901.

Intelligence Branch, Army Headquarters, India. *Frontier and Overseas Expeditions from India.* 1910.

Sir John Fortescue. *History of the British Army, Vol. xii.* 1927.

L. P. Nair. *Sir William Macnaghten's Correspondence relating to the Tripartite Treaty.*[1] 1942.

R. R. Sethi. *The Lahore Durbar*[1] 1950.

Other works consulted include: *The Letters of Queen Victoria; The Greville Memoirs; Up the Country* (Emily Eden); *The Oxford Hisotry of India; The Way to Glory* (J. C. Pollock); *Ladies in the Sun* (J. K. Stanford); *Ranjit Singh, Maharajah of the Punjab* (Khushwant Singh); *The Pathans* (Sir Olaf Caroe).

[1] For these I am indebted to Dr. H. Montgomery Hyde.

INDEX